Speaking
Treason
Fluently

ANTI-RACIST
REFLECTIONS
ANGRY WHITE
MALE

Speaking
Treason
Fluently

Tim Wise

SOFT SKULL
Brooklyn

Library of Congress Cataloging-in-Publication Data

Wise, Tim J.
  Speaking treason fluently : anti-racist reflections from an angry white male / Tim Wise.
     p. cm.
  1. Anti-racism—United States. 2. Racism—United States. 3. United States—Race relations. 4. Whites—United States—Attitudes. 5. Denial (Psychology)—Social aspects—United States. 6. Wise, Tim J. I. Title.

  E184.A1W57 2008
  305.800973—dc22

                        2008014083

1-59376-207-0
978-1-59376-207-0

Cover design by Brett Yasko
Interior design by Elyse Strongin, Neuwirth & Associates, Inc.
Printed in the United States of America

Soft Skull Press
An Imprint of Counterpoint LLC
2117 Fourth Street
Suite D
Berkeley, CA 94710

www.softskull.com
www.counterpointpress.com

Distributed by Publishers Group West

10 9 8 7 6 5 4 3 2

Contents

THE POWER OF PERSPECTIVISM 251

MEASURING THE COSTS 318

IV CONCLUSION—Being In (But Not *Of*) This Skin   353

Introduction

Why Treason?

"You speak treason!"

"Fluently."

—Maid Marian (Olivia de Havilland) to Robin Hood (Errol Flynn),
and his response, in the 1938 film *The Adventures of Robin Hood*.

Treason is defined in *Webster's New World Dictionary* as a "violation of the allegiance owed to one's sovereign or state." As such, to consider antiracist commentary treasonous may seem inappropriate, even hyperbole of the highest order. Given that the United States—though once, to be sure, a formally white supremacist nation—has transitioned over the past half century to one in which racism manifests more subtly, to think of antiracism as a slap in the face of the country itself may appear extreme. And yet, I think it fitting, so much so as to call forth the concept of treason in the title of this volume: a collection of essays, published over the course of the last ten years.

For my purposes, I use the concept of treason here in two ways. First, in the traditional sense of national betrayal, for indeed, although the nature of white supremacy in the United States has changed, the substantive fact of white racial power and privilege remains real enough as to suggest that at many levels, the nation's culture, politics, and many of its people are still committed to the maintenance of racial inequality. So, to speak against such forces is to commit treason, in so far as those purposes remain so intimately bound up with the national direction of the United States. And since any significant indictment of this nation and its institutions tends to bring down charges of treason, or at least "hating America" from those with small vocabularies and even smaller minds, it's frankly easier to just accede to the charge and say "so what?" than to try to convince others of one's deep and abid-

3

ing love of country. Bumper stickers that say things like DISSENT IS THE HIGHEST FORM OF PATRIOTISM may make those whose cars are adorned with such messages feel better (or at least more self-righteous), but it's doubtful they've ever convinced a single person who was inclined to feel otherwise.

But I am also thinking of treason in a different way: as a betrayal of one's expected allegiance to one's *race*. Although race treason may not be a concept as immediately recognizable to many, it is simply undeniable that over the course of USAmerican history, whites have been expected to fall in line, to accept the contours of racism, to remain quiet in the face of Indian genocide, the enslave-ment of Africans, the conquest of half of Mexico, and any number of racist depravities meted out against peoples of color. We were supposed to put allegiance to race, to whiteness, above allegiance to humanity. So, to speak against the prerogatives of whiteness, or merely to break the silence about white racism, is, at some level, to engage in "race treason." It is to break with the expected loy-alties, to cast one's lot with a larger purpose. It is to refuse to be limited by the definitions placed upon oneself by the guardians of the status quo.

Importantly, treason against whiteness should be differentiated from treason against people *called* white. If we believe, and I cer-tainly do, that whiteness is destructive to all, including even those who qualify for membership in the club known as the white race, then challenging whiteness becomes an act of profound love for those same people. To challenge white privilege and supremacy is to seek to redeem people of European descent as human beings and our true cultural selves, rather than as the "white people" we have become in a society that forced us into that identity as a way to organize a regime dedicated to profound inequities. In this sense, I plead both guilty and not guilty to the charge of being antiwhite. I am guilty if by "white" one means "the white race" as a collective social unit, with all the privileges that unit receives. But I plead not guilty to the same charge if by "white" one means white *people*, since it is my belief that those people, including myself, are not ultimately served by whiteness, but harmed by it.

In order to engage in race treason, becoming fluent in the language of resistance is a crucial first step. If whiteness is to be undermined as a dispenser of privilege and advantage—in other words, if we are to create a society of justice in which one's skin color or continental ancestry is of no consequence in determining one's station in life—one must learn the vocabulary of resistance, just as surely as one has previously been taught the vocabulary of collaboration. The vocabulary of collaboration is one that minimizes the crimes of racism, one that is rich with catchphrases like "playing the race card," "that happened a long time ago," "get over it," "I didn't mean anything by it; it was just a joke," "you're being hypersensitive," "I have black friends," "stop making excuses," "take personal responsibility," "this is the greatest country on earth," "anyone can make it if they try hard," and "my family came here with nothing and *we* made it, so why can't they?"

The language of resistance and race treason, on the other hand, sounds quite a bit different. It is a language rooted in a few key concepts: exposing white denial in its various forms, exploring white privilege in its material and psychological manifestations, and analyzing the way in which those privileges and the inequality they portend can prove deadly and destructive for all, including the very whites for whom they have proved so beneficial (in relative terms) for so long. It is a language that explores the relationship between past and present, rather than running from that relationship or denying it; a language that prioritizes outcome and impact over intent, so that racism is no longer seen as merely the deliberately bigoted acts of individual wrongdoers; a language that seeks to flip the script on mainstream race discourse by asking not what is wrong with people of color and *their* cultures or communities, but rather what is wrong with the *dominant* culture and its norms.

These essays represent nearly a decade of my own journey on

the road to speaking treason (and resistance) fluently. Some are no doubt more effective than others, and given the development of my own skills as a writer, and speaker of the language of treason, some will demonstrate a depth of thought and a fluency far greater than others. So be it. Being able to examine the trajectory of my own personal growth as an aspiring antiracist ally has been instructive (to me at least), and so as others travel on their own journey to fluent race treason, perhaps they will also find the process through which I have developed over time to be helpful for them. Either way, herein one will find a little more than forty of my essays, spanning a time frame from 2000 to the present. They were not necessarily chosen because they have been my "best" commentaries, either in terms of style, content, persuasiveness, or public impact. Some are pretty well written, others a bit hasty and intemperate; some are humorous, others pretty straightforward; some were read by millions, while others have barely been seen at all. Many of the pieces that do not appear in this book were excluded because they too-closely tracked segments of my previous books, *White Like Me: Reflections on Race from a Privileged Son* and *Affirmative Action: Racial Preference in Black and White*. Seeking not to be too redundant, I kept such pieces out, although even now there is some overlap between the concepts discussed and examples referenced in each volume.

It is my hope that unlike those longer offerings, the essays herein will prove short enough and digestible enough to be accessible to all readers, irrespective of their level of prior knowledge on these issues. Also, from a teaching perspective, it may be that a few of the commentaries, taken together, might prove more effective in a classroom setting than *White Like Me* would, given the greater time investment one must make to fully explore the latter. But even better would be for readers and teachers to use these essays in tandem with *White Like Me*, as a way to put social science and analytical meat on the memoir and first-person narrative bones of the earlier book. That way, those disinclined to listen to the stories offered in *White Like Me* (because, after all, it's just one person's "perspective" based on his own experiences) will have to contend with the same concepts, and the studies and analysis that give them weight. In other words, taken together, *White Like Me* and *Speaking Treason Fluently* form what I hope will be an effective one-two punch at the edifice of racism and white supremacy. May others add to them, critique them both, and further the language of resistance in the process, for the sake of us all.

Tim Wise
Nashville
February 2008

Challenging White Denial

(in Four Parts)

In order to address any social problem, the first and most important thing is to acknowledge its existence. Yet, when it comes to racism, it has long been the case that whites, in particular, deny its salience or seek to downplay the extent to which it can limit the success and accomplishments of its targets. The essays in this section explore the contours of white denial and the four primary ways in which it manifests itself: minimization, rationalization, deflection, and claims of competing victimization.

Minimization is fairly self-explanatory, in that it refers to the tendency for whites to make molehills out of what may, indeed, be mountains when it comes to racism and discrimination. Claims that people of color "play the race card," or that individual success stories (à la Oprah Winfrey or Barack Obama) signify the demise of racism as a persistent social problem are among the most common arrows in the quiver of white deniers. Additionally, claims that racist humor is taken too seriously are commonly heard from whites who seek to minimize the damage that racial subordination can wreak. Minimization is not only the work of reactionary and overtly racist types, however. As the essays in this section demonstrate, liberals have their own versions of minimization, such as focusing on the bigotry of individuals, for example, while ignoring larger structures of institutional inequity.

Rationalization, though it goes hand in hand with the tendency to minimize the problem of racism, stands apart from mere minimization in an important way. While minimizers seek simply to downplay the problem, rationalizers often acknowledge racial bias is real, even within themselves, but then seek to justify its existence by claiming that prejudice (and even discrimination) flows from logical and understandable thought processes, informed by personal experience. So, for instance, white folks will claim that our experiences with certain groups (blacks, Latinos, or Arabs, as a few examples) make the biases we often have toward members of these groups acceptable. Sure, we're racists, but so what? That's essentially the position of the rationalizers, who range from overt neo-Nazi types to respected academics to average, everyday folks who simply don't want to put in the time or effort needed to overcome their own biases or those of the society in which they live, and who would rather shrug them off with a dismissive "there's nothing we can (or should) do."

The essays in the section on deflection confront the way in which whites often seek to change the subject whenever racism is brought up. Some seek to shift the conversation to condemnations of hip-hop and rap music while others insist that the focus should be placed on cultural defects within the black community and the need for folks of color to "take personal responsibility" for their lives, rather than worry about discrimination. Still others seek to shift the public focus onto the issue of free speech—as with those who rush to defend every racist utterance with reference to the First Amendment, and in so doing fail to even strongly condemn the speech being defended—or, as with the case of immigration, onto the undocumented status of certain migrants, as if to suggest that their bias toward immigrants has nothing to do with race or ethnicity, but merely the legal status of those coming across the U.S. border. In each case, deflection serves to paper over the issue of racism and feed white denial of the existence of racism as a persistent problem.

Finally, the last six essays in this section on white denial address the notion of "competing victimization." Though whites typically decry the way in which people of color raise the issue of racism and discrimination—and refer to such discussions as "playing the race card"—we have actually been quite quick to claim the mantle of victimhood ourselves, as these essays demonstrate. From claims that whites are oppressed because we aren't encouraged to have "white pride" (the way people of color are) to the belief that college scholarships are going disproportionately to people of color to the idea that blacks are targeting whites for criminal victimization (or, in the case of the Duke lacrosse case, false claims of their own injury), whites are increasingly seeking to play victim and shift the focus away from the ongoing institutional obstacles in the way of people of color. The essays in this section dismantle the notion of white victimization so that we can keep out eyes on the bigger issue: structured white supremacy and systemic racism against those who are decidedly nonwhite.

MINIMIZATION

Uh-Obama:

Racism, White Voters, and the Myth of Color Blindness

By the time you read these words it may well be the case that the United States has elected—or is on its way to electing—a person of color as president. Make no mistake, I realize the way that any number of factors, racism among them, could derail such a thing from coming to fruition. Indeed, results from several Democratic primaries this summer suggested that a lot of white folks, especially rural and working-class whites, are still mightily uncomfortable with voting for such a candidate, at least partly because of race. In states like Ohio, Pennsylvania, and Indiana, about 15 percent of white voters were willing to admit that race was important to their vote, and three-quarters of these voted for Hillary Clinton. Indeed, in all three of these states, the number of whites casting votes for the white candidate because of self-professed racial reasons was equal to or larger than the margin of victory for Clinton in those primaries. In other words, white racism is more than capable of sinking Barack Obama's chances to become president.

But having said all that—and I think anyone who is being honest would have to acknowledge this as factual—as I write this, we are far closer to the election of a person of color in a presidential race than probably any of us expected. Barack Obama's meteoric rise from community organizer to law professor to Illinois state senator to the U.S. Senate and now, possibly, to the highest office in the land, is something that could have been foreseen by few if any just a few years ago. Obama's undeniable charisma, savvy political instincts, passion for his work, and ability to connect especially with young voters is unparalleled in recent decades. The fact that as a black man (or, as some may prefer, a man of biracial background) he has been able to catapult to the position in which he now finds himself makes the accomplishment even more significant. It does indeed mean something.

Of course, this is where things become considerably more complicated: the point at which one is forced to determine what, exactly, his success means (and doesn't mean) when it comes to race, race relations, and racism in the United States. And it is at this point that so-called mainstream commentary has, once again, dropped the ball.

On the one hand, many a voice has suggested that Obama's success signifies something akin to the end of racism in the United States, if not entirely, then surely as a potent political or social force. After all, if a black man actually stands a better-than-decent shot at becoming president, then how much of a barrier could racism really be? But of course, the success of individual persons of color, while it certainly suggests that overt and old-fashioned bigotry has diminished substantially, hardly speaks to the larger social reality faced by millions of others: a subject to which we will return. Just as sexism no doubt remained an issue in Pakistan, even after Benazir Bhutto became prime minister in the 1980s and again in the '90s (or in India or Israel after both nations had female premiers, or in Great Britain after the election of Margaret Thatcher), so too can racism exist in abundance in spite of the electoral success of one person of color, even one who could be elevated to the highest office in the world's most powerful nation.

More importantly, to the extent Obama's success has been largely contingent on his studious avoidance of the issue of race—such that he rarely ever mentioned the matter until forced to do so in the wake of white reaction to the remarks of his pastor, Jeremiah Wright—one has to wonder just how seriously we should take the notion that racism is a thing of the past, at least as supposedly evidenced by his ability to attract white votes. To the extent those whites have rewarded him in large measure for *not* talking too much about race (or, as with his Philadelphia speech on the subject, taking special care to temper remarks about the legitimacy of black anger with others that sought to legitimize white fear about affirmative action, as if these two were equally valid), we should more properly view Obama's success, given what has been required to make it possible, as confirmation of the ongoing salience of race in American life. Were race really something we had moved beyond, whites would be open to hearing a candidate share factual information about housing discrimination, racial profiling, or race-based inequities in health care (and not only because exigencies like the Wright affair made it impossible to avoid any longer). But we don't want to be reminded of those things. We prefer to ignore them, and many are glad that Obama has downplayed them too, whether by choice or necessity.

Erasing Race and Making White Folks Happy

The extent to which Obama's white support has been directly related to his downplaying of race issues simply cannot be overstated. Indeed, in the wake of the Wright controversy, white support for Obama fell, especially among so-called independents, who had previously been supporting him in large numbers. As of April 2008, support for Obama among whites in a hypothetical race against John McCain had fallen to 37 percent. Even before the dustup over Wright, however, the kinds of things being said openly by many white Obama supporters indicated a significant correlation between Obama's "post-racial" persona and their enthusiasm for the candidate.

So, consider the chant offered by his supporters at a rally in

March—and frankly, a chant in which whites appeared to join with far greater enthusiasm than folks of color—to the effect that "race doesn't matter, race doesn't matter," a concept so utterly absurd, given the way in which race most certainly still matters to the opportunity structure in this country, that one has to almost retch at the repeated offering of it. Or consider the statements put forth by Obama supporters in a November 2007 *Wall Street Journal* article, to the effect that Obama makes whites "feel good" about ourselves (presumably by not bothering us with all that race talk), and that Obama, by virtue of his race-averse approach, has "emancipated" whites to finally vote for a black candidate (because goodness knows we were previously chained and enslaved to a position of rejectionism). Worst of all was the comment of one white Obama supporter, an ardent political blogger in Nashville, to the effect that what he likes about the senator is that he "doesn't come with the baggage of the civil rights movement." Let it suffice to say that when the civil rights movement—one of the greatest struggles for human liberation in the history of our collective species—can be unashamedly equated with Samsonite, with *luggage*, with something one should avoid as though it were radioactive (and this coming from a self-described liberal), we are at a very dangerous place in our history, all celebrations of Obama's cross-racial appeal notwithstanding.

What does it say about the nation's political culture—and what does it suggest about the extent to which we have moved "beyond race"—that candidate Obama, though he surely knows it, has been unable or unwilling to mention that 2006 saw the largest number of race-based housing discrimination complaints on record, and according to government and private studies, there are between two and three million cases of housing discrimination each year against people of color? Indeed, though he addressed housing bias in his now-famous address on race in March, he did so almost exclusively from the perspective of a backward-looking commentary about how racism in the past had limited the ability of

African Americans to accumulate wealth—a true and vital point, but one that, in a vacuum, still allows whites to think of racism as an ancient sin, rather than as a contemporary reality.

What does it say that while on the campaign trail, Obama has failed to note that according to more than a hundred studies, health disparities between whites and blacks are due not merely to health care costs and economic differences between the two groups (a subject he does address), but also due to the provision of discriminatory care by providers, even to blacks with upper incomes, and black experiences with racism itself, which are directly related to hypertension and other maladies?

What does it say that Obama has never been able to bring himself to mention, for fear of likely white backlash, that whites are over 70 percent of drug users, but only about 10 percent of persons incarcerated for a drug possession offense, while blacks and Latinos combined are about 25 percent of users, but compose roughly 90 percent of persons locked up for a possession offense?

Why no mention—even in his seminal race speech—about the massive national study by legal scholars Alfred and Ruth Blumrosen, which found that at least a third of all businesses in the nation engage in substantial discrimination against people of color, hiring such folks at rates that are well below their availability in the local and qualified labor pool, and well below the rates at which they are to be found in nondiscriminating companies in the same locales and industries? Indeed, according to the Blumrosen study, at least 1.3 million qualified people of color will face job discrimination in a given year. Or what of the study of temporary agencies in California, which found that white women who are less qualified than their black counterparts are still three times more likely to be favored in a job search?

And while Obama has certainly blasted the Bush administration for its actions during the aftermath of Hurricane Katrina, he has studiously avoided mentioning the way that government at all levels and across party lines has engaged in ethnic cleansing in New Orleans. No mention of the bipartisan failure to provide rental assistance to the mostly black tenant base for more than a year, or the bipartisan plotting to tear down five thousand usable units of public housing, or the bipartisan decisions to keep the city's public health care infrastructure shut down, or the bipartisan directives to the Red Cross, ordering them *not* to provide relief in the first few days after the city flooded in September 2005, so as to force evacuation and empty out the city. Speaking of the failures of the Bush administration is one thing, but addressing the deliberate acts of cruelty that go well beyond incompetence, and which amount to the forced depopulation of New Orleans–area blacks, is something he has been unwilling to do for fear of prompting a backlash from whites, most of whom, according to polls, don't think the events of Katrina have any lessons at all to teach us about race in America.

Surely, that Obama has been constrained in his ability to focus any real attention on these matters beyond one speech—and even then a speech that, for all of its power and poignancy, he would never have given had he not been forced to do so—suggests that whatever his success may say about America and race, one thing it utterly fails to say is that we have conquered the racial demons that have bedeviled us for so long. And to the extent he has had to remain relatively silent about these issues, lest he find his political ascent headed in a decidedly different direction, it is true, however ironic it may be, that his success actually *confirms* the salience of white power. If, in order to be elected, a man of color has to pander to white folks—in ways that no white politician would ever have to do to people who were black or brown—then white privilege and white power remain operative realities. Obama's ascent to the presidency, if it happens (either in 2008 or at some point in the future) will happen only because he managed to convince enough whites that he was *different*, and not *really* black, in the way too many whites continue to think of black people, which according to every opinion survey is not too positively. None of this is Obama's fault per se, but all of it suggests that his electoral accomplishments take place against a cultural backdrop that limits his ability to address these important issues of race and racism.

Transcending Blackness, Reinforcing White Racism: The Trouble with Exceptions

Obama's rise has owed almost everything to his ability—and this, again, coming from people who support him and are willing to speak candidly—to "transcend" race, which is really a way of saying his ability to carve out an exception for himself in the minds of whites. But this notion of Obama "transcending race" (by which we really mean transcending his blackness) is a patently offensive and even racist notion in that it serves to reinforce generally negative feelings about blacks as a whole, feelings that the presence of exceptions cannot cancel out, and which they can even serve to reinforce.

To the extent Obama has become the Cliff Huxtable of politics—a black man with whom millions of whites can identify and to whom they can relate—he has leapt one hurdle, only to watch his white compatriots erect a still higher one in the path of the black masses. If whites view Obama as having transcended his blackness—and if this is why we like him so much—we are saying, in effect, that the millions of blacks who haven't transcended theirs will remain a problem. To praise the transcending of blackness, after all, is to imply that blackness is something negative, something from which one who might otherwise qualify for membership ought to seek escape, and quickly.

Note: Never has a white politician been confronted with questions about his or her ability to transcend race or, specifically, whiteness. And this is true, even as many white politicians continue to pull almost all of their support from whites, and have almost no luck at convincing people of color to vote for them. In the Democratic primaries this year, Obama regularly received between 40 percent and half of the white vote, on average, while

Hillary Clinton managed to pull down only about 15 percent of the black vote, yet the question was always whether *he* could transcend race. The only rational conclusion to which this points is, again, that it is not race in the abstract that needs to be overcome, but blackness. Whiteness is not seen as negative, as something to be conquered or transcended. Indeed, whereas blacks are being asked by our culture to rise above their racial identity, for whites, the burden is exactly the opposite: The worst thing for a white person is to fail to live up to the ostensibly high standards set by whiteness; it is to be considered white *trash*, which is to say, to be viewed as someone who has let down whiteness and fallen short of its lofty pinnacle. For blacks, the worst thing in the world, it seems (at least in the minds of lots of whites), is to be seen as black, which is no doubt why so many whites think it's a compliment to say things to black folks like "I don't even think of you as black," not realizing that the subtext of such a comment is that it's a damned good thing they don't, for if they did, the person so thought of would be up the proverbial creek for sure.

In what must prove among the greatest ironies of all time, for Barack Obama to become president, he will have to succeed in convincing a lot of racist white people to vote for him. Without the support of racists he simply can't win. While this may seem counterintuitive—that is, after all, what makes it ironic—it is really inarguable. After all, according to many an opinion survey in the past decade, large numbers of whites (often as high as three-quarters) harbor at least one negative and racist stereotype about African Americans, whether regarding their intelligence, law-abidingness, work ethic, or value systems. Without the votes of at least some of those whites (and keep in mind, that's how many whites are willing to *admit* to racist beliefs, which is likely far fewer than actually hold them), Obama's candidacy would be sunk. So long as whites can vote for a black man only to the extent that he doesn't remind them of other black people, it is fair to say that white people remain mired in a racism quite profound.

To the extent we view the larger black community in terms far more hostile than those reserved for Obama, Oprah, Tiger, Colin, Condoleezza, Denzel, and Bill (meaning Cosby, not Clinton, whose blackness is believed to be authentic only by himself nowadays), whites prove how creative we can be, and how resourceful, when it comes to the maintenance of racial inequality.

By granting exemptions from blackness, even to those black folks who did not ask for such exemptions, we have taken racism to an entirely new and disturbing level, one that bypasses the old and all-encompassing hostilities of the past and replaces them with a new, seemingly ecumenical acceptance in the present. But make no mistake, it is an ecumenism that depends upon our being made to feel good, and on our ability to glom on to folks of color who won't challenge our denial, let alone our privileges, even if they might like to.

In short, the success of Barack Obama has proven just how powerful race remains in America. His success, far from disproving white power and privilege, confirms it with a vengeance. It will be up to the rest of us—no matter the outcome of the 2008 election—to move the political culture in a different direction, so that his success, however far it goes, will amount to more than merely the placement of a brown face on a seat historically reserved for whites.

MAY 2008

What Kind of Card Is Race?

The Absurdity (and Consistency) of White Denial

Recently, someone in the audience of one of my speeches asked whether or not I believed that racism, though occasionally a problem, might also be something conjured up by people of color in situations where the charge was inappropriate. In other words, do folks sometimes play the so-called race card to gain sympathy or detract from their own shortcomings?

.It's a question I'm asked often, and which I answered this time in much the same fashion as I have done previously: First, by noting that the regularity with which whites respond to charges of racism by calling said charges a ploy suggests that the race card is, at best, equivalent to the two of diamonds. In other words, it's not much of a card to play, calling into question why anyone would play it (as if it were really going to get them somewhere). Furthermore, I pointed out that white reluctance to acknowledge racism isn't new and isn't something that manifests itself only in those situations where the racial aspect of an incident is arguable. Fact is, whites have always doubted claims of racism at the time they were being made, no matter how strong the evidence, as will be seen below. Finally, I concluded by suggesting that whatever "card" claims of racism may prove to be for the black and brown on occasion, the denial card is far and away the trump, and whites play it regularly: a subject to which we will return.

Turning Injustice into a Game of Chance: The Origins of Race as "Card"

First, let us consider the history of this notion that the "race card" is something people of color play to distract the rest of us, or to gain sympathy. For most Americans, the phrase "playing the race card" entered the national lexicon during the murder trial of former football star O.J. Simpson in 1995. Robert Shapiro, one of Simpson's attorneys, famously claimed in the aftermath of his client's acquittal that co-counsel Johnnie Cochran had "played the race card, and dealt it from the bottom of the deck." The allegation referred to the way in which Cochran had made an issue of prosecution witness Mark Fuhrman's regular use of the "n-word" and suggested that his racist tendencies indicated a propensity to frame Simpson. To Shapiro, whose own views of his client's innocence apparently shifted over time, the issue of race had no place in the trial, and even if Fuhrman was a racist, this fact had no bearing on whether or not O.J. had killed his ex-wife and her acquaintance Ron Goldman. In other words, the idea that O.J. had been framed because of racism made no sense, and to bring it up was to interject race into an arena where it was, or should have been, irrelevant.

That a white man like Shapiro could make such an argument, however, speaks to the widely divergent way in which whites and blacks view our respective worlds. For people of color, especially African Americans, the idea that racist cops might frame members of their community is no abstract notion, let alone an exercise in irrational conspiracy theorizing. Rather, it speaks to a social reality about which blacks are acutely aware. Indeed, there has been a history of such misconduct on the part of law enforcement, and for black folks to think those bad old days have ended is, for many, to let down their guard to the possibility of real and persistent injury.

So if a racist cop is the lead detective in a case, and the one who discovers blood evidence implicating a black man accused of killing two white people, there is a logical alarm bell that goes off in the head of most any black person, but which would remain silent in the mind of someone who was white. And this too is understandable. For most whites, police are the helpful folks who get your cat out of the tree, or take you around in their patrol car for fun. For us, the idea of brutality or misconduct on the part of such persons seems remote to the point of being fanciful. It seems the stuff of bad TV dramas, or at the very least *the past*, that always remote place to which we can consign our national sins and predations, content that whatever demons may have lurked in those earlier times have long since been vanquished.

To whites, blacks who alleged racism in the O.J. case were being absurd, or worse, seeking any excuse to let a black killer off the hook (ignoring, of course, that blacks on juries vote to convict other blacks of crimes every day in this country). And while allegations of black "racial bonding" with the defendant were made regularly after the acquittal in Simpson's criminal trial, no such bonding, this time with the victims, was alleged when a mostly white jury found O.J. civilly liable a few years later. Only blacks can play the race card, apparently; only they think in racial terms, at least to hear white America tell it.

Anything but Racism: White Reluctance to Accept the Evidence

Since the O.J. trial, it seems as though almost any allegation of racism has been met with the same dismissive reply from the bulk of whites in the United States. According to national surveys, roughly three out of four whites refuse to believe that discrimination is any real problem in America—at least not one that truly limits the opportunities of people of color relative to white folks. That most whites remain unconvinced of racism's salience—with as few as 6 percent believing it to be a "very serious problem," according to one poll in the mid-'90s—suggests that racism-as-card makes up an awfully weak hand. While folks of color consistently articulate their belief that racism is a real and persistent presence in their lives, these claims have had very little effect on white attitudes. As such, how could anyone believe that people of color would somehow pull the claim out of their hat, as if it were guaranteed to make white America sit up and take notice?

If anything, it is likely to be ignored or even attacked, and in a particularly vicious manner.

That bringing up racism is far from an effective "card" to play in order to garner sympathy is evidenced by the way in which few people even become aware of the studies confirming racism's existence. How many Americans do you figure have even heard, for example, that black youth arrested for drug possession for the first time are incarcerated at a rate that is forty-eight times greater than the rate for white youth, even when all other factors surrounding the crime are identical?

How many have heard about the massive study from MIT and the University of Chicago, which found that persons with "white sounding" names are 50 percent more likely to be called back for a job interview than those with "black sounding" names, even when all other credentials are the same? Or that this study found that in order to have the same odds of receiving a callback as a white person, a person with a black-sounding name would need eight years *more* experience than the white applicant?

How many know about the research by Princeton sociology professor Devah Pager, summarized in her book, *Marked: Race, Crime, and Finding Work in an Era of Mass Incarceration*, which found that white men with a criminal record are equally or even slightly *more* likely to be called back for a job interview than black men without one, even when the men are equally qualified and present themselves to potential employers in an identical fashion?

How many have heard that according to the Justice Department, in its 2005 report entitled *Contacts Between Police and the Public*, black males are three times more likely than white males to have their vehicles stopped and searched by police, even though white males are over four times more likely to have illegal contraband in our cars on the occasions when we are searched?

How many are aware that black and Latino students are about half as likely as whites to be placed in advanced or honors classes in school, even when test scores and prior performance would justify higher placement, and twice as likely to be placed in remedial classes? How many have seen the research from Indiana University, which looked at fourteen studies from across the nation and discovered that students of color are two to three times more likely than whites to be suspended or expelled from school, even though rates of serious school-rule infractions do not differ to any significant degree between racial groups?

The truth is that few folks have heard any of these things before, suggesting how little impact scholarly research on the subject of racism has had on the general public, and how difficult it is to make white folks give the subject a second thought.

Perhaps this is why, contrary to popular belief, research indicates that people of color are actually *reluctant* to allege racism, be it on the job, in schools, or anywhere else. Far from "playing the race card" at the drop of a hat, it is actually the case (again, according to scholarly investigation as opposed to the conventional wisdom of the white public) that black and brown folks typically "stuff" their experiences with discrimination and racism, only making an allegation of such treatment after many incidents have transpired about which they said nothing for fear of being ignored or attacked. Precisely because white denial has long trumped claims of racism, people of color tend to underreport their experiences with racial bias, rather than exaggerate them. Again, when it comes to playing a race card, it is more accurate to say that whites are the dealers with the loaded deck, shooting down any evidence of racism as little more than the fantasies of unhinged blacks, unwilling to take personal responsibility for their own problems in life.

Blaming the Victims for White Indifference

Occasionally, white denial gets creative, and this it does by pretending to come wrapped in sympathy for those who allege racism in the modern era. In other words, while steadfastly rejecting what people of color say they experience—in effect suggesting that they lack the intelligence, and/or sanity, to accurately interpret their own lives—such commentators seek to assure others that whites really do care about racism, but simply refuse to pin the label on incidents where it doesn't apply. In fact, they'll argue, one of the reasons that whites have developed compassion fatigue on this issue is precisely because of the overuse of the concept, combined with such things as affirmative action (which has, ostensibly, turned *us* into the victims of racial bias). If blacks would just stop playing the race card where it doesn't belong, and stop pushing for so-called preferential treatment, whites would revert back to our prior commitment to equal opportunity and our heartfelt concern about the issue of racism.

Don't laugh. This is actually the position put forward recently by James Taranto, of the *Wall Street Journal*, who has suggested that white reluctance to embrace black claims of racism was really the fault of blacks themselves and the larger civil rights establishment. As Taranto put it: "Why do blacks and whites have such divergent views on racial matters? We would argue that it is because of the course that racial policies have taken over the past forty years." He then argues that by trying to bring about racial equality, but failing to do so because of "aggregate differences in motivation, inclination and aptitude" between different racial groups, policies like affirmative action have bred "frustration and resentment" among blacks, and "indifference" among whites, who decide not to think about race at all rather than engage an issue that seems so toxic to them. In other words, whites think blacks use racism as a crutch for their own inadequacies, and then demand programs and policies that fail to make things much better, all the while discriminating against whites. In such an atmosphere, is it any wonder that the two groups view the subject matter differently?

But aside from the inherently racist implications of Taranto's claim that blacks and whites have "aggregate differences" in things like motivation and aptitude, his argument fails on a fundamental level. Simply put, his suggestion that prior to the creation of affirmative action, white folks were mostly on board the equal opportunity train and were open to hearing about claims of racism from persons of color flies in the face of the evidence. White denial is not a form of backlash to the past forty years of civil rights legislation, and white indifference to claims of racism did not only recently emerge as if from a previous place where whites and blacks had once seen the world similarly. The fact is—and though we might not like to acknowledge it, its veracity is simply not open to debate—whites in every generation have thought there was no real problem with racism, irrespective of the evidence, and in every generation we have been wrong.

Denial as an Intergenerational Phenomenon

So, for example, what does it say about white rationality that according to a Gallup poll taken in 1963 (when in retrospect all would agree racism was rampant in the United States, and before the passage of modern civil rights legislation), nearly two-thirds of whites said they believed blacks were treated the same as whites in their communities—almost the same number as say this now, forty-five years later? What does it suggest about the extent of white folks' disconnection from the real world, that according to a 1962 Gallup poll, 85 percent of whites said black children had just as good a chance as white children to get a good education in their communities? Or that in May 1968, 70 percent of whites said that blacks were treated the same as whites in their communities, while only 17 percent said blacks were treated "not very well," and only 3.5 percent said blacks were treated badly?

What does it say about white folks' historic commitment to equal opportunity—which Taranto would have us believe has only been rendered inoperative because of affirmative action programs—that in 1963, three-fourths of white Americans told *Newsweek*, "The Negro is moving too fast" in his demands for equality? Or that in October 1964, nearly two-thirds of whites told Gallup pollsters that the Civil Rights Act should be enforced gradually, with an emphasis on persuading employers not to discriminate, as opposed to forcing compliance with equal opportunity requirements? Or that in August 1969, 44 percent of whites told a *Newsweek*/Gallup National Opinion Survey that blacks had a *better* chance than they did to get a well-paying job: two times as many as said blacks would have a worse chance? Or that 42 percent said blacks had a better chance for a good education than whites, while only 17 percent said they would have a worse opportunity for a good education?

In other words, even when racism was, by virtually all accounts (looking backward in time) institutionalized, white folks were convinced there was no real problem. Indeed, even forty years ago, whites were more likely to think that blacks had *better* opportunities than to believe the opposite and obviously accurate thing: namely, that whites were advantaged in every realm of American life.

Truthfully, this tendency for whites to deny the extent of racism and racial injustice likely extends back far before the 1960s. Although public opinion polls in previous decades rarely if ever asked questions about the extent of racial bias or discrimination, anecdotal surveys of white opinion suggest that at no time have whites in the United States ever thought blacks or other people of color were getting a bad shake. White Southerners, for example, were all but convinced that their black slaves had it good, and were actually shocked when these same slaves ran away once slavery was abolished. After emancipation, but during the introduction of Jim Crow laws and strict Black Codes that limited where African Americans could live and work, white newspapers would regularly editorialize about the "warm relations" between whites and blacks, even as thousands of blacks were being lynched by their white compatriots.

From Drapetomania to Victim Syndrome: Viewing Resistance as Mental Illness

Indeed, what better evidence of white denial could one need than that provided by Dr. Samuel Cartwright, a well-respected physician of the nineteenth century who was so convinced of slavery's benign nature that he concocted and named a disease to explain the tendency for many slaves to run away from their loving masters. Drapetomania, he called it: a malady that could be cured by keeping slaves in a childlike state and taking care not to treat them as equals, while yet striving not to be too cruel. Mild whipping was, to Cartwright, the best cure of all. So there you have it: Not only is racial oppression not a problem, even worse, those blacks who resist it, refuse to bend to it, or complain about it in any fashion are to be viewed not only as exaggerating their condition, but indeed, as mentally ill.

And lest one believe that the tendency for whites to psychologically pathologize blacks who complain of racism is only a relic of ancient history, consider a much more recent example, which demonstrates the continuity of this tendency among members of the dominant group. A few years ago, I served as an expert witness and consultant in a discrimination lawsuit against a school district in Washington State. Therein, numerous examples of individual and institutional racism abounded: from death threats made against black students to which the school district's response was pitifully inadequate to racially disparate "ability tracking" and disciplinary action. In preparation for trial (which ultimately never took place, as the district finally agreed to settle the case for several million dollars and a commitment to policy change), the school system's "psychological experts" evaluated dozens of the plaintiffs (mostly students as well as some of their parents) so as to determine the extent of damage done to them as a result of the racist mistreatment. As one of the plaintiff's experts, I reviewed the reports of said psychologists, and while I was not surprised to see them downplay the damage done to the black folks in this case, I was somewhat startled by how quickly they went beyond the call of duty to actually suggest that several of the plaintiffs exhibited "paranoid" tendencies and symptoms of borderline personality disorder. That having one's life threatened might make one a bit paranoid apparently never entered the minds of the white doctors. That facing racism on a regular basis might lead one to act out, in a way these "experts" would then see as a personality disorder, also seems to have escaped them. In this way, whites have continued to see mental illness behind black claims of victimization, even when that victimization is blatant.

In fact, we've even created a name for it in the culture: "victimization syndrome." Although not yet part of the DSM-IV (the diagnostic manual of the American Psychiatric Association, used by its members to evaluate patients), it is nonetheless a malady from which blacks suffer, to hear many whites tell it. Whenever racism is brought up, such whites insist that blacks are being encouraged, usually by the civil rights establishment, to adopt a victim mentality and to view themselves as perpetual targets of oppression. By couching their rejection of the claims of racism in these terms, conservatives parade as friends to black folks, only concerned about them and hoping to free them from the debilitating mindset of victimization that liberals wish to see them adopt.

Aside from the inherently paternalistic nature of this position, notice too how concern over adopting a victim mentality is very selectively trotted out by the right. So, for example, when crime victims band together (and even form what they call "victims' rights" groups) no one on the right tells them to "get over it" or suggests that by continuing to incessantly bleat about their kidnapped child or murdered loved one, such folks are falling prey to an unhealthy and ignominious victim mentality. No indeed, crime victims are venerated, considered experts on proper crime policy (as evidenced by how often their opinions are sought out on the matter by the national press and politicians), and given nothing but sympathy. Nancy Grace, for example, regularly recounts during her wildly popular television show how her fiancé was murdered, yet the conservative "tough on crime" folks who have made her a hit all out of proportion to her level of talent seem not to fret about the way that her perpetual victimology may hinder her personal development and healing.

Likewise, when American Jews raise a cry over perceived anti-Jewish bigotry, or merely teach their children (as I was taught) about the European Holocaust, replete with a slogan of "Never again!" none of the folks who lament black "victimology" suggests that we too are wallowing in a victimization mentality, or somehow at risk for a syndrome of the same name.

In other words, it is blacks and blacks alone (with the occasional American Indian or Latino thrown in for good measure) who get branded with the victim mentality label. Not quite drapetomania, but also not far enough from the kind of thinking that gave rise to it: Both cases are rooted in the desire of white America to reject what all logic and evidence suggests is true. Further, the selective branding of blacks as "perpetual victims," absent the application of the pejorative to Jews or crime victims (or the families of 9/11 victims or other acts of terrorism), suggests that at some level, white folks simply don't believe black suffering matters. We refuse to view blacks as fully human and as deserving of compassion to the extent that we do these other groups, for whom victimization has been a reality as well. It is not that whites care about blacks and simply wish them not to adopt a self-imposed mental straitjacket; rather, it is that at some level we either don't care or at least don't equate the pain of racism even with the pain caused by being mugged, or having your art collection confiscated by the Nazis, let alone with the truly extreme versions of crime and anti-Semitic wrongdoing.

Conclusion: See No Evil, Hear No Evil, Wrong as Always

White denial has become such a widespread phenomenon that most whites are unwilling to entertain even the mildest of suggestions that racism and racial inequity might still be issues. To wit, a recent survey from the University of Chicago in which whites and blacks were asked two questions about Hurricane Katrina and the governmental response to the tragedy. First, respondents were asked whether they believed the government response would have been speedier had the victims been white. Not surprisingly, only 20 percent of whites answered in the affirmative. But while that question is at least conceivably arguable, the next question seems so weakly worded that virtually anyone could have answered "yes" without committing too much in the way of recognition that racism was a problem. Yet the answers given reveal the depths of white intransigence to consider the problem a problem at all.

So when asked if we believed the Katrina tragedy showed that there was a lesson to be learned about racial inequality in America—*any lesson at all*—while 90 percent of blacks said yes, only 38 percent of whites agreed. To us, Katrina said nothing about race whatsoever, even as blacks were disproportionately affected; even as there was a clear racial difference in terms of who was stuck in New Orleans and who was able to escape; even as the media focused incessantly on reports of black violence in the Superdome and Convention Center that proved later to be false; even as blacks have been having a much harder time moving back to New Orleans, thanks to local and federal foot-dragging and the plans of economic elites in the city to destroy homes in the most damaged (black) neighborhoods and convert them to nonresidential (or higher-rent) uses.

Apparently, to white America *writ large*, nothing has to do with race nowadays. But the obvious question is this: If we have *never* seen racism as a real problem, contemporary to the time in which charges of the same were being made, and if in all generations past we were obviously wrong to the point of mass delusion in thinking this way, what should lead us to conclude that at long last we've become any more astute at discerning social reality than we were before? Why should we trust our own perceptions or instincts on the matter when we have run up such an amazingly bad track record as observers of the world in which we live? In every era, black folks said they were the victims of racism, and they were right. In every era, whites have said the problem was exaggerated, and we have been wrong. Every single time. Without fail.

Unless we wish to conclude that black insight on the matter—which has never to this point failed—has suddenly converted to irrationality, and that white irrationality has become insight (and are prepared to prove this transformation by way of some analytical framework to explain the process), then the best advice seems to be that which could have been offered in past decades and centuries: If you want to know whether or not racism is a problem, it would probably do you best to ask the folks who are its targets. They, after all, are the ones who must, as a matter of survival, learn what it is and know when it's operating. We whites, on the other hand, are the persons who have never had to know a thing about it, and who, for reasons psychological, philosophical, and material, have always had a keen interest in covering it up.

In short, and let us be clear on it, race is not a card. It determines who the dealer is, and who gets dealt.

APRIL 2006

(Proto)Typical White Denial:

Reflections on Racism and Uncomfortable Realities

Not long ago, after I had written an article in which I discussed white denial—the tendency for most white folks to reject the notion that racism is still a significant obstacle for people of color in the United States—I received an e-mail from a white man who insisted that my argument was itself racist. His reason? According to his message, simply by stating that most white folks remain in denial about the extent of racism and discrimination against people of color, I had engaged in antiwhite bigotry, since I had made a generalization about a racial group: in this case, the one that both he and I share.

He went on to offer an analogy that he felt proved my argument to be racist. "What if I were to write an article where I said 'most black people are criminals'?" he asked. "Wouldn't that be racist against blacks?" In other words, he argued, to make any comments about racial groups is inherently racist, and so my saying that most whites were in denial was every bit as bad as saying that most blacks are criminals.

Of course, and as I explained to him at the time, such an argument makes no sense at all. The reason it is racist to say that "most blacks are criminals" is because such a position is based on racial stereotypes rather than factual information: It casts aspersions upon an entire group of people, based not on truth, but on the basis of ignorant prejudice. Most blacks are not criminals; indeed, the vast majority of black folks are not. There are about 28 million African Americans over the age of twelve in the United States (and thus eligible for inclusion in crime data), and only a small number of these (fewer than 3 percent) will commit a crime in a given year. So while it would not be racist to note that black folks have a higher official crime rate than whites—this is a fact borne out by evidence, and which doesn't necessarily cast a characterological judgment upon those it mentions—saying that most blacks are criminals is simply a lie, and to the extent it casts aspersions upon a racial group that can lead to their continued stereotyping, a racist lie at that.

To say that most white folks are in denial, on the other hand, is not racist, because such a belief is not based on stereotypes about whites; rather, the claim is supported by what white folks actually say when asked if we believe racism to be a significant problem: The vast majority, in poll after poll, answer that it is not, irrespective of the evidence to the contrary. And we have long believed that, so even in the early 1960s, at a time when in retrospect all would agree the nation was profoundly unequal in its treatment of people of color, whites told pollsters in overwhelming numbers (anywhere from 65 to nearly 90 percent) that blacks had equal opportunities in employment and education. White denial has been a hallmark of the nation's racial history. Saying that is not racist; it is an incontrovertible fact.

Apparently, and if recent events are any indication, the difference between mentioning a group tendency, on the one hand, and casting aspersions upon the group in question, on the other, is something lots of folks can't quite grasp. So, consider the uproar among many white Americans when presidential candidate Barack Obama stated that his grandmother had been a "typical white person," in that she would often have a negative reaction when encountering someone of a different race. The comment, made during a radio program the day after Obama's now-famous speech on race from Philadelphia, was taken by many whites to be a racist assault, a blatantly prejudicial example of antiwhite bigotry on the part of the U.S. senator. To many if not most whites, still in a lather over the comments made by Obama's pastor Jeremiah Wright, the "typical white person" remark was only further confirmation that Obama is racist against white people. The story dominated talk radio for days, as well as letters to the editor of local and national papers, and I received hundreds of e-mails from folks demanding to know when I was going to speak out against Obama's "defamation" of white people.

Interestingly, outrage over Obama's remarks has manifested, despite how easy it is to confirm the utter accuracy of his comment—accuracy which itself disproves the notion that the statement about "typical" white people was racist. The fact is, if by "typical" one means the norm, the average (and what else, after all, could be meant by it?), then whites indeed, by our own admission, hold any number of negative, prejudiced, and ultimately racist beliefs about black people. Evidence of this basic truth can be gleaned from any number of sources: opinion surveys, psychological tests like the Implicit Association Test, and several experiments that one can do (and I have done) time and again with white audiences, all with the same result: namely, confirmation that the "typical" white person (and I include myself in that by the way) does harbor internalized notions of white racial superiority or "betterness" vis-à-vis African Americans.

Looking first at public opinion surveys just over the past fifteen years or so, roughly six in ten whites, by our own admission, adhere to at least one negative racial stereotype about blacks. According to a National Opinion Research Center survey in the early '90s, more than 60 percent of whites believe that blacks are generally lazier than other groups, 56 percent say they are more prone to violence, and over half say that blacks are generally less intelligent than other groups. What makes these beliefs racist is that by assuming that blacks are more "prone" to violence and "less intelligent," respondents are not merely signaling that blacks have higher crime rates, or score lower on various indicia of academic achievement—both of which are true, for reasons owing to the opportunity structure and the location of black communities relative to that structure—but instead are making assumptions about the inherent abilities and characters of black people.

A similar survey from 1993, conducted by the Anti-Defamation League, found that three in four whites accept as true at least one racist stereotype about African Americans, regarding such items as general laziness, propensity to criminality and violence, intelligence, or work ethic. And according to a 2001 survey, 60 percent of whites, approximately, admit that they believe at least one negative and racist stereotype of blacks: for example, that they are generally lazy, generally aggressive or violent, or prefer to live on welfare rather than work for a living. In fact, the belief in black preference for welfare over work is typically the most commonly believed of the stereotypes; this, despite the fact that five out of six black folks receive no form of government assistance at all, and only one in seven receive cash assistance according to Census data.

Interestingly, whites often deny the importance of racism in determining the life chances of blacks, even as they give voice to beliefs that are themselves evidence of the very racial prejudice they deny. So, for instance, in one of the more respected opinion surveys from the 1990s, six in ten whites said that discrimination was less important in determining the position of blacks in society than the "fact" that blacks "just don't have the motivation or willpower to pull themselves up out of poverty." But if most whites believe that blacks as a group are unmotivated or lazy, that is itself a racial generalization amounting to racism: ascribing a negative characterological trait to blacks as a group. Of course the irony should be apparent to all: On the one hand, whites are saying that blacks are lazy, but on the other they insist that racism—including the kind that holds African Americans in this low regard—would be of very little consequence to their ability to succeed; as if people imbued with that kind of bias would be able to fairly evaluate job applicants or students who were members of the presumed defective group!

Other studies stretching back nearly forty years have indicated a significant degree of white racial bias toward blacks, which we are almost always loath to acknowledge. But in one set of studies, when whites were told (falsely as it turns out) that they were hooked up to functioning lie detectors that would be able to ascertain if they were being dishonest when they claimed not to have any racist beliefs about blacks, they were far more likely to indicate biases up front. In other words, whites often deny our racial biases, even when those remain deeply ingrained. Research has suggested, for example, that many persons will feign a more liberal and nonprejudicial attitude than that to which they actually adhere when asked questions about racial "others" on opinion surveys. Meaning that if roughly six in ten whites are willing to admit to serious antiblack prejudices of one form or another, the real percentages holding those beliefs are likely quite a bit larger.

Implicit Association Tests are even more decisive as to the extent of internalized and often subconscious, but nonetheless real, white racism. These tests, which measure response time to visual stimuli—specifically testing how quickly respondents associate briefly shown images of blacks or whites with either positive or negative words that are also briefly flashed on a screen—suggest that the typical white person does indeed harbor racial biases against African Americans. According to the research, chronicled in Joe Feagin's 2006 book, *Systemic Racism*:

> . . . When given a test of unconscious stereotyping, nearly ninety percent of whites who have taken the test implicitly associate the faces of black Americans with negative words and traits such as evil character or failure. That is, they have more trouble linking black faces to pleasant words and positive features than they do for white faces. Most whites show an antiblack, pro-white bias on psychological tests. In addition, when whites are shown photos of black faces, even for only thirty milliseconds, key areas of their brains that are designed to respond to perceived threats light up automatically.

In my own work I have often conducted word association exercises, in which I ask participants to honestly tell me the first thing that pops in their heads when they hear certain words. Although there is no way to verify their answers, since I am relying on them to be honest, even in this noncontrolled environment, in which participants could easily lie in order to seem less racist than they are in practice, the answers are quite revealing. When asked to envision a criminal, a person buying groceries with food stamps (or an electronic benefits card), a drug dealer or user, or a pregnant teenager, almost all white participants (and even large numbers of participants of color) respond that their first image was that of someone who was black or Latino/a. This, despite the fact that over half of all crime is committed by non-Hispanic whites, most people using food stamps are white, more than seven in ten drug users are white (as are most dealers), and most pregnant teens are white as well. Although people of color have higher rates of crime, or welfare receipt, or teen pregnancies, it is simply false that the typical representative of any of these groups is black or brown. Thus, for people to think of a person of color when those words are mentioned is to acknowledge implicit biases, rooted in the conditioning that comes from numerous sources, media first and foremost among them.

On the other hand, if I ask people to envision an "all-American boy or girl," or even worse, God, they invariably admit to envisioning white images (in the latter case, even those who admit to being atheists, because of the symbolic conditioning to which they have been subjected). Confirming my own experiments, researchers writing in the *Journal of Alcohol and Drug Education* note that when they have asked white focus group members to envision a "typical drug user," upward of 95 percent of whites report envisioning a black person; this, despite the fact that blacks only represent 13 percent of all drug users, according to the Centers for Disease Control, while whites compose approximately 70 percent of all drug users.

Of course, none of this should be interpreted to imply that whites are inherently racist, as if because of something intrinsic to our culture or biology. White bias against black folks is the direct result of environmental conditioning: media images that overrepresent blacks as criminals relative to the share of crime that they commit, and images that, at least since the early '70s, have overrepresented blacks as members of the welfare-dependent "underclass," relative to the percentages of the long-term poor who are actually black. If one is subjected repeatedly to images of God or all-American kids that are white, it ought not surprise anyone that such images would become ingrained in the minds of white folks, and many folks of color as well. Likewise, if one is repeatedly subjected to negative imagery of blacks—imagery that represents them as pathological and culturally defective—how shocking should it be that such images would influence the way in which whites come to view African Americans and their communities?

This is why it was ultimately so easy for whites to believe the stories coming out of New Orleans in the wake of Hurricane Katrina, which suggested that black folks were raping and killing people en masse in the Superdome and Convention Center. These reports, all of which turned out to be false, and which were exposed as false by the media about a month after the city flooded (retractions that many Americans never heard, it should be noted), were never questioned at the time they were being reported by any mainstream media outlet. Looking at the comment boards on Nola.com during the tragedy (the main website for the city's newspaper and media outlets) one could find hundreds of racist comments from whites who had bought the claims of black depravity and were advocating machine-gunning those responsible and letting the masses who were stuck downtown starve to death, because they were "animals" who didn't "deserve to be saved."

Needless to say, were a hurricane to take out Nantucket, or destroy the summer homes of the white and wealthy who vacation on Cape Cod, and were the media to broadcast rumors to the effect that rich white folks were raping and killing people in the local Episcopal church, no one would believe the reports without evidence, without bodies, without proof. But because of racism, you can say anything you like about black people, especially when they're poor, and others will believe it, every word of it, without question.

So until white folks can demonstrate that we have transcended our racist conditioning, and until we no longer confirm our anti-black biases in test after test, and survey after survey, our defensiveness (indeed, outright anger) at the comments of Barack Obama makes me wonder if we may be protesting just a bit too much, and giving away our hand in the process. To the extent there are some white folks who don't envision a black person when they hear the term "drug user," or who don't see a white man when they hear the term "God," or who don't automatically think of an Arab Muslim when the term "terrorist" gets thrown around (because after all, there have been hundreds of terrorist bombings and arsons at abortion clinics by white Christians in the United States in the last two decades, not to mention the Unabomber, the Olympic Park Bomber, or Tim McVeigh), then so be it. But such persons shouldn't get defensive on behalf of the majority of our white brothers and sisters who still think exactly those things: Rather, they should be challenging them, and encouraging them to break out of the racist box into which years of conditioning have placed us—all of us, to at least some extent.

Our anger should be aimed at those who, by virtue of their racism, implicate us all in the sickness, rather than at those who merely point out that we, indeed, are still carrying the virus.

APRIL 2008

The Oprah Effect:

Black Success, White Denial, and the Reality of Racism

"What about Oprah?"

So came the question from the middle of the crowded lecture hall, spat out from a contorted face whose owner had just sat through an hour-long talk, the substance of which I can only imagine he had found excruciating.

Needing a bit more information before I could confidently respond, I replied the only way I could, up to that point: "What about her?"

And then came the predictable soliloquy to which I have grown accustomed in the eleven or so years I've been speaking about racism around the country. It's the one that goes roughly like this: "If racism is really so bad, and blacks face so much discrimination, how come Oprah is one of the most loved people in America? How come she's been so successful, and has become so wealthy, and so powerful?"

Before I could respond, the questioner continued by throwing in a few other folks of color whose success he believed trumped any evidence of racism as a real and persistent problem: to wit, Tiger Woods, Bill Cosby, and Colin Powell.

I paused for a second, half expecting him to persist, perhaps by noting the professional accomplishments of Jackie Chan, Lucy Liu, Russell Simmons, and J-Lo as ironclad confirmation that racism had been eliminated, but at this point he fell silent, convinced that he had made his case well enough. The statistical evidence I had presented throughout my talk, not to mention the findings of several studies that have directly tested for racism in the job market, housing, and elsewhere (and found it to be a substantial impediment to equal opportunity) were all irrelevant to him; they meant

45

nothing in the face of individual success stories. Anecdote, in his mind, was not only proof; it was even better proof than social science research and quantitative data. That such thinking can survive a college education suggests that the concerns of reactionary crank David Horowitz, to the effect that leftist professors are brainwashing college students, are more than a bit misplaced. Apparently, this guy's professors hadn't even convinced him of the most basic strictures of research design and accepted scholarly interpretation, let alone turned him into a mouth-foaming revolutionary.

And speaking of Horowitz, the "What about Oprah?" trope was one he too had used in response to my work, when an AP reporter had asked him about me in 2005. According to Horowitz, I adhere to a "Marxist framework" when it comes to race because I believe in a "collective effort by white people to keep black people down" (not sure where Marx ever said that, nor I for that matter, but I digress), and that such thinking can't explain the success of someone like Oprah. When the AP reporter asked for my response to this statement, I remember being speechless for several seconds, stunned that such a rejoinder was all this leading light of the nation's far right had been able to muster—in fact, a little embarrassed for him that it was so. It's one thing to ask that kind of question when you're twelve, or even a college student. It's quite another to continue asking it while posing as a deep-thinking conservative intellectual (no joke intended here, by the way).

When Exceptions Prove the Rule

So, what about Oprah?

Well, here's an even better question, and one that pretty well answers the first: What about Madame C.J. Walker?

When I asked the agitated audience member this question, he looked puzzled, naturally never having heard of Walker before, and not understanding why I would have offered this reply to his original query about Winfrey. I quickly explained the point: namely, that Madame C.J. Walker had become one of the very first African American millionaires, by way of tapping into a largely ignored market for black beauty products. She had worked hard, persevered against the odds, and triumphed brilliantly: a real American success story!

"Exactly!" interjected the man from the audience. How do you explain someone like her, he wanted to know, if racism is really that bad?

Of course, what I hadn't shared up to that point was that Walker had become a millionaire in 1911, a year in which sixty-three black folks had been lynched in this country (more than one a week), and at a time when obviously all would agree that overt racial oppression of African Americans was the norm.

In other words, of course it's true that some black folks have done extraordinarily well in this society. No one ever suggested the impossibility of such a thing, even amid crushing bigotry. But surely no one would suggest that Madame C.J. Walker's success, even at a time of legally codified terrorism against black folks, should stand as evidence that anyone in the black community could have made it, and that those fighting against racism at the time were misguided, let alone that there was something wrong with all the other black folks for having failed to replicate Walker's singular achievements.

Yet the logic of a David Horowitz or the young man questioning me that day leads precisely in this direction, as if the fact of individual triumphs against great obstacles ends all debate about a society's degree of fairness. As if the success of a few, who have risen from the bottom, serves as the final proof of equal opportunity, despite the evidence of all the other millions who have labored equally hard and yet remained in roughly the same station as that into which they were born. As if we should conclude from the success of an Oprah that opportunity is equal, instead of wondering how many more Oprahs there might be, figuratively speaking, and how much more quickly they might have emerged, had the remaining obstacles been eliminated from their paths.

As James Baldwin so presciently put it, some forty-five years ago, responding even then to the same "anyone can make it if they try" mantra commonly heard today:

[T]he inequalities suffered by the many are in no way justified by the rise of a few. A few have always risen—in every country, every era, and in the teeth of regimes which can by no stretch of the imagination be thought of as free.

Which brings to mind the obvious question: If whites were willing, even in 1961, at which time Baldwin wrote those words, to insist upon the meritocratic nature of what was, after all, a formal apartheid system, what spectacular level of irrationality would allow us to think that this kind of argument was persuasive, or that those putting it forth had even the faintest inkling as to what they were talking about?

Whites, as it turns out, have always said that racism wasn't that big a deal, and that the "determined will," as Baldwin put it, was sufficient to make all obstacles vanish in its wake, even when the evidence to the contrary was incontestable. You need only go back and read the Gallup polls of white racial attitudes, even before the passage of civil rights legislation, to see this fantastical vision of America on full display. Therein you can find most whites, even in the early '60s, insisting that blacks had fully equal opportunity in education, employment, housing, and the like—a position that all would recognize as borderline delusional now, but which prompted no concerns for the mental health of the white masses at the time.

And then as now, those who sought to downplay or flatly ignore the reality of racism would point to the success stories—perhaps Sammy Davis Jr., or Sidney Poitier—as confirmation that all was right with the world, and that those crusading to end segregation were wasting their time. After all, with a little effort, all black folks could have an act at the Copa or star in motion pictures, just as today, presumably, they can all have a talk show empire or a clothing line, or become secretary of state.

But just as such argumentation was the textbook definition of foolishness in Baldwin's era (and before, seeing as how it reaches back well before his lifetime), so too does it fail the laugh test today, despite what progress has been achieved. Until such successes become so common that we can no longer name all the power brokers with dark skin, their triumphs will stand as a stark reminder that exceptions can indeed prove the very rules against which they have been deployed.

The Superstar Fallacy (or Why Entertainers Aren't a Good Gauge of Social Fairness)

Of course, there's an even more basic flaw in the thinking of the "What about Oprah?" crowd. The simple fact is, very few people of any color ever become superstar celebrities or high-ranking political officials. Very few people become millionaires, let alone billionaires. So to think that any person who has attained these heights of fame and fortune, by dint of their existence, says something about the larger society and its openness to talent is by definition absurd. If these statistical outliers teach us anything about the larger society, it would be that their relative infrequency indicates their exceptionality, rather than suggesting that hard work and effort are all that really matter. I mean, do we really think that Bill Gates worked that much harder than everyone else? And if others have also worked incredibly hard, why is it that almost no one approaches his level of wealth (indeed, many *nations* fail to do so)?

To judge the openness of a society by examining the outcomes obtained by the elite is tautological in the extreme. It is to say, we know we live in a meritocracy because of the existence of superstars, and we have superstars because we live in a meritocracy—the ultimate in circular logic. Rather, to determine larger social realities we must examine the relative outcomes for the typical white person or family, compared to the typical person or family of color. Averages and medians tell us far more about the norm than the extremes at either end. To judge a nation by looking only at those at the top (or, for that matter, the bottom) is ignorance on stilts. Surely, conservatives would balk (and rightly so) if someone were to visit an Appalachian coal town and then declare that what they'd seen had proven the United States to be a nation where opportunity was altogether lacking. Yet, they seem comfortable proclaiming opportunity to be as open as the top of Mt. St. Helens after examining only those at the society's pinnacle.

But what is more telling about the extent of equal opportunity: the fact that Oprah could buy and sell the land out from under most all of us, or the fact that the typical white family has eleven times the net worth of the typical black family, and eight times the net worth of the typical Latino family, thanks to past and present barriers to wealth accumulation, income, and equal housing? To ask the question is to answer it.

Not to mention, the powerful persons of color my questioner had rattled off are almost entirely from the worlds of entertainment or sports, which, important and culturally influential though they may be, are hardly like the industries in which most people find themselves. After all, when it comes to athletic ability or musical aptitude, or any kind of performing art, one either "has it," so to speak, or one doesn't. Such areas of life are among the most meritocratic in any society, by necessity, as the standards used to judge ability in those areas are relatively objective.

But in the regular private sector workforce, this is far from the case. Old boys' networks still skew opportunity to those with the best connections (found by several studies to be overwhelmingly white and male), and the criteria used to determine ability are inherently subjective: Will this person "fit in" with the company? Does he or she have "enough" experience? Will he or she be able to relate to the customer base? All of these evaluations are judgment calls and, according to the evidence, the kind of judgment calls that are often susceptible to internalized race, class, and gender biases. Whether or not a person can hit a three-pointer, carry a tune, or make you laugh is not nearly as subjective (though of course, even there, success still depends on getting certain breaks, and occasionally, being in the right networks to be discovered). Not to mention, whites have always been willing to let black people entertain us, even at the height of segregation. But how have we felt about blacks being our bankers, doctors, bosses, colleagues, neighbors, or in-laws for that matter?

Only Certain Blacks Need Apply:
The Importance of Making Whites Comfortable

And there is something else too. With very few exceptions, those black and brown folks who have made it to the top of the nation's political or economic elite have been those who have done one of two things: either parroted the line of whites, especially those in power, or avoided controversy altogether, taking few political stances on anything, such that they can be seen as having "transcended" their race. In other words, black folks will do just fine, so long as they don't remind us about the issue of racism, don't remind us of their blackness too often (or in the case of some, like Tiger Woods, deny it altogether in favor of some made-up category like "Cablinasian"[1]), and don't wear their hair in an identifiable "ethnic" hairstyle or "sound too black," whatever that's taken to mean.

So Oprah is OK, because although she occasionally tackles racism on her show, and certainly never tries to run from her heritage, she is careful about not seeming to overdo it, and with good reason, from a professional perspective. In fact, the one time she recently claimed to have been the victim of racism—alleging she was kept out of a Paris boutique because of racial profiling by the staff—public reaction was swift and furious. Even those who had always liked Oprah were blasting her on chat room boards and talk radio, accusing her of "playing the race card" and alleging victim status, which they insisted she had no right to do (irrespective of what had happened), since, after all, she was so rich. And when Oprah decided to then tape an episode about racism, in part because of her experience in Paris, and in part because of having seen the movie *Crash*, she spent a significant amount of time not talking about racism, but challenging one of the film's stars, rapper Ludacris, about bad language in rap music, which is no doubt a more comfortable topic for her white viewers.

Bill Cosby is fine too, so long as he's selling Jell-O, playing a nice, safe, affluent father figure on TV, or even more so if he's criticizing other black folks for their shortcomings, which is his current trip, going on four years now. But back in the early '90s, when he ruminated about the possibility that the government had created AIDS in a lab to get rid of folks deemed "undesirable," most never heard the statement at all (the media didn't think it newsworthy to spend much time on), and whites who did catch wind of his comments were outraged. Likewise, when Camille Cosby wrote a widely circulated column after their son was killed, in which she blamed America for teaching his Russian-born murderer to hate (a column with which her husband showed no signs of disagreement), white folks blasted the Cosby duo for not appreciating all they'd been "given" in this country. And one can only imagine the storms of shit that would come down upon Cosby's head, irrespective of how much white folks loved Cliff Huxtable, were he to openly and publicly express the views he put forward in his doctoral dissertation, wherein he explained:

> The "American Dream" of upward mobility is just another myth ... Far from being prepared to move along an established career ladder, black children are trained to occupy those same positions held by their parents in a society economically dominated and maintained by a white status quo.

Moving on, Condoleezza Rice is OK, because she does the bidding of white men in power, without seeming to ever question them (and even better, came from a family that saw no need for Dr. King's protest activities in Birmingham in 1963). Clarence Thomas is better than OK, because not only does he not question white folks about racism, he denies that it's an issue at all, and blames blacks openly for whatever problems they may have. So too Larry Elder, Shelby Steele, Walter Williams, Thomas Sowell, and a gaggle of black conservatives whose acceptance by whites is inversely proportional to their support from others in the black community. In other words, the less you're identified with the black freedom struggle, historically or today, the better from the perspective of white America.

Colin Powell is a textbook example here: So long as he was seen as a team player, especially on a white-led team, folks were touting him as a hero, and someone who might make a great presidential candidate one day. After all, he had never been involved in any civil rights activism to speak of. Even better, when others were leading that fight, getting beaten in the streets of Alabama or murdered in Mississippi, he was killing brown-skinned folks on the other side of the world for America—the same nation that wouldn't even guarantee federal protection for civil rights workers in the South, and in which the human rights of black people were being violated daily, while most white folks couldn't have cared less. Such is the stuff that white folks' heroes are made out of, apparently. But then let that black soldier suggest that he actually supports affirmative action, and let his wife suggest that the reason she doesn't want her husband to run for president is because of a fear he might be shot by some white racist, and let him show insufficient enthusiasm for his boss's war plans (even as he was willing to go and prevaricate about them to the UN), and watch how fast he gets kicked to the curb, first by the public—notice, no more talk of presidential runs—and then by the administration for which he worked, from which perch he unceremoniously retired, to be replaced by a black person who wouldn't make waves.

Barack Obama proves the point even more viscerally. His support among whites has been directly related, according to many of the white folks who support him, to his general avoidance of issues of race during his campaign, and his apparent "transcendence" of race as an issue. It is precisely his deracialization—partly manufactured by others and partly embraced by the senator himself—that has brought him to the point of being a viable presidential candidate.

That the success of people of color has been so highly correlated with the pleasing of whites actually proves the ongoing salience of white power and the relative lack of its black and brown counterpart. After all, if people of color really had equal opportunity with white folks, there would be no logical reason to expect any significant differences in achievement between blacks with more liberal views as opposed to blacks with more conservative views, no reason for the ideological one-sidedness of black conservative success (or merely apolitical success, à la Oprah, or Tiger, or Michael Jordan). If whites didn't have the ultimate power in this society, black folks who refused to play to the tastes of white audiences, and who indeed ignored such audiences altogether, could prove every bit as successful as the Oprahs of the world. Certainly there are plenty of white politicians, advertisers, and companies that routinely ignore the black demographic, either because it isn't necessary for their success, or because they are simply too disconnected from it to know how to attract its members; yet they suffer no penalty as a result. But if blacks ignore what white folks want, need, and respond to (either as voters or consumers), they'll generally go nowhere, Madame C.J. Walker notwithstanding.

Thus, hip-hop execs, black or white, pander to white youth, who purchase the vast majority of hip-hop merchandise and rap CDs, so that even in one of the industries where African Americans probably have the most strength (albeit not as much as many think), the ultimate power still resides in the hands of whites. As a result, there is never a shortage of songs about black folks killing other black folks, slingin' drugs, or partying in the club—what better way to make young white boys in the suburbs feel "street?"—but political and revolutionary MCs, who are often far more skilled, stay mostly in the underground, without major label support, radio play, or distribution deals. After all, very few white folks are looking to embrace artists who rhyme about overthrowing their dads or the established order from which they profit so handsomely.

Electoral politics are no different. Whites will vote for blacks on occasion, but only those, as with Obama, who make them comfortable. To this, many would say, so what? After all, no one can be expected to vote for a candidate with whom they disagree. And that's true, so far as it goes, but note the larger point. Black folks cannot stop white politicians from being elected if those politicians take stances with which the overwhelming majority of blacks disagree. On the other hand, to be elected anywhere other than the 'hood, black and brown candidates do have to please white voters or else they will lose and lose badly. If whites can control the outcome of elections in this way, but blacks can't, then the former have power and the latter don't.

Green Isn't the Only Color That Matters:
Racism and the Black Middle and Upper Class

Of course, the underlying premise of the "what about Oprah?" line of questioning is itself false: namely, that people of color who are successful are somehow immune to racism. According to this line of reasoning, not only does the success of such individuals, or of the much larger black middle class, indicate that racism is pretty much a thing of the past, generally, so too, it indicates that those who are members of the black and brown middle class and above have become insulated from racism themselves. Yet, not only is racism a problem for those who haven't "made it," indeed, it remains a problem, even for those who have: an important point to understand, given the tendency for even well-meaning people to insist that in the United States, "the only color that matters is green." As it turns out, nothing could be further from the truth.

Though it may seem counterintuitive, racism might actually be more of a unique burden for the black middle class and affluent than for the black poor. After all, African Americans at the bottom of the class structure face economic obstacles that are related to racism, especially historically, but which now also operate as part of the class system, with or without the presence of racial bias. On the other hand, black middle class and affluent professionals, who have largely navigated the class structure successfully, regularly find themselves—despite that success, or even because of it—wondering if perhaps they might be racially profiled or stereotyped, assumed to be a bad credit risk, a criminal, or less capable, despite mountains of evidence to the contrary.

Black professionals live with the knowledge that historically it has been precisely when persons like them began to "make it" that they were most vulnerable to attack. Lynching and mob violence by whites was often rooted in jealousy toward successful African Americans and black communities. The poor were "in their place" already, but the middle class and professional class of blacks were seen as having apparently forgotten theirs.

Additional research, originating from the Stanford University Psychology Department and its chair, Claude Steele, confirms the damage that racism can do to the black middle class. Specifically, research on black student performance—especially but not exclusively on standardized tests—has found that it is precisely those black children from upwardly mobile families, who place an extraordinarily high premium on education, who so often underperform relative to their previously demonstrated ability. And why? Because, according to the available evidence, such youth are so desperate to disprove the negative stereotypes held about their group that they experience additional anxiety in testing situations, thereby causing their scores to suffer.

The pressure felt by the black middle and upper classes to achieve above and against commonly held stereotypes about blacks as a group may also explain, at least in part, the persistent health disparities between whites and blacks. Indeed, although poor folks of color receive even worse care than poor whites—hard to imagine, given the lousy care received by low-income persons generally—it is among those with more money and access where we see the largest racial disparities in health outcomes emerge. So, according to a study at Meharry Medical College, in Nashville, hypertension differences between whites and blacks virtually disappear when you exclude upper income whites and blacks from the sample. But when those who are doing well economically are included in the analysis, the racial gaps become stark. This suggests that for blacks who are middle class and above, even though they are likely to have decent health care coverage, they will typically fare worse than their white counterparts. Among the logical explanations for such disparities between white and black affluent folks, one might consider the stress experienced by African American professionals, striving to overcome negative stereotypes and prove themselves against a backdrop of racism and inequality about which they are acutely aware.

So while the emergence of the black middle class may indeed signify progress on many levels, it nonetheless remains true that members of that middle class are in a far more precarious position than their white counterparts, not only with regard to educational and health outcomes, but also in regard to income, occupation, and net worth. Consider the position of the black business class, for example. For blacks seeking to start their own businesses, or who already operate their own firms, opportunity is far from truly equal. Studies have found that African Americans are less likely than whites to have their business loan applications approved, even when their collateral and credit records, as well as other factors, are comparable with their white counterparts. Likewise, even with affirmative action requiring good faith efforts to include so-called minority contractors in government-funded initiatives, folks of color receive a minuscule proportion of said work: about 6 percent of federal contract dollars, despite owning 15 percent of all businesses in the United States. Unequal access to the most lucrative markets explains in part why black middle class businesspersons remain so much more vulnerable than their white counterparts. So, for example, the average white business takes in forty-five times the annual receipts of the average black-owned business, and eighteen times the average for Latino-owned businesses.

As for black workers generally, even those who are college-educated and part of the middle class typically earn less and are in less lucrative occupational positions than their white counterparts. According to Census data, black college graduates are only two-thirds as likely as whites to be employed in a professional or managerial position, while Latino college grads are only 44 percent as likely to be employed in such jobs. Furthermore, black men with college degrees earn, on average, about $20,000 less annually than their white counterparts, which is a difference of almost 50 percent; whites with masters degrees earn about 10 percent more than comparable blacks, on average, and whites with professional degrees (like medical or law degrees) earn, on average, about $30,000 more than their black counterparts each year. These gaps persist, despite the fact that whites and blacks receive college degrees in the same disciplines at roughly the same rates, and even when their ages, experience levels, and prior academic performance records are similar.

Most telling, on those occasions when black families have achieved middle class status, it is typically only after having worked far harder than whites in the same position. Indeed, the average black middle class family has to work twelve more weeks per year than its white counterpart, simply to earn the same as the average white middle class family. This generally means that black middle class families will be dependent on having two wage earners to make the same as white families with only one. And sadly, when black folks do attain middle class status or above, they have a much harder time transmitting that status to their children intergenerationally. Melvin Oliver and Thomas Shapiro have shown in their book, *Black Wealth/White Wealth*, that the children of black middle class professionals are more likely to move downward on the class ladder than to move up, and far more likely to move downward than similarly situated whites.

As if these disparities were not bad enough, income gaps are only one part, and typically the smallest part, of the overall picture when it comes to racial disparity, even among the white and black middle classes. When income disparities are relatively small, wealth gaps remain massive, in large measure because of accumulated advantages among whites going back several generations. Today's young black couples, even if professionally successful, are starting out well behind their typical white counterparts because of the legacy of unequal access to wealth going back many decades and centuries, and which has now provided inherited head starts to the latter and headwinds to the former. Even white families with incomes below the poverty line are more likely to own their own home than black households with incomes that are two to three times higher, according to the data compiled by Oliver and Shapiro. Likewise, white households with incomes below $15,000 annually (and as low as $7,500), actually have a greater average net worth than black households with incomes as high as $60,000 per year. Various explanations exist for such disparities, not least of which is the way that the government itself subsidized white home-ownership in the middle of the twentieth century, via FHA and VA loans that were almost entirely off-limits to blacks, and which created billions of dollars in equity for the new white middle class: wealth that is today being handed down to a new generation of white Americans.

As noted before, the typical white family has nearly 11 times greater net worth than the typical black family, and 8 times greater net worth than the typical Latino family. But even more tellingly, if we exclude home equity from the calculation of assets and net worth—since home equity is not as easily liquidated as stocks, bonds, commercial real estate, or other financial instruments—the median white household has almost 20 times the net worth of the median black household and 12 times that of the typical Latino household. And these gaps exist at every income level, including among those whose incomes suggest they are "making it." According to the Census Bureau report *Net Worth and Asset Ownership of Households: 1998 and 2000*, published in 2003, even among middle class families (in terms of income), whites have 5.2 times more net worth, on average, than blacks (nearly $60,000 compared with less than $12,000). Among the wealthiest fifth of income earners, whites average 3.2 times the net worth of blacks ($208,000 compared to $65,000). In other words, typical members of the white middle class have almost the same net worth as typical members of the black upper class, irrespective of the latter group's higher income and occupational status.[2]

Conclusion: So, What about White Denial?

Taken together, the conclusion to which all of this leads is simple: The real question is not what individual black and brown successes mean in terms of the existence or nonexistence of racism. Rather, the question is why whites are so quick to point to these anecdotal examples of achievement as a way to deny what all of the data suggests is true, and which study after study for years has found to be the case: namely, that racism is a real problem, even for successful folks of color, and that the ability of some to achieve despite it hardly negates that larger structural truth.

Since there is no reason to assume that whites are incapable of separating truth from fiction in this regard, there must be some other factor motivating the phenomenon of white denial. There must be some need that is met by that denial, which makes it largely impervious to fact. Perhaps it is the psychological need to believe in meritocracy so as justify one's own successes and the social dominance of those from one's own group. Perhaps it is the related need to believe in meritocracy, even if one hasn't "made it," so as to allow oneself to hold on to the hope that with just a little more effort things will

all work out. Perhaps white denial stems from the very real material advantages that have come from the system of white privilege
and racial subordination, and which whites fear either consciously
or subconsciously would be threatened in a more equitable system.
After all, acknowledging unfairness then calls decent people forth
to correct those injustices. And since most persons are, at their core,
decent folks, the need to ignore evidence of injustice is powerful: To
do otherwise would force whites to either push for change (which
they would perceive as against their interests) or live consciously as
hypocrites who speak of freedom and opportunity but perpetuate
a system of inequality.

Of course, the sad fact is that by holding on to the faith in
meritocracy—in this case as a way to justify racial inequities that
have pretty well worked to our benefit—whites also commit
ourselves to the perpetuation of an economic order that is disem-
powering and harmful for most everyone, including most of us.
After all, if you believe that anyone can make it if they try, but then
notice that you're constantly struggling to make your bills and
save for your kids' education or your own retirement, and never
seem to have enough money at the end of the month (which is
the case for millions of whites in this country), you have no way
to explain your seeming inadequacies except by way of internalized self-blame and self-doubt. Oh sure, outwardly you can blame
affirmative action for a while, or immigrants, or taxes (the benefits
of which you're convinced go only to "those people" whose skin
tone is several shades darker than your own). But in the back of
your head the voice keeps reminding you that people who aren't
living up to their expectations need only to buckle down, pull
themselves up, and stop complaining.

In other words, belief in meritocracy becomes over time a psychological dagger pointed at the very heart of all but the elite in a
society. For everyone else, it becomes a way to keep them in line,
encourage them to blame only themselves when their job is unful-
filling; their wages inadequate; their benefits pathetic; their lives an

overscheduled, hypertense mess. In short, meritocracy is a fraud, belief in which fraud is tailor-made for justifying not only the maintenance of racial inequality but economic inequality as well. In the long run, the vast majority of whites, as with folks of color, would be far better off facing the facts and losing their faith in this utterly stultifying system to which they have pledged allegiance.

It's one thing, after all, for Oprah to believe in meritocracy. It's quite another for a young white man in a cash-strapped community college, who uses her as proof of society's fairness, to do so.

JULY 2006

---

1 While one can certainly respect Woods's desire to honor all parts of his heritage, on both sides of his family tree (which includes Irish, American Indian, Thai, and African American), his decision to call himself "Cablinasian" ignores a fundamental racial reality in the United States: namely, that whatever you choose to call yourself, or whatever it is that you *think* you are, racially speaking, you are still most likely to be perceived as (and treated as) whatever others think you are. And in this country, no one sees someone who is part black as a complex multiplicity of ethnicities and heritages. Rather, those who can be seen as black are black, in every functional sense. If one is black and anything else, one tends to be seen as black. In fact, racism operates in such a way as to more or less ensure that one will be viewed as a member of whichever group is least "desirable" in one's particular mix, in the eyes of the dominant culture. So if Tiger Woods goes on the wrong side of New York City, at the wrong time of night, and fails to wear his Nike cap, or forgets to bring along his caddy, and then fails to flash that trademark smile of his when confronted by the Street Crimes Unit, well, let's just say, he could easily end up like Amadou Diallo in the morning, "Cablinasian" notwithstanding.

2 In response to those who would claim that the differences in wealth and net worth between whites and blacks are due to whites saving more, and blacks engaging in too much conspicuous consumption—an argument that has been made by white and black conservatives alike, with some regularity—please note that according to economist Ed Wolff, in a report for the Levy Economics Institute of Bard College, as well as additional academic studies, black families have equal or higher savings rates than whites, at each level of income. The only reason that net savings is higher for whites is because, in the aggregate, whites are better off, and more affluent folks tend to be able to save more, by definition. But when income levels are controlled, so that we are comparing only similar white and black families, blacks actually have the same or slightly higher savings rates.

Majoring in Minstrelsy:

White Students, Blackface, and the Failure of Mainstream Multiculturalism

Sometimes you just have to ask, "What the hell is wrong with you?"

I've been asking this question a lot lately, given the almost monthly reports that white college students at one or another campus have yet again displayed a form of racist ignorance so stupefying as to boggle the imagination.

For some, it means dressing up in blackface. For others, a good time means throwing a "ghetto party," in which they don gold chains and Afro wigs and strut around with forty-ounce bottles of malt liquor, mocking low-income black folks. For still others, hoping to spread around the insults a bit, fun is spelled "Tacos and Tequila," during which bashes students dress up as maids, landscapers, or pregnant teenagers so as to make fun of Mexicans.

The last few years have seen at least two dozen such events transpire, bringing to well over forty the number of such incidents in recent years. Among the institutions where white kids apparently think this kind of thing is funny, we have the University of Texas School of Law, Trinity College, Whitman College, the University of Virginia, Clemson, Willamette University, Texas A&M, the University of Connecticut School of Law, Stetson University, the University of Chicago, Cornell, Swarthmore, Emory, MIT, Macalester, Johns Hopkins, Dartmouth, the University of Louisville, the University of Wisconsin at Whitewater, William Jewell College, Oklahoma State, Auburn, the University of California at Irvine, Syracuse, Tarleton State, Union College, and the Universities of Colorado, Tennessee, Arizona, Alabama, Illinois, Delaware, and Mississippi.

Whether racist parties like this are happening more frequently or whether they're just gaining more attention thanks to websites like Facebook, MySpace, and others that allow the sharing of photo files is unclear. But in either case, the question remains: Why do so many whites engage in these kinds of activities without giving their appropriateness a second thought?

There are generally two theories put forward to answer this question. The first holds that these students are ignorant about the history of blackface and the racist implications of mocking the so-called ghetto. The second suggests that the whites involved are anything but ignorant. According to the latter theory, the students know exactly what they're doing and are deliberately trying to make a statement against students of color on their campuses.

While it may be tempting to accept one or another of these explanations, both might contain a partial truth. For some—such as those who have thrown these parties on the Martin Luther King Jr. holiday, as happened a half-dozen times this past year—it is hard to believe they were unaware of the racial message they were sending. On the other hand, persons dressing in blackface as part of a Halloween costume, while offensive, may well be acting from sheer stupidity, absent malicious intent.[1]

The truth is probably somewhere between the two theories. It's certainly true that most whites are unaware of the way that blackface has been used historically to denigrate the intellect and humanity of blacks. And most probably know little about the history of how ghetto communities were created by government and economic elites to the detriment of those who live there. Yet, at some level, most of those engaged in these activities had to know they were treading on offensive ground. After all, never did the sponsors of these parties make the mistake of inviting real black people to the ghetto celebration. They knew better, apparently, than to approach their campuses' Black Student Associations and ask them to cosponsor the events. They didn't ask Latino students to come to "Tacos and Tequila" to lend authenticity to the fun. Had they been acting out of pure ignorance, they wouldn't have hesitated to try and make the events into multicultural funfests.

But they never made this mistake, suggesting that even if only subconsciously, they had to know something was wrong.

There are several potential causes of racist theme parties. Among the more obvious would be the insular nature of the Greek system, from which a disproportionate number of these events have emanated. After all, fraternities and sororities mostly choose members based on how much alike they are to those already in the club. They are not, in other words, natural incubators for diversity. Nor are they the kinds of places where dissent typically flourishes. So if one's brothers or sisters were planning a racist party, even those who were bothered by it might not speak up, for fear of being ostracized. But as easy as it might be to beat up on the Greeks, there are much larger institutional issues involved. Not to mention, there has also been a massive failure of white students, including those not involved in fraternities or sororities, to take a stand against these kinds of events.

Watered-Down Multiculturalism as a Cause of White Racist Behavior

For the past two decades, most colleges have engaged in various types of diversity efforts, from affirmative action policies to the creation of multicultural affairs offices to diversity-related programming. Yet the way in which diversity and multiculturalism have typically been approached leads one to wonder if the messages being sent might actually contribute to the kinds of racism on display in ghetto parties or blackface incidents. Sadly, diversity on campus is still most often approached as it has been for the past twenty years. In most instances, schools push the "celebrate differences" paradigm of diversity, in which everyone is encouraged to be tolerant and to appreciate the cultural contributions of all the different racial and ethnic groups. While this may sound good, in practice it creates problems.

First, "tolerance" can be used as a weapon to insist that we should be tolerant of racist humor too. As such, emphasizing toleration rather than equity of treatment may contribute to a climate where students feel comfortable throwing these kinds of parties, because, after all, "it's just a joke." Secondly, by implying that race issues are about culture (and not power differences between whites and folks of color), most diversity efforts allow whites to think of blackness as little more than style, which can be appropriated, copied, or mimicked, without making fun of black people per se, or furthering inequity. In this kind of multiculturalism, the power dynamic that makes racially insensitive humor hurtful isn't discussed. Students are encouraged to see how "We're all different" (and gee, isn't that interesting?), but are not asked to reflect on the biggest difference of all: in this case, the one regarding who's on top and who's not in the larger society.

Even worse, these students are just as likely to consider their copying of what they see as black culture and style as celebratory and positive as they are to consider it negative and demeaning. In other words, it's as if they were saying, "Hey, we're just celebrating difference! Look at me, I'm a rapper!" Sure, they may have a horribly stunted view of what constitutes both celebration and true cultural difference (seeing as how they clearly equate blackness with the gangsta image), but their assumptions in this regard make sense, stemming from a context-absent analysis in which issues of power are largely missing.

Additionally, by avoiding issues of power, mainstream multiculturalism makes it possible for whites who see no harm in blackface or ghetto parties to respond to their critics by saying things like "Well, what about that movie *White Chicks*, where the Wayans brothers put on white face makeup and made fun of people like us?" In other words, whites see all groups as equally capable of objectifying each other, so what's the big deal? Indeed, if you're being taught to view issues of race as the mere pluralistic existence of different groups, perhaps competing for resources and attention, but without a discussion of power, this kind of argument has a certain logic to it. Of course, once the social context is brought in, it makes no sense at all. There has been no history of whiteface as a mechanism for denigrating the intelligence of whites, whereas blackface served precisely that purpose. *White Chicks* conjures up no painful memories and is so devoid of the historical "umph" of blackface that to consider it in the same category as minstrelsy is to call into question one's ability to think rationally at all.

What's more, because mainstream multiculturalism rarely explores the historical or sociological roots of what some now think of as cultural phenomena, it is also possible for whites to view "the ghetto" as an authentic expression of black culture, rather than understanding it as a geopolitical space occupied by persons whose opportunities have been constricted. To most whites, ghettos are culturally specific spaces, either to be feared, turned into style, or even romanticized as more "real" than the places from which most of them come. If they had an understanding of how the ghetto became the ghetto—a history of residential segregation; urban "renewal," which destroyed black homes and neighborhoods; and deindustrialization, beginning in the '60s—many of the whites who have participated in these kinds of activities might have thought twice about it. If they understood that the ghetto is something that has been *done* to millions of black people—that indeed it is more an expression of white supremacist culture than anything authentically black—many might recognize that throwing parties celebrating or mocking ghetto life would be hardly different from throwing concentration camp or internment camp parties. But if whites think of the ghetto as an authentic expression of blackness, they'll be less likely to feel shame while making fun of such a place. Indeed, they may not even view a ghetto party as making fun at all, so much as being a romanticization of a place that both fascinates and terrifies them.

So long as diversity talk avoids issues of power and privilege, opting instead for cultural tourism, whereby we're encouraged to sample one another's stuff, from food to clothing to hairstyles—note the phenomena of white boys wearing dreadlocks, and white girls with tight braids—we can expect this kind of thing to continue. After all, what could be more "touristy" than dressing like the people whose culture you're sampling? To many whites, blackface, or putting on an Afro and fake bling, is just a more up-to-date and hipper version of the Hawaiian shirt their dad wears every time the family goes to Honolulu.

Until colleges include discussions of power, inequality, and privilege (and how these can misshape the campus climate) during first-year orientation programs, and with all students, they really can't feign shock or outrage when some proceed to act out their ignorance on a public stage. Until schools clearly define what a racially hostile environment is, and what is to be viewed as con-tributing to such a climate—and what kinds of acts will therefore not be tolerated, just as they would not be in the workplace—they can't be surprised when students feel they can get away with virtu-ally anything, no matter how offensive. Finally, so long as colleges turn a blind eye to the overwhelmingly white student pathology of epidemic binge drinking that has served as the backdrop for most, if not all, of these racist parties—indeed, white students are 130 percent more likely to binge drink than blacks, and 300 per-cent more likely to do so on a regular basis—not much is going to change. This means attacking problem drinking as an abuse of privilege, and not just alcohol.

White Protectionism and the Need for Ally Behavior

In addition to the need for school officials to take action, stu-dents must also take responsibility for addressing these occurrences head-on. In particular, whites who are not involved in these acts need to stand up against those who are. Although some whites have joined with students of color to condemn these events when they've happened, quite telling has been the speed with which others have sought to downplay the racism evinced in such instances.

At Oklahoma State, one young man minimized the seriousness of the incident in his fraternity (in which one of his "brothers," wearing a Klan hood, posed for a picture while holding a rope around the neck of another member who was dressed in black-face) by noting that the perpetrators were just "young men, having fun, no one was hurt, and above all nothing was meant by their actions." At Stetson, a group of young women who dressed in blackface claimed that their event had the blessing of the mostly black basketball team, and at Illinois, white sorority girls defended their "Tacos and Tequila" event by noting that their two Latina members were "cool with it" (as if a handful of black and brown folks can speak for their entire groups). The attorney for a group of white frat boys at Auburn even suggested that his clients had actually been trying to be "inclusive" by dressing in blackface, since the party theme was to come dressed as something you might see in the Auburn community.

Or consider the internet posting of a University of Texas law student, who didn't participate in last year's "ghetto fabulous" party, but who found more fault with those critiquing it than those who threw it in the first place:

> Get over it. You were offended. You complained . . . Prolonging the drama only makes you look like attention whores—you aren't trying to educate people, and you aren't trying to create an atmosphere of inclusion, where people can understand your point of view. You want to continue to spank the naughty 1Ls. The Dean gave you recognition. Everyone in the law school received that email. Do you honestly think that prolonging the drama is going to do anything productive? And for the record, equating ghetto fabulous with blackface is really fucking stupid.

In other words, the students who engaged in the racist objectification of blacks are "naughty," but the students of color who complained are "attention whores" and "fucking stupid." Other whites at the law school voiced their displeasure at the possibility that the school may now alter its curricula, thereby forcing them to learn about racism. Imagine, having to learn about such an irrelevant subject while studying law. Still others criticized the black students for going public about the event instead of handling things internally, since it might harm the careers of whites who didn't participate, but who would now be tainted by the actions of a few. Instead of being upset at their white peers for throwing the racist party, and thereby tainting them as whites, their anger was focused on the black students for discussing it openly!

And in keeping with the tendency for white folks to seek out black scapegoats whenever one of ours engages in racism (as happened with radio personality Don Imus), many students have sought to shift the blame for things like ghetto parties onto hip-hop and rap music. In other words, white kids are just copying what they see on MTV, and if black folks can glamorize the ghetto, why can't we? That rappers, for good or ill, are often telling stories about their own lives and the communities from which they come (or at least with which they have some familiarity) while white coeds are engaging in vulgar voyeurism devoid of authenticity escapes them. Not to mention, rap can hardly be blamed for the ignorance here: After all, black students, who last time I checked often liked hip-hop too, don't throw these parties. Not ever.

Then there's the tendency to redefine racist incidents as something else, like simple bad taste, or even political satire. The latter of these was offered as the excuse last year, after one Willamette student came to a party in blackface to mock the school's president, and another dressed as an indigenous woman who had been raped. Funny stuff.

Until white students become less concerned about hurting the feelings of a bunch of racists or drunks (or both) by calling them out, and more committed to the creation of a respectful and equitable environment on campus, those whites who engage in acts of racism will feel no need to change their behaviors. Unless whites ostracize such students, those who find racism humorous will continue to push the envelope. Only by our making clear that these kinds of things are unacceptable to us will other whites apparently get the message that their actions are inexcusable. It's obvious by now that they won't respond to black and brown protests alone.

Perhaps we should think of it as an updated version of the white man's (and woman's) burden: not, as with the original and racist version, to "civilize" others, but instead to civilize ourselves, to grow up, and to enter into the world of adults as more functional human beings, rather than as the walking, talking stereotypes into which we too often turn ourselves.

JUNE 2007

---

1 Putting aside whether or not blackface incidents or ghetto parties are intentionally racist (rather than being mostly the result of ignorance), there is little question but that overt racism poses a serious problem on college campuses. Data going back to the 1980s suggests that there are thousands of instances of ethnoviolence (ranging from assaults to graffiti to racial slurs) directed toward students of color each year. A study at the University of California at San Diego in the '90s found that over 80 percent of white students admitted to having seen or heard racial slurs or acts of race-based discrimination aimed at students of color. And a 2004 survey at the University of Virginia found that 40 percent of all black students at the school had been the target of a direct racial slur, while 91 percent had either experienced or witnessed an act of racial discrimination or intolerance since coming to the college. Additional research by Joe Feagin and Leslie Picca, published in their recent book, *Two-Faced Racism,* finds that white students often use racial slurs and express blatantly racist beliefs around their white friends and colleagues, even though they would rarely if ever do so publicly, or in front of the persons to whom the slurs are directed.

Racism, White Liberals, and the Limits of Tolerance

Let me get this straight: If three white guys chain a black man to a truck and decapitate him by dragging him down a dirt road, *that's* a hate crime, but if five white cops pump nineteen bullets into a black street vendor, having shot at him forty-one times, that's just "bad judgment"? And what's more, we should pass hate crime laws that require enforcement by the *police*? Call me crazy, but something about this brings to mind the one about the foxes and the henhouse.

Don't get me wrong. I realize there are horrible acts of bias-inspired violence perpetrated every day in America against people of color, gays, lesbians, trans-folk, and religious minorities. And I have no problem in principle with passing special laws to send a message that such hatred won't be tolerated. But is this really the point? Does it do anything to address the larger issues of racism, sexism, or straight supremacy that plague our society? And will it save Amadou Diallo, or prevent Abner Louima from getting a toilet plunger shoved up his ass by bigots in blue uniforms? Of course not. Hate crime laws make us feel better, but in the end, the biggest injuries suffered by people of color continue: job and housing discrimination, unequal access to health care, and the development of a prison-industrial-complex that is locking up black and brown bodies faster than you can say "three strikes and you're out," all of which could and would persist, even if there were never another cross-burning on a black family's lawn, or another violent assault on an immigrant.

Ultimately, this is what has long been so troubling about our national dialogue on race: It only seems to take place in a comfort zone where pretty much everyone can agree. So when James Byrd gets dragged to death in Jasper, everyone is quick to condemn the atrocity. But when the Centers for Disease Control reports that tens of thousands of people of color die each year because they receive inferior health care and are exposed to greater levels of toxic chemicals relative to their white counterparts (people who, in other words, wouldn't die were they simply white), few say anything.

When we hear about people of color harassed by neighbors in white communities and forced to move due to the bigotry of a few, most react with horror. "How terrible," we insist, "People should be able to live wherever they choose." But when study after study indicates that people of color are denied home mortgages at twice the rate of whites, and considerably more often, even when they have similar credit and higher incomes, and that they face housing discrimination over two million times a year because of more subtle biases—far less blatant than the racist neighbor—few raise their voices indignantly, and no one thinks to send bankers or real estate agents to jail for bias crime.

And when we turn on some talk show and see a Klansman or skinhead ranting about the inferiority of black and brown people, we laugh, or perhaps yell at the TV, and collectively condemn them. But when two well-respected social scientists named Murray and Herrnstein write a book like *The Bell Curve*—which argues pretty much the same thing, only with footnotes—we not only fail to condemn them but whites go out and make their book a bestseller: Half a million copies sold in the first eighteen months. Furthermore, Murray gets interviewed on every major news show in America, and is then asked to speak to the GOP Congressional delegation one month after the Republicans took over Congress in 1994.

In other words, the problem of racism is not to be found at the extremes. It's not about "intolerance" and a need to "love your neighbor," hold hands, and sing Pete Seeger songs. The problem is the everyday discrimination, inequity, and mainstream silence about these things by folks who pretend to care about racism, and think they can prove it by condemning lynch mobs—an act that ceased to be courageous about forty years ago.

Extremism and the Focus on the "Other"

Ask any white person what a racist looks like, and you're likely to get a response involving men and women wearing sheets, hoods, and swastikas, yelling slurs at people of color. So, for instance, consider one of the women interviewed by Joe Feagin and Hernan Vera for their 1995 book, *White Racism*, who when asked her opinion of blacks replied: "They look like apes . . . I dislike them, except when they treat me with respect . . . I don't say I hate every black person, [just] the majority," but then went on to explain, "I don't consider myself racist. When I think of the word racist, I think of the KKK, people in white robes burning black people on crosses . . . or I think of the skinheads . . . "

Indeed, it's doubtful that the 17 percent of white Americans who readily tell pollsters that "Blacks lack an inborn ability to learn" would consider themselves racists, nor the 31 percent who claim "most blacks are lazy," nor the 50 percent who believe blacks are "more aggressive and violent" than whites, nor the three-quarters who express the belief that "Most blacks would rather live off welfare than work for a living." In fact, despite these numbers, only 6 percent of whites admit they are "racist or prejudiced," which is about half as many as will say they believe Elvis is still alive.

Even more disturbing than these individuals' own denial of their racism is the seeming disregard paid such everyday prejudice by "antibias" organizations. Despite the fact that 17 percent of the white population (the percentage admitting they believe in black genetic inferiority) comprises thirty-four million white Americans, and despite the fact that this number is equal to the size of the entire black population of the United States, groups like Klanwatch, the Anti-Defamation League, and others seem to care little about challenging these folks' racism, unless of course they join a hate group or kill someone, in which case they will then become a problem worth addressing.

Again, call me crazy, but I'm more concerned about the 44 percent who still believe it's alright for white homeowners to discriminate against black renters or buyers, or the fact that less than half of all whites (according to polls in the early '90s) think the government should have *any* laws to ensure equal opportunity in employment, than I am about guys running around in the woods with guns, or lighting birthday cakes for Hitler every April 20. Sure, folks like that can do serious damage (just witness Oklahoma City for example), but the fact remains that the Tim McVeighs of the world get these ideas somewhere, long before they stumble across white power websites or read racist hate novels like *The Turner Diaries*.

Where Would They Get Such a Crazy Idea?

Ever notice how people seem genuinely amazed whenever yet another vicious hate crime takes place, or when they hear about an increase in the number of openly racist organizations in the United States? Each time one of these "isolated incidents" like Jasper occurs, the teeth-gnashing begins and the tears flow anew, and the sense of confusion as to how anyone could become such a hateful racist in a nation like *ours* begins to set in.

But is it really that hard to understand? Is it that hard to imagine that young white people who look around and see police locking up people of color at disproportionate rates might conclude there was something wrong with these folks, something to be feared, and if feared then perhaps despised? Is it so difficult to believe that whites who hear politicians blame immigrants of color for "taking American jobs" or "squandering welfare dollars" might conclude that such persons were a threat to their own well-being? Is it that difficult to believe that someone taught from birth that America is a place where "anyone can make it if they try hard enough," but who looks around and sees that, in fact, not only have some not made it but that these unlucky souls happen to be disproportionately people of color might conclude that those on the bottom deserve to be there because they just didn't try hard enough, or didn't have the genetic endowment for success?

When police in Riverside, California, shoot Tyisha Miller in her car because, after they pounded on her window and woke her from a diabetic stupor, she reached for a gun to protect herself, what message is sent regarding the value of black life? And how does it differ from that of the Klan?

When police in Philadelphia shoot Dontae Dawson in his car because he raised his hand and they "thought he had a gun" (which he didn't), what message is sent about the value of black life? And how does it differ from that of White Aryan Resistance?

When New Jersey State Troopers pump eleven shots into a van occupied by four black and Latino students on their way to basketball tryouts, simply because the van, after being pulled over, started to slowly roll backward and they thought the young men were "trying to run them over," what message is sent about the value of black and brown life? And how is it different from that of the skinheads?

When a cop in Chicago shoots Carl Hardiman for refusing to drop his "weapon" (which turned out to be a cell phone); or when Brooklyn officers shoot fifteen-year-old Frankie Arzuega in the back of the head, kill him, and then don't report the incident for three days, at which time they're never disciplined; or when Anibal Carrasquillo is killed by yet another Brooklyn cop, shot in the back, for no identifiable reason; or when Aswon Watson is killed by still another of New York's finest, shot eighteen times sitting in a stolen car, unarmed, and the grand jury indicts no one; or when Aquan Salmon, age fourteen, is shot in the back by an officer in Hartford, after being chased for a crime he didn't commit, what message is sent about the value of the lives of people of color, and how does it differ from the message of neo-Nazi David Duke?

And lest anyone think these are isolated incidents, it should be noted there are over fifteen thousand cases of alleged police brutality on file with the Justice Department, languishing for lack of funds to investigate. Brutality complaints in New York City alone have risen by more than 60 percent since 1992, costing over $100 million in damage payouts to victims, and national studies have found that more than 80 percent of brutality victims are people of color, while the overwhelming majority of officers involved are white, and in three out of four cases where police kill someone, the person killed was unarmed.

But the message that people of color are different, dangerous, and need to be controlled is sent out by more than just local police. The criminal justice system from start to finish inculcates such a mindset. Even though African American and Latino crime rates have remained roughly steady for two decades, the numbers of persons of color incarcerated has tripled, thanks to intensified law enforcement in communities of color. The war on drugs, fought mostly in poor and person of color communities (despite the fact that whites are more than 70 percent of all drug users) has contributed dramatically to the growth of a prison-industrial-complex that is quickly sapping resources from education, job training, and other vital programs.

Nationwide, spending for job creation and training has fallen by more than half since the 1980s, while spending on "corrections" has exploded by 521 percent. In California, spending on higher education as a share of the state budget has fallen by more than 90 percent since 1980, while spending for prisons has mushroomed by nearly 800 percent. In New York, spending on prisons has increased by $761 million since 1988, during which time funding for the city and state university systems was slashed by $615 million. A decade ago, New York spent twice as much on higher education as it did on prisons. Now, the state spends almost $300 million more annually locking people (mostly of color) away than it does on higher education. Since 1980, the number of whites incarcerated for drug offenses increased by 103 percent, while the numbers of blacks incarcerated for drug offenses during this time grew by 1,311 percent, and the number of Latinos incarcerated on drug charges grew by over 1,600 percent.

What message does our society send when we allow (and even cause by a combination of policies) the kind of housing segregation, isolation, and poverty that confront all too many persons of color? When blacks who work full-time year-round are still three times as likely to be as poor as whites who do the same, and Latino/as working full-time year-round are still four times more likely to remain poor? When unemployment rates for persons of color remains in double digits and twice the white rate even in times of economic recovery? When whites with only a high school diploma are just as likely to have a job as an African American or Latino with a college degree? Why should we be surprised that at least some persons, witnessing the way the larger institutions of our society neglect (at best) and oppress (at worst) people of color, might reach the conclusions that they were superior, more deserving of opportunity and perhaps even life than those same persons?

Simply put, any nation that allows corporate polluters in communities of color to get away with fines only one-fifth the amount they would pay in white neighborhoods is going to have a hard time convincing me it's serious about cracking down on hate or racism of any kind. Any nation that thinks nothing of strip-mining uranium on American Indian land, thereby causing Navajo teens to develop reproductive organ cancer at seventeen times the national average, doesn't have much moral capital to expend lecturing Klansmen who burn down black churches. Any nation that funds education mostly through property taxes, thereby guaranteeing massive inequity between the schools and resources available in poor urban and rural areas relative to more affluent suburbs, deserves to be laughed at when it proclaims itself committed to fairness, tolerance, and equity.

In other words, even to the extent that we should concern ourselves with combating "hatred," or "intolerance," be it of the individual or organized type, it is still necessary to consider the ways in which such overt bigotry is instilled by the larger workings of the dominant culture, and by institutions run not by extremists, but by acceptable, respected, and mainstream Americans. This is the vital context to the politics of hatred which is rarely explored, let alone addressed by the organizations who proclaim themselves dedicated to an antiracist mission.

DECEMBER 2000

More of a Thud, Really:

Racism, Crash, *and the Perpetuation of White Denial*

I remember the first time I heard about the movie *Crash*. It was several months before the film's release, and my introduction to it came in the form of an e-mail, sent from a friend and professional colleague. Therein, my friend, a multicultural affairs coordinator at a small liberal arts college, asked rather excitedly if I had heard about this great new movie that dealt with racism. I had not, I told her, which admission of ignorance then prompted her to excitedly send along a link to the film's official prerelease website. She also mentioned that she was planning to use *Crash* as a teaching tool for her students on the issue of race, once it became available on DVD.

Though I was a bit skeptical, given the way in which Hollywood has traditionally tackled issues of race and racism, I immediately clicked on the link to find out more. The website was vague to the point of virtual irrelevance, with no real trailer and only a brief description of the plot. But the cast was impressive, and so I figured I would surely want to see the movie upon its release. Maybe this time a race film would really be different.

In retrospect, it seems telling that my friend and I, and many others to whom I spoke before the film hit theatres, had such high hopes for *Crash*. It says something about how desperate those of us in the antiracist and civil rights communities are for a tool that can assist our endeavors, especially if that tool is mass-marketed to the general public as opposed to being merely an educational documentary seen by far fewer. That my colleague, without having even seen the film, was already committing to using it as an antiracist teaching tool speaks to how badly we long for that perfect instrument that will get students and others to take seriously the problem of racism in this country. The statistics we offer haven't done it, the studies documenting the problem haven't done it, and the personal stories offered up by folks of color as to their experiences obviously haven't proved sufficient. So maybe, just maybe, this film could accomplish what heretofore we had been unable to, on our own.

Even before it won Best Picture at the 2006 Academy Awards, *Crash* was being screened at innumerable college campuses, often cosponsored by organizations dedicated to raising issues of racism, diversity, and multiculturalism, in the hopes that it might begin a productive dialogue on those subjects. Often these screenings were followed by extensive talk back sessions, where audience members could share their reflections on the movie, and their views about the touchy racial subject matter that was at the heart of its narrative. Everywhere I went during this period to give a speech or conduct a workshop on racism, I was asked the same thing: Had I seen *Crash* yet, and if so, what had I thought? At first, having been taken in by the film's artistry, I would answer that not only had I seen it but that indeed I thought it to be an excellent, even compelling narrative, which, though far from perfect, was a useful tool for beginning a conversation on race and racism. In fact, I went so far as to praise it, in almost glowing terms, in front of a large audience of actors, producers, cinematographers, and other Tinseltown types, during an event in Hollywood in early 2006.

Shortly thereafter, I watched the film for a second, third, and fourth time. And after each concurrent viewing, I felt a pit growing in my stomach. Each time, things started to jump out at me that I had oddly missed before. Now, after viewing *Crash* seven times, I have a much different appraisal of the film than I did at first blush. Though it is difficult to deny the artistic merit of the film—its cinematography, direction, editing, and acting are all spectacular throughout—its usefulness as an educational or consciousness-raising tool is considerably less clear. Indeed, for those of us trying to educate others about racism as a persistent social phenomenon, and to inspire others to join the larger struggle for racial equity and justice, it is quite possible that *Crash*, improperly used and viewed without a critical lens, may frustrate our efforts, rather than aid them.

To understand why this is so, it may help to recall that according to every public opinion survey of white Americans, dating back to the 1960s, racism isn't really a major social problem in need of being addressed. Even at the height of the civil rights movement, most whites, according to polls, thought people of color had fully equal opportunity. Today, only a very small percentage of whites say we believe that racial discrimination against persons of color is still a major issue. So what does it say that a movie about racism should become so popular and so critically acclaimed in a nation whose majority overwhelmingly refuses to acknowledge the significance of the very subject dealt with in that film? What does it say that against a backdrop of white denial as to the problem of racism, white moviegoers, white critics, and ultimately the disproportionately white Academy of Motion Picture Arts and Sciences should bestow such praise upon a film that deals with the very thing those whites, every other day, largely dismiss as a nonissue?

At the risk of sounding cynical, it seems safe to say that for a movie about racism to receive such a positive response from people who, in general, don't see racism as a particularly pressing concern, the film in question must tread quite lightly on white racial sensibilities. And so it does. *Crash*, for all of its strengths as art, largely reinforces various aspects of the dominant white racial narrative in this society. As such, it makes challenging racism more difficult. *Crash* reinforces the way in which most whites appear to understand the issue of racism, and this it does in a number of ways: first, by presenting racism as more or less an issue of individual bias and bigotry, rather than institutional or systemic inequality; secondly, by presenting racism as if it were an equal opportunity pathology to which all persons—white or of color—were equally likely to fall prey; and third, by playing into several white fears and insecurities about black crime and so-called reverse discrimination. Let us examine these one at a time.

Racism as an Individual, Rather than Institutional, Phenomenon

While most persons of color conceive of racism as an issue of structural injustice, whites often view it as nothing more than a personality flaw, present in only a small handful of especially damaged individuals, and hardly worth worrying about in the larger social sense. I first came to understand the difference between white, as opposed to black and brown, understandings of racism when I worked in the campaigns against neo-Nazi political candidate David Duke in the early 1990s. Even the white folks who opposed Duke and voted against him—sadly to say, a minority of whites in Louisiana at the time—largely viewed the problem to be Duke himself. If we could just derail *his* efforts to become a U.S. senator or governor of the state, then we'd done our job and all was right with the world. The notion that Duke was merely symbolic of a larger problem with white racism in the state and nation—and that indeed, his policy ideas (welfare cutbacks, ending affirmative action, immigration restrictions) were coming to be viewed as legitimate, and even implemented in one form or another around the nation as systemic realities—was clear to blacks in the state. But to whites, Duke wasn't symbolic of anything larger. *He* was the issue. The fact that persons of color were facing racism every day from police, the schools, and employers, among other sources, rarely and barely intruded into the consciousness of white Louisianans at the time.

More recently, with high-profile cases of individual bigotry surfacing, as in the examples of actor/comedian Michael Richards and radio personality Don Imus, the nation's awareness of individual-level racism has been raised yet again. But at the same time that these men's personal biases were made visible to anyone with a television, the media was almost entirely ignoring the persistent evidence of racism as an institutional phenomenon. So there was no coverage, nationally, of the report from the Department of Housing and Urban Development, to the effect that 2006 had witnessed the highest level of housing discrimination complaints in recorded history. Nor had there been any national coverage of, or outrage over, the 2004 study in a respected medical journal, which noted that between 1991 and 2000, there had been nearly one million African Americans who had died, who wouldn't have died had they merely had health care equal to that of their white counterparts. Though persons of color are painfully aware of these structural injustices, whites are largely oblivious, convinced that individual bad people are the problem to be solved: convenient, of course, since it allows those whites to avoid responsibility for our involvement in a system of inequality. So long as we don't toss around racial slurs or burn crosses, everything is presumed to be fine.

Crash plays to that individualistic understanding, by presenting racism in only its interpersonal, rather than institutional, forms. Racism plays out in the film as a personal problem between given individuals. Even when the racist Officer Ryan is portrayed (and devastatingly so by Matt Dillon), he is presented as a lone rogue cop (protected in his racism by a black lieutenant of all persons), but not as a symptom of a larger systemic problem. Surely for black and brown moviegoers in Los Angeles who went to see *Crash*, the idea that racism in the LAPD is merely a problem for a few individual bigots must seem fanciful. This, after all, is a department that is not only infamous for its participation in the Zoot Suit Riots in 1943, the brutality that touched off the Watts rebellion of 1965, and the Rodney King beating, but also various scandals involving the planting of evidence on suspects of color in the mid-'90s, and the defense of fatal chokeholds by then police chief Darryl Gates, who said the reason blacks tended to die more readily from this maneuver was because the arteries in their necks were defective and didn't open up to allow the proper flow of blood that would otherwise be evident in "normal" people.

By presenting racism as an individual malady, rather than a social issue of great import, *Crash* allows white viewers to default to our preexisting understanding of the issue, rather than having to deal with the way in which every structure of American society continues to treat people of color as inferiors, be it in housing, employment, education, or criminal justice. When characters in the film are the victims of racism, it is only the racism of a handful of "bad apples." So Officer Ryan (Dillon) sexually molests the wife of the black movie director (Terrence Howard) because *he* is a racist. And when his behavior is covered up by the black superior, it is because the latter seeks to make his job easier, not because the LAPD is, and has long been, a racist institution, infamous for this kind of behavior, and worse.

When Sandra Bullock's character (the wife of the district attorney, played by Brendan Fraser) lashes out about the Latino locksmith who has come to their house to change their lock, her assumptions of his likely gang membership are hers and hers alone. They are divorced from any larger narrative that virtually permeates Los Angeles at this point, regarding immigration and the way in which Chicanos have come to be viewed by the white majority. And even better, from the perspective of white viewers, not only is Bullock's prejudice symbolic of nothing larger but if anything, it's justified. After all, the precursor to the lock-changing scene, and Bullock's fear, is a carjacking at the hands of black criminals earlier that evening. So even when whites express racism, there's a reason for it, and one that much of the audience will likely view as rational, a subject to which we'll return shortly.

In keeping with the individualization of racism, *Crash* also manages to diminish the audience's understanding of racism as an institutionalized phenomenon, by way of its tendency to present the subject as almost a random matter, as if there were no systemic force behind it at all. The film's central metaphor of the automobile accident, repeated at both the beginning and ending of the movie, leaves viewers with the sense that racism and racial conflict, as with fender-benders, just happen, perhaps inevitably. And isn't that interesting? Well actually no, because that isn't how racial tension operates. It isn't random. The drivers, so to speak, on the racial highway have vastly unequal degrees of power, and some drive far more recklessly than others.

Racial conflict has emanated from a very particular history, which has been anything but random, whether in Los Angeles or anywhere else in the United States. Racial conflict in L.A. hasn't just happened, as if by accident. Particular patterns of oppression, including police brutality, the exploitation of immigrant labor, racist housing patterns that have kept people of color isolated from opportunities, and deindustrialization, have all conspired to produce the toxic mix of hostility and desperation that has so often played out in the city. So too with America more broadly: We are not randomly crashing into each other, as if by coincidence. We are not suspicious of one another by accident. The history of the United States has been one in which opportunities have been racially contingent, in which whites have been favored in every avenue of life, and people of color relegated to either de jure or de facto second-class citizenship. Against that backdrop, it is little surprise that whites and people of color would have, as the saying goes, beef with one another. That *Crash* gives us little in the way of insight as to that backdrop—and as such utterly decontextualizes the conflict that plays out for the audience in the movie theater viewing it—only reduces the likelihood that audience members will come to appreciate how deeply ingrained the damage of racism is.

The Ecumenism of Blame:
How Crash *Ignores the Special Power of Whiteness*

Crash further reinforces the white perspective on racial issues by seeking to present the problem as something of an equal opportunity offender. In other words, racism is something that infects us all: white, black, Latino, Asian, it doesn't matter. All are biased, and in roughly equal proportions. This ecumenism of blame comports nicely with the mainstream white perspective on racism, which holds that racism is a problem of individuals, and that people of color are just as racist, perhaps more so, than whites. In an era of backlash against rather minor affirmative action efforts, and at a time when whites can become hysterical over the comment by New Orleans mayor Ray Nagin to the effect that New Orleans, post-Katrina, would remain a "chocolate city" (because to them, such verbiage was racist against whites, as the vanilla), it is clear that whites are quick to feel victimized. *Crash* does nothing to alleviate that mentality, and in several ways, feeds it.

In the film, virtually every character, regardless of race or ethnicity, displays racial and ethnic biases. Likewise, most all are at some point the target of racial stereotypes. How does this egalitarian portrayal, which implies that racism infects us all and injures us all, fit with the reality of racism in the United States, or even Los Angeles? Has racism in the United States been an "equal opportunity" infection, in the sense that all persons have been equally likely to act on the basis of it, or equally likely to be its target?

The answer of course is that racism has not been an equal opportunity infector. Although it is likely true that prejudice resides in all groups to similar degrees, racism, by definition as a word ending with the letters "ism," is more than prejudice. Racism, as with all "isms," is a system (think capitalism, socialism, communism, fascism, etc.). So to suggest that racism is a problem for all groups in roughly equal degrees is to paper over the fact that not all groups have had, or have now, anywhere near the equal ability to put their prejudices into action, via systemic policy. Blacks, for example, cannot racially profile whites, or deny housing or jobs to whites in the way that whites can do these things to blacks, because blacks are rarely in positions of power sufficient to allow for that kind of imposition. But by individualizing racism, as discussed previously, and then "equivalizing" it as well, *Crash* makes it difficult to see the power differentials and the way that these differentials determine who the real victims of racism are likely to be at any given time. *Crash* allows us to see the problem as racism, writ generically, as opposed to white supremacy, operationalized specifically.

Even when the viewer might have gotten the message that the racism of white folks, in the end, does have more power behind it—say, after seeing the police officer played by Ryan Philippe kill Lorenz Tate's character because the former jumped to conclusions as to the danger the latter posed—the film manages to bring us back to the ecumenical narrative of the previous two hours. In the closing scene of the movie, in fact, *Crash* sends us out with a brief but strangely important throwaway line, by office manager Shaniqua Johnson (Loretta Devine), who yells at an Asian driver with whom she's had a car accident that unless the driver speaks "American," she doesn't want to hear any excuses for the fender bender. So see, the audience can think to themselves, Shaniqua's a racist too. *Whew!* Thank goodness.

Without understanding the role that power plays in the dispensing of racist discrimination, audiences (and especially whites for whom the power-averse analysis is already the default position) can leave a film like *Crash* no more enlightened as to the way racism really operates than they were when they walked in. Although the film can inspire many good conversations on the subject of personal prejudices and stereotypes—and perhaps a good dialogue facilitator could link those to the issues of power and systemic oppression—in and of itself, *Crash* is unlikely to help viewers make sense of the racial drama playing out every day in the United States with regard to immigration, profiling, job discrimination, or housing.

By presenting racism as an equal opportunity infector, *Crash* further validates color-blind formalism as the best solution for racism and racial tension. If we could just stop seeing each other as racialized beings, it seems to say, everything would be better. Noticing race can come to no good, at least if one accepts the metanarrative offered in *Crash*, for inevitably, noticing another's color will result in bigoted stereotyping and likely discrimination. But what does such a narrative mean for efforts to remedy discrimination in housing, employment, or education? After all, programs that seek to undo the effects of racial bias, or ensure that bias is rooted out in the present, all require that we consider race and think about it, by making deliberate efforts at inclusion, for example, or by conducting race-conscious and deliberate recruitment of persons of color for certain jobs or educational opportunities on which they otherwise would miss out. Color blindness, as scholars like Eduardo Bonilla-Silva have noted, has become the new mechanism for the perpetuation of glaring racial inequities, for it leaves in place the status quo of white racial advantage cemented over generations, and which legacy can only be uprooted by efforts that take account of race in fashioning social remedies. So by ignoring power, and making racism about personal biases shared by all, *Crash* encourages radical color blindness as the answer, whether or not that is the intent of its creators.

Reinforcing White Fear: How Crash *Actually Feeds Racial Resentment*

But even worse, there are actually parts of the film that may increase, rather than alleviate, white racism. Part of the dominant white racial narrative for years has been the notion of "reverse discrimination," whether from affirmative action programs, multicultural education efforts, or diversity policies at companies. Whites, according to the available evidence, are far more likely to believe that reverse discrimination against us is a problem than we are to believe that discrimination against people of color still is.

So against this background noise about white victimhood, what does *Crash* give us? It presents us with a narrative that feeds that noise directly, allowing it to grow even louder, and virtually unchallenged. Indeed, there is only one scene in *Crash* that deals directly with the subject of systemic racism at all, and in so doing, reinforces the idea that race-conscious efforts like affirmative action are misguided and unfair forms of reverse discrimination against more-deserving whites. So we have Dillon's Officer Ryan verbally lashing out at the insurance company office manager (Devine's Shaniqua Johnson), implying that she only had her job because of affirmative action, and that there was likely a "more qualified white male" passed over on her behalf. He then insists that his father "lost everything" when the city was forced to give preference to minority contractors, and he could no longer operate his previously successful waste disposal business. How does this narrative, devoid of any response (other than Johnson throwing Ryan out of her office), allow, or even encourage white viewers to remain hostile to affirmative action efforts, and to blacks more generally? There is no counterpoint to Ryan's anti-affirmative-action tirade. So viewers are left with the sense that although Ryan may be a bigot and have serious anger management issues, as for that whole quota thing, hey, he was right! Much as *American History X*—another film about racism, from several years ago, starring Edward Norton—allowed the anti-immigrant, anti-affirmative-action soliloquies of Norton's skinhead character to go unchallenged (even as his violence was clearly condemned), so too does *Crash* allow the viewer to remain convinced of the unfairness of the racial status quo for whites, thanks to affirmative action. The fact that roughly 94 percent of government contracts go to white-male-owned businesses—so that the story Ryan tells Johnson is utterly contradicted by the way affirmative action actually operates—is irrelevant, one supposes. The white belief in reverse discrimination is allowed to trump the social fact of white privilege.

And of course, in one of the early scenes in the movie, yet another white fear is validated, when the two young black men played by Tate and Ludacris carjack the DA (Fraser) and his wife (Bullock). And this right after Bullock's character had been talking about the likelihood of being victimized by such persons. Not only that, but when the two men discuss their crimes later,

Ludacris's character justifies his crime spree by noting that he only robs whites, almost as a political act! So now whites have had their fear of black men (however loquacious and hyperliterate they may be between holdups) reinforced, and are left to wonder if perhaps blacks really are targeting us as some form of payback for hundreds of years of oppression. That this is hardly a significant or common motivation for black crime in the real world matters not: To the creators of *Crash* it becomes the principal stimulus for black criminality.

Fact is, data in the real world suggests that although whites think we are likely to be the victims of black crime, few of us will be, and less than 1 percent of blacks will violently victimize a white person in a given year. But *Crash*'s portrayal of black-on-white crime reinforces white fear of black males, and thus may well undermine efforts to eradicate racism, and especially racial inequality in the justice system.

Conclusion: Bringing Context to Crash *Is the Only Way to Redeem It*

In closing, none of what I have said should be seen as invalidating the use of *Crash* as one tool among many for getting people to think about and discuss racism. But unless such dialogues are facilitated, and specifically by trained and skilled facilitators who can bring to light the various shortcomings of the movie, I fear its use would do more harm than good. Discussed with the above caveats, *Crash* might actually provoke a productive exchange, and prove to be enlightening. But without an analytical frame that discusses systems, rather than merely individuals, and power, rather than merely bias, and challenges the film's dominant white gaze, audience members will likely experience the film as nothing more than a fine piece of art, which ultimately leaves in place many of their preconceived notions on the subject.

The lesson for those of us involved in antiracism work is clear: We cannot wait for others, especially Hollywood moviemakers, to produce the tools we'll be using as we go about our work.

Hollywood is in the business of making money. And so long as this culture is one in which the dominant majority sees racism as a minor problem at best, any film that really seeks to challenge that perspective will likely flop. It surely won't win a Best Picture Oscar. So let us move forward, prepared to challenge *Crash* and all other films like it, and insist on a more in-depth reading of the movie. Only by doing our jobs better can we tease out the positives in this kind of art, while making sure all are aware of the negatives.

MAY 2007

RATIONALIZATION

Rationalizing the Irrational:

Racism and the Fallacy of Personal Experience

To paraphrase a line from the movie *Forrest Gump* (which film I never liked much, actually) "E-mail is like a box of chocolates. You never know what you're gonna get." And here, I'm referring not so much to the bevy of ads for porn or weight loss remedies that seem to sneak through whatever spam filter I supposedly have on my browser. Rather, I mean the daily torrent of hate mail, sent my way by folks who feel the burning desire to tell me not only of their disagreements with my antiracist views, but also to inform me of how badly I need to die, or to invite me to perform various sexual acts upon myself which I feel fairly certain are impossible.

Occasionally the message-writers feign a bit more substantive critique, supplementing their slurs with semicoherent rationalizations for their racist views. Among these, in recent weeks, have been the following:

> If you'd ever lived around black people or Mexicans you wouldn't think the way you do. You'd see how trashy they were, and how loud. You'd see the drug-dealing and the crime up close, and once you'd been attacked by one of them, the way I have, you'd change your tune.

Or this, from someone who said we should "wall off" inner city communities from the places where "decent people" live:

If you think minorities are so great, why don't you go walk through the ghetto and see how long you last?

Or this, from someone who said he hated all blacks and would "gladly pay for the tickets for all niggers and mescans [*sic*]" to go back where they came from:

I own rental properties ... this is what caused me to become so mad. I got checks from the government for almost all my tenants but received no thanks, no courtesy, just racial slurrs [sp] when I was late to have the yard mowed or wouldn't change a light bulb.

I wish I could say that these were the only such messages I'd ever received, but sadly, they are not. I could fill a book with these kinds of notes, sent to me by folks who have read one or another of my articles, or perhaps come to one of my speeches, and then felt compelled to chime in about how naive I am to advocate for racial equity, or to criticize racial stereotyping. After all, their personal experiences have demonstrated to their satisfaction that those stereotypes are justified, and that racial bias is a normal and natural reaction to those experiences. Presumably, they insist, I've just been lucky to avoid getting mugged by a person of color (probably because I've lived in a sheltered, suburban environment all my life, they typically speculate—wrongly of course), but if *I'd* seen what *they'd* seen, I would change my views.

Yet, as it turns out, to generalize about entire groups of people based upon one's personal (and by definition limited) experiences with persons from those groups is illegitimate on several levels.

Personal Experiences and the Problem of Selective Memory

First, those who rationalize their racism on the basis of their personal experiences with members of the group they dislike are being highly selective when it comes to the experiences from which they think we should draw conclusions. After all, if their negative experiences with blacks "prove" that blacks are bad people, then by definition, anyone who had had good experiences with black people would be able to say that all blacks are good people: an argument every bit as silly, but just as logical, given the original line of reasoning.

Or, if having been violently victimized in a black neighborhood by a black person proves that black people are dangerous, I could reply that since I have never been victimized by a black person in a black neighborhood—even when I worked in nearly all-black public housing projects, or lived in a neighborhood that was 70 percent African American—that blacks are therefore guaranteed to be no threat to me, ever. In fact, since I *have* been the victim of black criminals, but only in neighborhoods that were mostly white and fairly affluent, following the rationale of those who think personal experience is all that matters, I could argue, incorrectly of course, that poor black neighborhoods are the safest ones around, and that people should avoid affluent white areas at all costs.

Second, to draw conclusions about large groups (in the case of black folks, some thirty-six million people, and for Latinos, another thirty-seven million or so in the United States) based on one's experiences with a handful of people from those groups is the very definition of statistical illiteracy. Even if you had encountered dozens of folks from a particular group who, for whatever reason, had rubbed you the wrong way, this would be such a small and obviously unrepresentative sample that to reach any conclusions about that group as a whole would be absurd. This is among the reasons that it's nonsensical to harbor generalized dislike or suspicion of Muslims *as* Muslims, or Arabs *as* Arabs, in the wake of 9/11. After all, nineteen such persons out of 1.5 billion Muslims on planet Earth and hundreds of millions of Arabs is the walking, talking definition of an unrepresentative sample. Not to mention, we never reach generalized conclusions about whites when we engage in acts of terrorism, and indeed, did not in the wake of Oklahoma City, or the crimes of the Unabomber, or the Olympic Park Bomber, or any of the dozens of abortion clinic bombings or arsons over the past two decades, all of which were committed by whites, so far as we can tell.

Which points up the biggest flaw in the thinking of racist whites who call upon their personal experiences with people of color to justify their bigotry: namely, how many bad experiences with other whites are such folks forgetting, which didn't lead them to generalize about white folks as a group? Studies have found that we tend to remember stereotype-confirming behavior in those who are considered different, while ignoring the many times members of our own group did the same things, because in the latter instance, such behavior doesn't trigger a preexisting mental schema, or set of beliefs, that can be applied to explain the behavior. So whites can do all the same things as blacks, but still be viewed as individuals, while blacks who do anything negative are viewed through a racial group lens. Social conditioning is critical here: By training our minds to not only see differences—which they would see anyway and categorize, as a matter of evolutionary psychology—but also to attach dualistic value judgments to those categories in terms of better/worse, superior/inferior, etc., the culture in which we live has led us away from the ability to think critically about these kinds of things.

After all, how many whites who say they fear blacks—perhaps because of a fight they got in at school with someone who was black—also have gotten in fights with other whites? Or worse: How many of these folks have been physically or even sexually assaulted by a member of their own white family? In other words, how many white folks who claim their dislike of blacks is justified because of a handful of negative experiences with African

Americans have had years of bad experiences with other whites, but in none of those cases drew an inference about whites as a group?[1]

Think about it: The landlord who ripped us off and refused to give us back our deposit was probably white. The boss who fired us or regularly gave us a hard time was probably white. The girlfriends or boyfriends who dumped us were probably white. White people probably ran the companies that made the shitty products we bought over the years. The service technicians who worked on our air-conditioning, or our cars, or our plumbing, and never could quite seem to fix things, but always charged us plenty for their time? Mostly white. The politicians who lied to us were almost all white. The teachers who scared us, talked down to us, and tried to control our every move in school were probably white. In my case, most everyone who ever did anything to hurt me was white, but I would never think of holding that fact against whites as whites, because their whiteness had nothing to do with it.

Oh, and returning now to my electronic detractor's accusations, that I only believe what I do because I've never really been around people of color, nothing could be further from the truth. The fact is, I have lived in neighborhoods that were mostly black and mostly Latino (in New Orleans and Houston respectively), and the loudest and most obnoxious people on the block were always white, often college students, who could count on their behavior not being held against their entire racial group. Just this summer, my family and I moved from a neighborhood where the folks of color engaged in such mundane activities as mowing their lawns twice a week to keep them looking nice, but where white drug dealers kept us constantly guessing when police cars were going to roll up and raid their house, or when one of their inevitably white customers was going to break into our house looking for cash to spend across the street (they tried three times, actually). The dealers were brothers (how sweet), named Justin and Dustin (no,

I'm not making this up), who counted among their best clients a suburban soccer mom who would come all the way into the city to buy her OxyContin (or to trade sex for it, more often than not) after dropping her kids off at one of the area's elite private schools. So by the logic of the folks who write to me, I should therefore assume that white neighbors are all pill pushers, and that rich SUV-driving mothers of students at the Ensworth School are all Oxy-heads. Seems fair, no? No, of course not, but precisely where the illogic of racists leads us.

And I have been threatened and/or victimized by black folks before. A black guy stuck a gun in my face when I was a sophomore in college, in Uptown, New Orleans, and a few years later, I had another gun pointed at me from across the street, also by a black guy, whom I had just witnessed trying to murder someone. Why he ran off and didn't actually shoot at me (and at the woman I was dating at the time, whose car I was in), I'll never know. And although I won't deny my own internalized racist views, which occasionally have caused me to respond to a person of color fearfully—a subject about which I have written extensively before—I make a point of trying to recognize the ultimate irrationality of those moments. After all, I have also been victimized by whites, including the two guys who broke into my apartment my senior year and stole everything they could grab. And I was once shot at by a white guy in a car who was leaning out the window, shooting at people for the hell of it. And then there were the three guys who broke into my wife's car several years ago, who according to the police were a veritable rainbow coalition of criminals: one black, one white, and one Latino. The point being, if I were to use these personal experiences to justify generalized racial prejudices, I would have to be afraid of pretty much everyone except Asians. So, based on the logic of the racists who write to me, I should move to the nearest Chinatown as quickly as possible, lest I be victimized again by some predatory white, black, or Latino thug.

...And No, Data Doesn't Strengthen the Argument Either

It is typically at this point that unapologetic racists shift gears, noting that their beliefs are not solely the result of personal experiences, but rather are also rooted in an appreciation of crime statistics indicating that black folks commit a disproportionate share of violent crime, relative to their percentage of the population. While this is true (because of the high correlation between concentrated poverty and crowded urban conditions on the one hand, and crime on the other), it still doesn't mean that fearing black people as a group makes sense. After all, with 30.1 million African Americans over the age of twelve in the United States (and thus, eligible for consideration in crime data), if blacks commit a million violent crimes a year (the rough total for the most recent year on record), this means that even if we assumed each crime had a unique perpetrator (in other words, if there were no multiple offenders—obviously not the case), the maximum percentage of blacks who were violent criminals, as a share of all blacks, would be 3.3 percent. Meaning that at least 96.7 percent will not commit a violent crime this year, let alone against a white person, let alone against a white stranger, let alone against us.

So, if the 3 percent of blacks who will commit a violent crime in a given year somehow prove that blacks are dangerous and to be avoided, then why don't the 97 percent who *won't* commit such a crime equally prove that blacks are nonviolent and perfectly safe to be around? After all, why should the acts of a maximum of a million people be seen as a better indicator of what the group is like than the non-acts of the other twenty-nine million or so?

And of course, if we are to take statistics such as these to indicate a group's dangerousness, then whites should have intense bias against other whites. After all, we are five times more likely to be victimized violently by another white person than by a black person, according to Justice Department data, and each year, far more people are killed by occupational diseases and injuries resulting from inadequate safety and health standards in white-owned corporations than are killed in street-level homicides, let alone those committed by blacks. Yet rarely do whites seek to avoid other whites because of our documented predisposition to corporate fraud and misconduct (think Enron; think the S&L swindle; think Bhopal, India).

Pit Bulls, Poodles, and Pitifully Weak Analogies

Oh, and I know the response that will be coming here, from those seeking to hold on to their well-nurtured bigotry. It's always the same. It's the one about the different dog breeds. The one that goes like this: "If we know that certain breeds of dogs are more likely to bite than other breeds, doesn't it make sense to avoid the more dangerous breeds, and to be more fearful of them than others?"

Putting aside the biological and genetic fallacy of comparing dog breed differences to the differences between whites and African Americans (given that pit bulls are typically far larger than poodles, and that the former were also bred for behavioral and temperament differences over many centuries, unlike people of different "races"), there are several other flaws in the dog breed analogy.

To understand why, let's take an extreme example: Consider a person who had actually been bitten by a particular kind of dog. In other words, let's consider someone who was not only aware in a vague sense that certain breeds might be more dangerous than others, but someone who had actually experienced that danger up close, by having been bitten. Would it be rational for that person, after that point, to fear any and all other dogs that were members of that same breed? While we may certainly expect such fear to manifest in the person who had been bitten, the fact that something is predictable doesn't make it rational, if by rational we mean rooted in a logical assessment of actual risk. What would be rational would be to fear other dogs like the one who bit us if those others were behaving in the way the biter had been prior to the attack, giving off the same kinds of signs that they were agitated, for example.

And this points to the fundamental reason why we might naturally recoil from a particular kind of dog, or other animal, but still shouldn't do the same with regard to other people. The reason we respond fearfully to an animal of a different species when one of its kind has attacked us is because we are responding in large measure to our fear of the unknown. We don't know how to read dog behavior, instinctively, the way we can read the behavior of other people. We are socialized among other humans whose body language, facial expressions, and verbalizations give off clues as to when they are dangerous or unstable, or some such thing. Although nonhumans no doubt give off similar signals, most of us are not trained to read them, so we are naturally skittish, in ways that it would make no sense to be with regard to others of our same species. To view others of our human family as if they were as species-foreign to us as a hyena makes no sense whatsoever. Dogs that bite almost always do so because they were agitated. Avoiding agitated dogs makes sense, as does avoiding agitated people. But avoiding people who are black irrespective of their level of agitation is nonsensical.

Additionally, we wouldn't respond with this kind of generalized hysteria to children, if a child bit us. Occasionally kids do bite of course—they bite other kids; they bite teachers or child-care workers; they even bite their parents—and yet we don't tend to respond to this fact by saying "Well, that's it, I'm getting rid of my kid," or "quitting my job at this school," or "sequestering myself in my home, never to play with a child again!" If we can see that individual behavior says nothing about the group from which the individuals come, in this case, why not see the same truth with regard to race?

Not to mention, while it may be true that pit bulls as a breed are more dangerous than poodles (the most common comparison made by those who really want to make their case), to analogize pit bulls to blacks and poodles to whites is ludicrous. Whites commit nearly three million violent crimes a year, which is far more than are committed by blacks (even though the per capita crime rate is higher in the latter case). Needless to say, that is hardly poodlelike behavior. And since whites are five times more likely to be attacked by another white person than a black person, the only way the dog analogy holds is if we are also five times more likely to be bitten by a poodle than a pit bull. And if that is the case, then why should we be sweating pit bulls? It would make more sense, at that point, to get the hell away from poodles. And if you wanted to reduce the net number of dog bites each year, given the raw numbers, you'd euthanize the poodles, or separate them from polite society, rather than taking out your frustration on the pit bulls, who may indeed have higher bite rates, but who compose a relatively small share of overall bites or attacks. (Note: No actual poodles were harmed during the writing of this sentence.)

Understanding the Difference Between Logic and Rationality

So why do people seek to rationalize their biases, either with reference to limited personal experiences or by appealing to ostensibly objective data? Are those who do this simply bad people, or perhaps unstable? While it might be easy and comforting to classify racists in this fashion, doing so would be not only unfair—after all, none of us can be free from racist conditioning and thoughts in a society that has studiously inculcated the same in its people for generations—but also flatly inaccurate. Despite the ultimate irrationality of racist thinking, such thoughts are far from illogical. Though it may seem counterintuitive to suggest that something can be both logical and irrational at the same time, there is nothing particularly radical about the suggestion. Racist beliefs, like any other set of beliefs, have their own internal logic, and make perfect sense, given certain realities and conditions to which persons in a social order are subjected. Exploring the conditions that make racism "logical," even if ultimately irrational in a larger cosmic sense, is a critical step in the process of figuring out how to dismantle racism, whether at the individual and personal level or the systemic and institutional level.

To understand why people may, quite logically, come to develop biases toward others, and even act out in a racist fashion against them, consider the example of Irish immigrants to the United States. At the time of the most intense Irish immigration to America (the mid to late 1800s), the Irish had had almost no experience with blacks, so they would not have had an opportunity to develop antiblack biases rooted in firsthand negative experiences. Yet, they had had considerable experience with the English, most all of which had been negative: centuries of overt oppression, virtual enslavement, and state terror imposed upon the Irish by Anglos.

Given that history, and applying the kind of thinking that says personal experience can justify prejudices, it would have made sense for Irish immigrants to the United States to detest and fight against the Anglo elite. It would have made sense for them to join the fight against slavery—indeed, they were implored to do so by their religious leaders in the mother country—because they had been the "slaves of the British" for generations. But in fact, after a very short time in the states, Irish immigrants were rioting against blacks (as with the New York draft riots during the Civil War), joining in the barring of blacks from labor unions, and seeking to "become white" by assimilating to the WASP system that was firmly in place. However irrational this racial bonding might have been in the long run—after all, it divided the Irish working class from the black working class, when both would have been better off joining together to push for more opportunities for all—it was hardly illogical: The Irish recognized the status differences between those who were white and those who were not, and, desiring to be closer to the top than the bottom, swallowed their pride, joined the club of whiteness, and collaborated with the oppression of black folks.

So engaging in racist behavior and rationalizing one's racist thoughts makes perfect sense from the perspective of people hoping to improve their status, relative to a despised "other." Likewise, for whites who have accumulated various advantages and privileges, racism (and the rationalization of the same) becomes a mechanism by which those advantages can be justified, and viewed as earned, as opposed to being the outcome of an unfair process of unequal opportunity. Not to mention, the rationalization of racism becomes a means to maintain those advantages and privileges, and to protect them from being "taken." After all, civil rights protections force more equal opportunity and fairer competitions, both of which, by definition, reduce the hegemony of white dominance and force whites, for the first time, to compete openly for things they would have simply been given before. If persons of color can be denigrated, however, and made to shoulder the blame for their economic condition and status in society, the pressure to equalize opportunity is lessened, and white privilege is maintained. So the logic of racism, in a profoundly unequal society, is nearly unassailable, at least at first blush.

Conclusion: The Danger of Rationalizing Racism

But however logical it may be to harbor and rationalize racist views, and to defend racism in practice, in the long run, doing so is detrimental and counterproductive, even to those whites who, in the short run, reap the benefits. After all, when folks start believing that a certain group is the dangerous one, to be avoided or repressed in some way, they are likely to let down their guards to the dangers posed by others—dangers that might, for them in fact, be greater than those about which they are hyperalert.

So when white middle class families take up residence in Littleton, Colorado, or Santee, California, or any of a dozen or so other "nice, safe" places to live and raise kids, and in the process pat themselves on the back for having gotten away from the city, they let their guard down to the emotionally disturbed young white men in their midst: boys who are plotting to blow up the school, or mow down everyone with a heartbeat, or some such thing. They let down their guard to the even more dangerous middle-aged, middle-class white men, who, upon losing their jobs or watching their stocks take a tumble, then tweak out and kill their whole family, not to mention coworkers. And then when the shit hits the fan, they're the first ones on TV, wide-eyed with amazement at the realization that white people from families with money can actually manage to kill. Imagine: murder from a people who can count among their number Columbus, Andrew Jackson, Hitler, and Stalin, just to name a few. Speaking of which, I guess according to racist logic, these men indicate ironclad confirmation that whites are mass murderers and genocidal maniacs.

Unless we begin to think critically about the way we respond to our personal experiences, in large measure due to socially ingrained biases, we'll continue to seek explanations and justifications for beliefs that are not only unjustified and irrational, but ultimately harmful, and which put us in greater danger.

In this regard, we must come to see racism (and for that matter all other forms of bias) as not merely issues of ethical concern, though they are surely that, but also practical matters of safety and personal well-being. To hold socially defined and categorized groups of people up to scorn or derision, or to fear them en masse on the basis of limited personal experience or horribly misinterpreted and misunderstood data, is to put not only those "others" at risk for mistreatment but ourselves at risk as well: at risk of failing to see the dangers posed by nonstereotypical threats, while we stay on guard against the dangerous "other." It means worrying about Islamic hijackers, but not so-called Christian warriors seeking to impose their version of faith upon unbelievers by blowing up clinics or government buildings. It means worrying about carjackers, but not drunk drivers (85 percent of whom are white, by the way, according to the FBI), who kill and maim far more white people each year than all the black and brown street thugs combined. It means worrying about being killed by a gang member, but ignoring the risk of death or injury from corporations cutting corners on workplace safety or product quality, or from hospitals and doctors engaging in unnecessary medical procedures and botching them terribly. Or from secondhand smoke, or air and water pollution, neither of which risk has been contributed to mostly by folks of color.

In this regard, racism should be seen as a toxin, the first victims of which are folks of color, to be sure, but which then claims as collateral damage millions of whites as well. It does this by initially sapping the critical thinking abilities of the latter, and then by exposing us to the consequences of our own sloppy mental processing. Hopefully, we will come to our senses, before too much more damage is done. But if my e-mail browser is any indication, that hope may be more wishful thinking than anything else.

JULY 2006

---

1 This also plays out with regard to child sexual molestation and hetero/ homosexuality. Even though the vast majority of persons who have been molested were molested by persons whose adult sexual orientation was/is clearly heterosexual, it is homosexuals, especially gay men, who are labeled as particularly deviant with regard to pedophilic urges. Not to mention, if a person's dislike of gay men is to be justified on the basis of having been molested by a man who happens to be gay, does that mean that persons who were molested by straight men should now dislike all straight men, or fear them all, or disallow their own child, if they have one, to be around straight men? And would such a bias be fair or justified? My guess is that very few homophobes and heterosexists would say yes to the latter scenario.

Working for the Man Every Night and Day:

Black Conservatives and the Politics of Self-Abuse

A few weeks ago, a young man approached me after a speech and handed me a small piece of paper. On it, he said, was the name of a book he thought I should read. Given that the student and I had previously gotten into a bit of a row over the issue of racial profiling, I didn't have high expectations as for what I would find scribbled on his note to me. And it's a good thing, for there I discovered the name of a book by black conservative Larry Elder, whose only real claim to fame is that he does a bad imitation of Judge Wapner on a pedantic little courtroom reality show called *Moral Court*. Oh, and that white folks like the student in question really like him. Which, as it turns out, is all it takes to become a best-selling author in this country.

Elder, like Shelby Steele, and Walter Williams before that, and Ken Hamblin before that, and Thomas Sowell before him, and Clarence Thomas always, says the kinds of things that most white folks love to hear: essentially that blacks are the source of their own problems in life. Black cultural pathology and bad behavior, according to these types, explain everything from black poverty rates to the gaps between blacks and whites in income, wealth, and incarceration figures. Racism? What racism? To the Larry Elders of the world, and the whites who have made them stars entirely out of proportion to their scholarly credentials (or decided lack thereof), racism is just an excuse black people use to explain away their own internal shortcomings.

Two of the most popular arguments from black conservatives and the white people who love them are that blacks spend too much on luxury items they can't afford and refuse to save money the way responsible white folks do and that blacks place little value on education, preferring to critique learning as selling out, or "acting white," and thereby sabotage their own achievement. That the evidence for both of these positions is painfully thin makes little difference, it appears. After all, when one is saying what the man wants to hear, the man requires no footnotes or actual corroboration.

Taking these one at a time, first comes a recent article in *USA Today* by Yolanda Young, whose forthcoming book, *SPADE: A Critical Look at Black America*, will serve as the latest installment in an emerging cottage industry of pseudoprose, issued by African Americans intent on soothing white consciences about racism and reassuring us that blacks are their own worst enemies. In her *USA Today* piece, Young claims that blacks have been spending exorbitant amounts of money despite the tough economic times in which the larger black community finds itself. In other words, instead of "belt tightening," African Americans have been on a spending spree: the implication being that black folks are "motivated by a desire for instant gratification and social acceptance" and care more about their own selfish desires than "our future." To back up her claims, Young turns to Target Market, a company that tracks spending by black consumers. But a careful glance at the source of her claims makes it apparent either that she is incapable of interpreting basic data or that she deliberately deceives for political effect. In fact, not only do the figures from Target Market not suggest irresponsible spending by blacks in the face of a bad economy, they tend to suggest the opposite.

According to Young, blacks spent nearly $23 billion on clothes in 2002, and this, one presumes, is supposed to signal a level of irresponsible profligacy so obvious as to require no further context or clarification. That such spending occurred in an economic downturn, according to Young, is especially disturbing. But in fact, the very tables on which Young bases her position indicate that from 2000–2002 (the period of a slowing economy), black expenditures on clothes fell by 7 percent, even before accounting for inflation. In other words, as the economy got worse, blacks reined in their consumption.

Young also chastises blacks for spending $11.6 billion on furniture in 2002, especially since many of the homes into which these furnishings were placed "were rented." Aside from the bizarre non sequitur here (after all, even renters need furniture, and its not as if black folks merely choose to rent, having foresworn home ownership due to their own laziness), the larger problem with Young's point is that it is brazenly dishonest. For example, during the period of economic slowdown, black spending on furniture fell 10 percent, even before inflation, and by 2002 was only a little higher in current dollars than it had been in 1996. In other words, blacks did exactly what would make sense in a tightening economy: They spent less on the kinds of presumably "frivolous" items that Ms. Young claims her people just can't resist. Not so irresponsible after all, it seems.

Next, Young berates blacks for their consumption of cars and liquor, which she labels "our favorite purchases." Unfortunately, the evidence she marshals to support such silliness is embarrassingly weak. She notes that although blacks make up only 12 percent of the population, they account for 30 percent of the nation's Scotch consumption. But what does that prove? It certainly says nothing about overall use of alcohol by blacks, which actually is quite low. Indeed, contrary to Young's claim, liquor is not among the favorite purchases of blacks, ranking instead behind eighteen of the twenty-five categories listed in the tables from *Target Market News* that she relied upon for her article. In fact, in just the past year black expenditures on alcoholic beverages fell by almost one-fourth, Scotch consumption or no. And of course, blacks spend far less than whites, per capita, on alcohol, and drink far less often and less heavily than whites according to all the available data from the Centers for Disease Control, National Institutes on Drug Abuse, and others. Indeed, African Americans spend less than half as much as whites per capita on booze each year, and 47 percent less on whiskey. In other words, if blacks are polishing off Dewar's like it's going out of style, white folks are doing more than our fair share when it comes to downing the Jack Daniels.

As for cars, Young's proof of black profligacy is limited to the fact that Lincoln had P Diddy design a limited edition Navigator for them, with DVD players and plasma screens all around. And yet, the amount spent by African Americans (not P Diddy, mind you, but the other thirty-five million or so black folks) on various vehicles, still amounts to less than that spent, per capita, by whites, whose consumption of such items is roughly 30 percent above that of blacks. Oh, and it should also be pointed out that sales for the Diddy Navigator were fewer than two dozen, so apparently black folks are fully capable of thinking for themselves (surprise, surprise) and don't merely go out and buy a product because it's endorsed by a famous rapper after all.

Likewise, Young tweaks blacks for spending $3.2 billion on consumer electronics, but fails to note that even before inflation, this is down roughly 16 percent from 2000, when blacks spent $3.8 billion on the same. Once again, as the economy slowed, so did black spending on these items, indicating that black consumers are every bit as rational as anyone else, and no more spendthrifty.

Young then attempts to skewer black America for cutting back on expenditures for books. Indeed, she claims that book purchases are "the only area where blacks seem to be cutting back on spending," having purchased $53 million less in books in 2002 than they had spent two years earlier. But once again, this claim is dishonest in the extreme. As noted before, books are not the only area where black consumption fell during this period. Instead, it fell in ten of the twenty-five categories listed by Target Market from 2000–2002. More to the point, while black book purchases did indeed drop from 2000–2002, this decline took place between 2000–2001 (a year in which book purchases fell nationwide and among all demographic groups), after which point book spending by blacks began to rise again despite the slowing economy, and grew by 3 percent between '01 and '02.

Next, Young insists that blacks fail to save money the way whites do, the implication being that this, and not racism and unequal access to capital, explains the wealth gap between whites and African Americans. As with her previous inaccuracies, however, she once again mangles the data. Young cites the 2003 *Black Investor Survey* from Ariel Mutual Funds and Charles Schwab, to suggest that black households with comparable upper middle class income to whites save nearly 20 percent less than whites for retirement. Furthermore, she claims that blacks are far less likely to invest in the stock market, thereby hindering their own ability to develop wealth. Yet a look at the Ariel/Schwab data (which itself is limited to five hundred individuals from each racial group with upper-level incomes) indicates a far different set of conclusions from those reached by Young. For example, according to the report in question, while whites are more likely to have an IRA, there is little difference between blacks and whites in terms of whether or not they have other types of retirement plans, and overall, while 89 percent of whites have money in a retirement program, so do 85 percent of blacks.

As for the amounts of money being saved among this upper-income group, although whites indeed save more, on average, the difference, according to the report itself, is not statistically significant. Indeed, whites are a third more likely than blacks to be saving nothing for retirement at this time, and roughly two-thirds of both groups are saving at least $100 or more monthly for retirement. As for investments, while there are small differences between upper-income blacks and whites, the Schwab study itself claims in its notes that those differences in monthly investments and savings are, once again, not statistically significant, amounting, as they do, to less than $60 per month. This kind of "behavioral" gap hardly explains the fact that upper-income white households, on average, have about three times the net worth of upper-income black households. Instead, that is the residual effect of generations of racism that restricted the ability of people of color to accumulate assets, while whites were allowed, encouraged, and even subsidized to do the same.

While it is true that black investment in the stock market lags behind that of whites, the reasons for this can hardly be decoupled from the history of racism. After all, even upper-income blacks tend to have far less wealth to begin with than whites of similar income. As a result, the level of wealth such persons are willing to put at risk is going to be less than for those with more of it to spare. Especially in the last few years, the volatility of the stock market has tended to scare away all but the most experienced investors, and certainly those whose assets are limited from the get-go. Surely, this describes much of black America, which has never had the excess wealth available to whites, which would allow them to roll the dice on Wall Street in the same way.

In much the same fashion, black conservative claims that African Americans don't properly value education are based on faulty (if any) data, and tend to rely on anecdotal experiences rather than hard social science. From Shelby Steele's early '90s bestseller *The Content of Our Character* to Berkeley linguist John McWhorter's near-hysterical rant in *Losing the Race: Self-Sabotage in Black America*, right-wing black commentators have turned cocktail party chit-chat into social science research for the sake of peddling antiblack propaganda.

The evidence, of course, for those who still care about such things, indicates the duplicity of these hucksters in their crusade to blame blacks for their own academic and economic condition. First, high school (and even college) graduation rates for blacks and whites are today roughly equal to one another, once family economic background is controlled for, according to longitudinal data presented by Dalton Conley in his groundbreaking book, *Being Black, Living in the Red*. In other words, whatever differences exist in black and white educational attainment are completely the result of blacks, on average, coming from lower-income families. Comparing whites and blacks of truly similar class status reveals greater or equal educational attainment for blacks. Although it should hardly have been necessary—after all, the entire history of black America has been the history of attempting to access education even against great odds and laws prohibiting it—there have been a number of recent studies, all of which prove conclusively that blacks value education every bit as much as their white counterparts.

An examination of data from the 1980s and early 1990s found that blacks were just as likely as whites to aspire to college and expect to attain a college degree. Furthermore, and contrary to the common claims that black youth harass other blacks who do well in school for "acting white," blacks do not appear to incur social penalties from their peers for doing well in school, any more so than students who are white. An even more recent study, conducted by the Minority Student Achievement Network, looked at forty thousand students in grades seven through eleven and found little if any evidence that blacks placed lesser value on education than their white peers. For example, according to the study, black males are more likely than white, Hispanic, or Asian males to say that it is "very important" to study hard and get good grades: indeed, white males are the least likely to make this claim. The researchers also found that blacks were just as likely to study and work on homework as their white counterparts.

Even in high-poverty schools, disproportionately attended by inner-city students of color, attitudes toward schooling are far more positive than generally believed. Students in high-poverty schools are four and a half times more likely to say they have a "very positive" attitude toward academic achievement than to say they have a "very negative" attitude. There is also no evidence that black parents take less interest in their children's education, or fail to reinforce the learning that takes place in the classroom. Once again, NCES statistics indicate that black children are more likely than whites to often spend time with parents on homework.

In their groundbreaking volume, *The Source of the River*, social scientists Douglas Massey, Camille Charles, Garvey Lundy, and

Mary Fischer examined data for students of different races enrolled in selective colleges and universities. Their purpose was to determine the different social context in which students of color grew up as compared to white students in these top schools. Among the issues examined was the degree to which differential performance in college could be attributed to blacks or their families placing less value on academic performance than their white and Asian counterparts. After all, this claim has been made by some like McWhorter, Steele, and a plethora of white reactionaries who seek to explain the persistent GPA gaps between blacks and others in college. Yet, as Massey and his colleagues discovered, the black students had parents who were *more* likely than white or Asian parents to have helped them with homework growing up, *more* likely than white or Asian parents to have met with their teachers, *equally* likely to have pushed them to "do their best" in school, *more* likely than white parents to enroll their kids in educational camps, and equally or more likely to have participated in the PTA. Black students' parents were also more likely than parents of any other race to regularly check to make sure their kids had completed their homework and to reward their kids for good grades, while Asian parents were the least likely to do either of these. Likewise, the authors found that black students' peers in high school had been more likely than white students' peers to think studying hard and getting good grades were important, and indeed white peers were the *least* likely to endorse these notions. Overall, the data suggests that if anything it is *white* peer culture that is overly dismissive of academic achievement, not black peer culture.

While many of these studies have focused on middle-class and above African American families, and while it is certainly possible that lower-income and poor blacks may occasionally evince a negativity toward academics, this can hardly be considered a racial (as opposed to economic) response, since low-income whites often manifest the same attitudes. Indeed, longitudinal research by sociologist Judith Blau of the University of North Carolina has found that lower-income whites are far less likely to espouse a commitment to academic success than lower-income blacks.

The fact that lower-income youth might come to devalue academic accomplishment, though certainly a dysfunctional tendency in the long run, is also not particularly surprising, seeing as how young people from low-income backgrounds can see quite clearly the way in which education so often fails to pay off for persons like themselves. For youth in the black community, for example, they can see how over the past few decades black academic achievement has risen, and the gap between whites and blacks on tests of academic ability has closed, often quite dramatically. Yet during the same time, the gap in wages between whites and blacks has often risen, sending a rather blatant message to persons of color that no matter how hard they work, they will remain further and further behind.

In other words, the question remains to be answered, to the extent that blacks, to any real degree, occasionally manifest anti-education attitudes and behaviors, where did they pick up the notion that education was not for them? Might they have gotten this impression from a curriculum that negates the full history of their people, and gives the impression that everything great, everything worth knowing about came from white folks? Might they have gotten this impression from the tracking and sorting systems that placed so many of them, irrespective of talent and promise, in remedial and lower-level classes, because indeed the teachers themselves presumed at some level that education wasn't for them? Might they have gotten this impression from the workings of the low-wage economy, into which so many of their neighbors and family members have been thrown—even those with a formal education? Or better yet, maybe they got this impression from the black conservatives who regularly bash them: persons who demonstrate that an education doesn't necessarily make you smart after all.

Whatever the case, let it be said clearly and regularly that the propaganda dispensed by such folks is not only poisonous in its implications, and in the way it reinforces existing beliefs of white Americans vis-à-vis people of color, but also based on an utterly false analysis, distorted data, and the hope on the part of its pur-veyors that the rest of us will never wise up to their game.

JULY 2004

A God with Whom I Am Not Familiar

This is an open letter to the man sitting behind me at La Paz today, in Nashville, at lunchtime, with the Brooks Brothers shirt.

You don't know me, but I know you.

I watched you as you held hands with your tablemates at the restaurant where we both ate this afternoon. I listened as you prayed, and thanked God for the food you were about to eat, and for your own safety, several hundred miles away from the unfolding catastrophe in New Orleans.

You blessed your chimichanga in the name of Jesus Christ, and then proceeded to spend the better part of your meal (and mine, since I was too near your table to avoid hearing every word) morally scolding the people of that devastated city, heaping scorn on them for not heeding the warnings to leave before disaster struck. Then you attacked them, all of them, without distinction it seemed, for the behavior of a relative handful: those who have looted items like guns or big-screen TVs.

I heard you ask, amid the din of your colleagues' "Amens," why it was that instead of pitching in to help their fellow Americans, the people of New Orleans instead (again, all of them in your mind) chose to steal and shoot at relief helicopters.

I watched you wipe salsa from the corners of your mouth, as you nodded agreement to the statement of one of your friends, sitting to your right, her hair neatly coiffed, her makeup flawless, her jewelry sparkling. When you asked, rhetorically, why it was that people were so much more decent amid the tragedy of 9/11, as compared to the aftermath of Katrina, she had offered her response, but only after apologizing for what she admitted was going to sound harsh.

"Well," Buffy explained. "It's probably because in New Orleans, it seems to be mostly poor people, and you know, they just don't have the same regard."

She then added that police should shoot the looters, and should have done so from the beginning, so as to send a message to the rest that theft would not be tolerated. You, who had just thanked Jesus for your chips and guacamole, said you agreed. They should be shot. Praise the Lord.

Your God is one with whom I am not familiar.

Let me just say, it is a very fortunate thing for us both that my two young children were with me as I sat there, choking back fish tacos and my own seething rage, listening to you pontificate on subjects about which you know literally nothing.

Have you ever even *been* to New Orleans?

And no, by that I don't mean the New Orleans of your company's sales conference. I don't mean Emeril's New Orleans, or the New Orleans of Uptown Mardi Gras parties.

I mean the New Orleans that is buried as if it were Atlantis, in places like the Lower Ninth Ward: 97 percent black, 40 percent poor, where bodies are floating down the street, flowing with the water as it seeks its own level. Have you met the people from *that* New Orleans? The New Orleans that is dying as I write this, and as you order another sweet tea?

I didn't think so. Well I have.

Your God—the one to whom you prayed today, and likely do before every meal, because this gesture proves what a good Christian you are (even though Jesus told folks to pray in their closets, but hey, why let Jesus interfere with your self-indulgent display of sanctimony?)—is one with whom I am not familiar.

Your God is one who you sincerely believe gives a shit about your lunch. Your God is one who you seem to believe watches over you and blesses you, and brings good tidings your way, while simultaneously letting thousands of people watch their homes be destroyed, or even die, many of them in the streets for lack of water or food.

But did it ever occur to you just how truly evil such a God would have to be, such that he would take care of the likes of you, while letting babies die in their mother's arms, and old people perish in wheelchairs at the foot of Poydras or Canal Street?

No, I'm fairly certain it isn't God who's the asshole here, Skip (or Brad, or Braxton, or whatever your name is).

God doesn't feed you, and it isn't God who kept me from turning around and beating your smarmy white ass today either.

God has nothing to do with it.

God doesn't care who wins the Super Bowl.

God doesn't help anyone win an Academy Award.

God didn't get you your last raise, or your SUV.

And if God is even half as tired as I am of having to listen to self-righteous blowhards like you blame the victims of this nightmare for their fate, then you had best eat slowly from this point forward. I've heard that people have been known to choke on tortilla chips before.

Why didn't they evacuate like they were told?

Are you serious?

There are a hundred thousand people in that city without cars, folks who are too poor to own their own vehicles, and who rely on public transportation every day. I know this might shock you. They don't have a Hummer H2, or whatever gas-guzzling piece of crap you either already own or probably are saving up for. And no, they didn't just *choose* not to own a car because the buses are so gosh-darned efficient and great, as Rush Limbaugh implied yesterday, and as you likely heard, since you're the kind of person who hangs on the every word of such bloviating hacks as these.

Why did they loot?

Are you serious?

People are dying in the streets, on live television. Fathers and mothers are watching their babies' eyes bulge in their skulls from dehydration, and you're begrudging them candy bars, diapers, and water?

If anything, the poor of New Orleans have exercised restraint. Maybe you didn't know it, but the people of that city with whom you likely identify (the wealthy white folks of Uptown) were barely touched by this storm or the flooding that followed. Yeah, I guess God was watching over them, protecting them, and rewarding them for their faith and superior morality. If the folks downtown who are waiting desperately for their government to send help—a government whose resources have been stretched thin by a war that I'm sure you support, because you love freedom and democracy—were half as crazed as you think, they'd march down St. Charles Avenue right now and burn every mansion in sight. That they aren't doing so suggests a decency and compassion for their fellow man and woman that, sadly, people like you lack.

Can you even imagine what you would do in their place?

Can you imagine what would happen if it were well-off white folks stranded like this without buses to get them out, without nourishment, without hope?

Putting aside the absurdity of the imagery—after all, such folks always have the means to seek safety, or the money to rebuild, or the political significance to ensure a much speedier response for their concerns—can you just imagine?

Can you imagine what would happen if the pampered, overfed corporate class, which complains about taxes taking a third of their bloated incomes, had to sit in the hot sun for four, going on five days? Without a margarita or hotel swimming pool to comfort them, I mean?

Oh, and please, I know, I'm stereotyping you. Imagine that. I've assumed, based only on your words, what kind of person you are, even though I suppose I could be wrong. How does that feel, Biff? Hurt your feelings? So sorry. But hey, at least my stereotypes of you aren't deadly. They won't affect your life one little bit, unlike the ones you carry around with you and display within earshot of people like me, supposing that no one could possibly disagree.

But I'm not wrong, am I Chip? I know you. I meet people like you all the time, in airports, in business suits, on their lunch break. People who will take advantage of any opportunity to ratify and reify their preexisting prejudices toward the poor, toward black folks. You see the same three video loops of the same dozen or so looters on Fox News and you conclude that poor black people are crazy, immoral, and criminal.

You, or others quite a bit like you, are the ones posting messages on chat room boards, calling looters subhuman "vermin," "scum," or "cockroaches." I heard you use the word "animals" three times today: you and that woman across from you—what was her name? Skyler?

What was it you said as you scooped that last bite of black beans and rice into your eager mouth? Like *zoo animals*? Yes, I think that was it.

Well, Chuck, it's a free country, and so you certainly have the right, I suppose, to continue lecturing the poor, in between checking your Blackberry and dropping the kids off at soccer practice. If you want to believe that the poor of New Orleans are immoral, greedy, and unworthy of support at a time like this—or somehow more in need of your scolding than whatever donation you might make to a relief fund—so be it.

But let's leave God out of it, shall we? All of it.

Your God is one with whom I am not familiar, and I'd prefer to keep it that way.

SEPTEMBER 2005

They Shoot Black Men, Don't They?

Sean Bell and the Internal (and Eternal) "Logic" of Racism

In case you were still wondering, black and brown lives count for very little in this country.

Were this not the case, then the officers who killed Sean Bell wouldn't have walked away free men last week, deemed by the judge in their case to have done nothing wrong—not even to have engaged in reckless endangerment—by shooting fifty times at the unarmed man and his friends outside a Queens, New York, nightclub in November 2006.

Fifty times. Like this—count 'em out:

Bam, Bam, Bam, Bam, Bam,
Bam, Bam, Bam, Bam, Bam,
Bam, Bam, Bam, Bam, Bam,
Bam, Bam, Bam, Bam, Bam,
Bam, Bam, Bam, Bam, Bam,
(Halfway done now, let us continue)
Bam, Bam, Bam, Bam, Bam,
Bam, Bam, Bam, Bam, Bam,
Bam, Bam, Bam, Bam, Bam,
Bam, Bam, Bam, Bam, Bam,
Bam, Bam, Bam, Bam, Bam.

Yeah, that ought'a do it.

That Joseph Guzman, Trent Benefield, and Bell were shot by officers Oliver, Cooper, and Isnora was "a tragedy" we are assured by the judge, but not one for which there is any legal remedy in the criminal courts. Just as there was no remedy for those who murdered Amadou Diallo, or Patrick Dorismond, or Frankie

Arzuega, or Anibal Carrasquillo, or Aswon Watson before them. Or, in places other than New York: Tyisha Miller, Dontae Dawson, Carl Hardiman, Tim Thomas, Michael Carpenter, Roger Owensby, Aquan Salmon, or Adolph Archie, the latter of whom in 1990 was driven around New Orleans and beaten for over two hours by cops there, who suspected him of having killed one of their own. By the time they took him to the hospital, they had broken every bone in his face. He would soon die, and the cause of death would be listed by the coroner as "homicide by police intervention." But no one would ever be punished for the murder: no prison time, no suspension, no anything.

Just like nothing is typically done whenever cops kill unarmed civilians—and indeed most of the time when cops kill, the persons whose lives they take *are* unarmed, and disproportionately they are black or brown.

Because black and brown lives do not matter.

In case you were still wondering.

Or if they do, they matter far less than the lives of whites. What seems "reasonable" to officers when confronting black men—that they probably have a gun, and hey, didn't that one there just mention going to *get* a gun?—would never seem reasonable, and apparently never *does* seem reasonable when officers confront young white men.[1] Because never—or at least so rarely as to constitute a level of occurrence too remote to notice—do cops seem to jump to such fatal conclusions when the men in front of them are lacking melanin. White boys don't get blown away at traffic stops, and they don't get shot in the back of the head like Arzuega was in Brooklyn over a decade ago, after which crime the cops didn't even report the incident for three days. They aren't felled in a hail of bullets while reaching for their cell phones because police naturally and "reasonably" assume that the object to which they will soon be clutching is a firearm.

And the benefit of the doubt—the presumption of innocence and the assumption that white lives count for something—is why white folks get to keep breathing, even when they *do* pose a threat to police, unlike Diallo, or Dorismond, or, in the instant case, Sean Bell.

So, for instance, how long do you think cops would wait before opening fire on a black man who was throwing bricks at them? If you're looking for an answer, you might want to ask Lorenzo Collins. Only you can't, because he's dead, his last moments spent encircled by fifteen of Cincinnati's finest, while holding a single solitary brick, and merely *threatening* to throw it their way. On the other hand, there have been more than 150 riots by drunken, white college students since 1995—mostly because of such earth-shattering events as the outcome of a sporting event or crackdowns on underage drinking—during which white males (and pretty much *only* white males) have chucked bricks, bottles, chunks of concrete, frying pans, rocks, frozen beer cans, and entire beer kegs at police. And not once have the cops shot a live round at anyone. Indeed, even at Washington State University, where twenty-three cops were sent to the hospital because of injuries done to them in a late-'90s white riot (including some sustained when a manhole cover was thrown at officers), none of the violent whites were shot. None of their families were left to grieve. No "unfortunate tragedies" befell them, because they never do.

Indeed, at the 1999 Michigan State riot—one of several at the campus in the past decade, in which a white mob did $150,000 worth of property damage, all because their team lost a basketball game—a group of white students were actually seen by police trying to pry a loaded shotgun out of a cop car. One guess as to how long a black person doing the same would have remained a living organism. But in the case of the white boys, tear gas was sufficient, along with a gentle "step away from the car please," shouted over a bullhorn.

Likewise, when thousands of whites at Woodstock '99—a three-day music festival in Rome, New York—began looting ATM machines, overturning lighting scaffolds, setting multiple fires throughout the venue, and committing dozens of sexual assaults in the mosh pit, there weren't even any cops on the premises to deal with the chaos for nearly two hours: Apparently no one thought that a quarter million mostly white people needed to have police around to maintain order. Once things began to get out of control, law enforcement had to be called in from surrounding communities, delaying the response and allowing things to proceed unabated far longer than would have been the case had the event been one at which a large percentage of the crowd had been black. Of course, once they arrived, the cops shot no one.

Nor did white folks taste police lead when they rioted over inadequate beer supplies in Salt Lake City during the Winter Olympics in 2002. Nor last month at yet another riot at Michigan State, this one captured on YouTube, during which young whites (many of whom had had riot T-shirts printed up before the event, indicating the premeditated nature of their criminality) destroyed public property, threw rocks and bottles at the cops, and chanted alternately "fuck the police" and "we want tear gas, we want tear gas." Because, after all, they have the luxury of viewing police brutality as some kind of a game—a rite of passage, if you will— unlike folks of color, who know that saying "fuck the police" too loudly brands you a thug, and inviting an attack from cops might well end with folks straight slaughtered by those who are frankly all too willing to oblige.[2]

To cops, it is reasonable *not* to shoot at white people, no matter what they throw at you, because even when they are aiming right at your head with that brick, their humanity remains visible. Even when their alcohol-addled Girls Gone Wild little brains spit venom your way, their humanity remains visible. Even when they reach for your shotgun, their humanity remains visible.

Even when they open up and fire on you, their humanity remains visible, as it did in Nashville back in 2001, when Sergeant Mark Nelson, angry at his ex (also a cop) for dumping him, went to the house of her new boyfriend to confront the couple. Unable to get into the house, Nelson began firing on officers when they arrived, who had been called by the ex from inside the home. Nelson shot at police in their cars and shot at a police helicopter overhead, all just down the road from an elementary school—in effect, holding the entire neighborhood hostage—and this for an amazing *four hours*, after which, and after police engaged in calm and rational discussions with the shooter, Nelson gave up and was taken in peacefully. That he would be pushing up daisies right about now were he black (even if he *were* a cop, let alone a "mere" civilian) should be so apparent as to warrant no further explanation.

White people's lives, it seems, are always worth the benefit of the doubt. Black folks' lives—especially those of black men—rarely are. Any false or sudden move, or any attempt to flee the scene because you have men pointing guns at you (who you can't even be sure *are* cops, seeing as how they're undercover and haven't announced their employment status), becomes a rationale, in the eyes of the law, to kill.

And no, the fact that two of the cops who shot Bell and his friends were black does not acquit them or the incident of being racially motivated. Racism does not require that the perpetrator of the deed be white, merely that the direction of the oppressive institutional behavior be aimed at members of a racial group due to biases held about that group. Black folks are surely capable of internalizing and then acting upon the same antiblack prejudices and stereotypes as whites. Indeed, when I have done trainings with officers, I have often found little difference between the way that white officers and officers of color view communities of color and the people who live there. With some notable exceptions, the culture of law enforcement encourages a siege mentality among its members, and this mentality often plays out in a blatantly racist fashion, no matter the color of the person wearing the uniform.

So, in closing, let us review the lessons borne out by the killing of Sean Bell and the acquittal of those who ended his life: Most importantly, we are to allow cops to get away with killing black people because they had reasonable suspicions about them (according to the white norms of the law). However, we are *not* to allow young black men to act reasonably: to be afraid and act nervous in front of cops, or to run away from them, even though doing so makes a lot of sense when police are known to *kill you*. No indeed. Reasonability is a one-way street.

And then a second lesson is this: If you're a black male, you'd best not say anything that might even remotely sound like "gun" in the presence of police.

Do not say "Let's go have some *fun*" to your friends at the beginning of the evening.

Do not say "I gotta *run*" when you're looking to head home at the end of it.

Do not say "I wish we were getting more *sun* this week" or "Man, I can't believe the Jets *won*," ever (not that you'll likely have to worry about this latter one all that often).

Because if you do, you might die.

Because black and brown lives do not count.

In case you were still wondering, that is.

MAY 2008

---

1 To Judge Cooperman, the shooting of Bell, Guzman, and Benefield was reasonable because the officers had a legitimate reason to suspect they posed a danger to them. Why? Because they supposedly heard one of them mention that he was going to get a gun. But is this claim by the officers actually reasonable? Is it reasonable to believe that someone would claim to have a gun, and be going for it, when they obviously knew they had no gun to retrieve? After all, there was no gun found in the victim's car.

2 Not only do lots of whites seem to think riots are a game, they appear also to view them as just another part of growing up. According to research by Iowa State University sociology professor David Schweingruber, one in four white males and one in ten white women at the college say they would like to participate in a riot before graduating. This level of endorsement for mass violence would provoke howls of condemnation—even platitudes about the pathologically detached values of young people—if those aspiring to riot were black or brown. We would question their families and their cultures, and we would condemn them as a deviant underclass of thugs. But because they are white, and mostly middle class or above, no one says anything.

The Tyranny of Common Sense:

Examining the Faulty Logic of "Terrorist" Profiling

Growing up in the South, I often heard folks criticize others for being "common." To be called common was to be vilified as trashy and unworthy of respect. Putting aside the elitist implications of such a slur, the pejorative nature of the term has always stuck with me, so much so that when I hear something described as "common sense," I instinctively assume that while it may indeed be the former, it is rarely ever the latter.

Perhaps there is no better example of this truth than the desire of so many to endorse racial and religious profiling of Arabs and Muslims in an effort to thwart terrorist attacks. In the wake of recent subway bombings in London, the call for profiling is being heard once again (as it was after 9/11), and once again those proposing such measures are cloaking their demands in the garb of "common sense," while mocking as politically correct fools anyone who dares criticize the idea. To wit, two separate editorials, published on two successive days: first, a recent op-ed in the *New York Times* by Paul Sperry of the conservative Hoover Institution, and then a syndicated piece by Charles Krauthammer the next day, both of which criticize New York's subway security efforts for not focusing on young Arab and Muslim males.

To hear Sperry tell it, plans to search roughly one out of five passengers make no sense, given that "we know what we're looking for" when it comes to suicide bombers. He conjures up the image of cops going through the bags of Girl Scouts and grandmothers, while letting the real threats slip through their fingers, so as not to be accused of intolerance. Krauthammer calls random searches "idiotic" and also resorts to the imagery of the elderly grandma (although in his rendering she is specifically "from

Poughkeepsie"), searched so as to "assuage the feelings of minority fellow citizens."

But in fact, resisting racial and religious profiling has nothing to do with political correctness: after all, the NYPD has never flinched from profiling black men for drugs, even though whites are equally or more likely to possess them. Rather, avoidance of this "common sense" prescription is smart policy. As it turns out, profiling is not only ethically questionable but also unlikely to prevent terrorism.

Sperry's insistence that profiling young Muslim men is no less rational than insurance agencies charging different premiums to persons of different groups (on the basis of age, for example) is rooted in a profound misunderstanding of statistical probability. In the case of actuarial data used by insurers, there are millions of data points used to calculate risk, thereby ensuring fairly accurate predictions. But with terrorism, the sample size of the subjects in question is much smaller: depending on which incidents you include, between a few dozen or a few hundred people over the past decade. With so few persons involved, to draw conclusions about who is likely to be the next person to blow up a subway or hijack a plane would be to engage in what experts call sampling error. It seems rational, but it's not, no more so than assuming that because most all sniper mass murderers have been white men, the next one will be too, only to discover that (as in the case of the DC snipers), they were actually black.

While Sperry views it as obvious that suicide bombers and terrorists are "most likely to be young Muslim men," this fact (even if true) hardly validates profiling in practice. To begin with, how does one know a Muslim man from his outward appearance? The 9/11 hijackers and London bombers typically dressed in Western apparel, were mostly clean-shaven, and in every respect blended in with the communities in which they carried out their attacks.

As for profiling young men of Arab or South Asian descent, there are followers of al-Qaeda and Islamist extremism in as many as sixty-five nations, including the Philippines, Indonesia, and several nations in Africa, none of whose citizens would fit the desired profile. Indeed, it hardly takes a leap of imagination to believe that groups like al-Qaeda would work around any profile we adopted, by recruiting only those who wouldn't trigger suspicion as readily for operations in the United States. Even now we've seen would-be shoe bomber Richard Reid (a British and Caribbean black guy) slip through security in France because he didn't fit the profile. Then there's John Walker Lindh, white as snow, but attracted to the ideology of radical Islam as well.

And this is where Sperry and Krauthammer's derision of searching old ladies and kids becomes especially dangerous, for, what better place to hide an explosive than in the backpack, luggage, or purse of such unsuspecting characters? Just last year, officials discovered a gun hidden in a child's teddy bear, coming through airport security. What makes us think explosives couldn't be similarly camouflaged?

Sperry and Krauthammer would apparently have us believe that persons who are ready and willing to blow themselves up would simply ditch their plans in the face of profiling. But terrorists are either motivated or they aren't. If we assume the former to be true (and if we don't, what are we worried about?), then we can hardly expect such folks to fold up shop this easily. Indeed, why wouldn't someone who saw they were going to be searched go ahead and detonate their bomb at the checkpoint, killing just as many people, and still ensuring themselves the martyrdom we are told they seek? Or perhaps just say to hell with the subway, and instead blow himself up in the TKTS line in Times Square, thereby massacring dozens of would-be theater patrons and striking fear in the heart of one of the most visible intersections in the world?

Among the reasons Sperry objects to the searches in New York, one is especially peculiar: namely, the fact that officials will be focusing on people who act suspicious. On the one hand, it is certainly true that "suspicious behavior" is in the eye of the beholder. Furthermore, all available evidence suggests that law enforcement tends to see dangerous or suspicious behavior more readily in the actions of persons of color than whites, even when the whites they ignore are more likely to be engaged in nefarious activity (possession of guns or drugs, for example). So on that level, searching folks based on their behavior may indeed lead to abuses, will not likely prevent terrorism, and should probably be considered as illegitimate as targeted profiling. But of course, it is not for fear of possible abuse that Sperry dislikes such searches. If anything, he would likely welcome them if such abuses could only be guaranteed.

Rather, Sperry thinks that searches based on behavior would be far less effective than his preferred method, which is to focus on people "praying to Allah and smelling like flower water." Sperry suggests that suicide bombers douse themselves with perfume in anticipation of paradise, so this should be the basis for a search, but is he serious? With all the malodorous scents of a subway, how would one even be able to distinguish "flower water" in the first place? Or to tell it apart from the overbearing scent of patchouli some white Deadhead has slathered on their clothing in lieu of taking a bath for the past week?

Krauthammer, to his credit, at least foresees the possibility of attempted circumvention by groups like al-Qaeda. Yet he insists we should proceed to profile anyway, since attempts to work around the profile will force terrorist groups to waste energy on finding less suspicious bombers. And, he crows, "By reducing the pool of possible terrorists from the hundreds of millions to . . . at most, tens of thousands, we will have reduced the probability of an attack by a factor of 10,000."

But this is lunacy of the highest order. To begin with, Krauthammer is assuming that all young males from what he calls the "Islamic belt" are possible terrorists (thus the hundreds of millions reference), a conclusion that is not only absurd but demonstrates his own long-standing religious chauvinism. To argue such a thing is no more logical than to suggest all white male Christians are possible terrorists because every abortion clinic bomber has been a white male Christian, as were Tim McVeigh and Terry Nichols. Secondly, Krauthammer assumes that by profiling young Muslim men, we would truly eliminate the threat from such persons. But as noted above, it's not as if they couldn't switch to other targets like open streets or cafés, where constant searches are obviously impossible, not to mention unacceptable in a free society. To then conclude that profiling would reduce the probability of attack by a factor of ten thousand is to make a fanciful calculation on the basis of these two previously ridiculous assumptions. In fact, if there are several million young Muslim males, only a few hundred of whom have been involved in these kinds of bombings or hijackings, the more proper calculation would be to say that the risk of attack by such persons is already infinitesimally small, and that even if we shot every other young Muslim male in the head, we would only reduce the risk by an incalculable amount, in practical terms.

Not to mention, what the supporters of profiling ignore is how such actions might increase the risk of terrorist attack, not only by causing us to let down our guard to other types of threats than those posed by the usual suspects, but also by reducing the willingness of law-abiding Muslims or Arabs to cooperate with law enforcement for fear of being arrested, detained, or suspected of criminal activity. If such persons hear of pending attacks but are afraid to come forward, the intelligence needed to thwart such bombings would be diminished, to the detriment of public safety.

So while white reactionaries like Sperry and Krauthammer prattle on about how racial profiling is just good common sense, it might do the rest of us well to remember the alternative definition of "common" that I learned as a child: trashy, and unworthy of respect indeed.

AUGUST 2005

No, Not Everyone Felt That Way:

Reflections on Racism and History

I remember my maternal grandmother defending Richard Nixon for the crimes of Watergate when I was a kid, because, as she put it: "He didn't do anything any worse than what every other president did." Frankly I knew, even at six, that this was hardly a morally compelling justification for one's actions, even if true, and I recall how it infuriated me to hear it over and over again, whenever politics were discussed in my grandparents' home.

Little did I realize that such obfuscation was hardly unique to certain members of my family. Indeed, throughout the years, it seemed like whenever Watergate came up in conversation (as it would for a long time after 1974, and Iran/Contra after that), someone would pull out this same canard, repeating with the precision of an atomic clock that "so-and-so didn't do anything that every other president/senator/congressman, or whatever, didn't also do." And invariably, those who would say these things were always staunch supporters of whomever was being criticized, whether it was Nixon, Reagan, or Bill Clinton. It's almost as if stupid arguments spread by osmosis, or some such thing. So we end up with people who have never met each other nonetheless miraculously spewing the same apologetics, as if they had gotten some kind of memo instructing them on what to say whenever one of their personal heroes stepped in it.

So, too, the oft-heard argument that one shouldn't be too harsh on this nation's founders, or other early USAmerican presidents when it comes to slaveholding, or involvement in Indian genocide, because, after all, they were "products of their time," and shouldn't be judged by the moral standards of the modern world. I heard this one again recently, after an article of mine hit the Internet, in which I discussed, among other things, the depredations of Andrew Jackson, who was among this nation's premier Indian killers. The person who wrote to attack me as a "PC liberal" who "hates America" insisted that Jackson and others, like Thomas Jefferson, shouldn't be evaluated on the basis of today's moral "underpinnings." And as with every other instance in which something like this has been said to me, in this case too, the comment was made absent any awareness on the part of its author as to the position's utter absurdity.

The most infuriating thing about the "men of their times" defense is that by insisting Jackson, Jefferson, and the rest were in line with the standards accepted by all in their day, apologists ignore, in a blatantly racist fashion, that to the blacks being enslaved, or the Indians being killed, the treatment they received was hardly acceptable. In other words, the "everybody back then felt that way" argument assumes that the feelings of nonwhites don't count. Some folks always knew mass murder and land theft were wrong: namely, the victims of either. That lots of white folks didn't hardly acquits them in this instance. It's not as if the human brain were incapable of recognizing the illegitimacy of killing and enslavement.

Secondly, the belief that killing and stealing are wrong hardly emerged only in the twentieth or twenty-first centuries. Indeed, the very people who suggest we should cut the founders slack because of the standards of their day are overwhelmingly the kind of Bible-thumping conservatives who insist morality is timeless, and who clamor for the posting of the Ten Commandments in the public square for this very reason. Yet they appear to have forgotten that among those Commandments (which were not, after all, handed down to Billy Graham in the 1950s, but rather to someone else a bit earlier) are prohibitions against murder and theft. In other words, the founders don't merely offend by today's moral standards; they offended by the moral standards set in place at least by the time of Moses.

But there's something else troubling about this kind of argument, the kind that seeks to paper over past crimes against humanity by insisting we can't hold old-timers to today's standards (as if today's standards were really all that much better when it came to justifying war, racism, and oppression). Namely, despite the apparent belief to the contrary, there were also whites in Jackson's time and before who opposed the extermination of Native peoples and who supported the abolition of slavery, not only on grounds of political pragmatism but on moral grounds as well. In other words, even using the fundamentally racist limitation suggested by the apologists as to whose views mattered, it is simply not the case that all whites stood behind racist landgrabs, killings, and the ownership of other human beings. Thus, Jackson, Jefferson, and whomever else one cares to mention can hardly seek refuge in the notion of a universal white morality either.

That the apologist (and for that matter, most everyone else) knows little of this history is as tragic as it is infuriating. Because the history of white dissent from the crimes of our kinfolk is so rarely told, too many of us become invested in a view of history that is thoroughly bound up with the narratives and interpretations of elites. So not only is the history we remember a white history, it is a very specific, narrow, and cramped white history at that, one that normalizes contributing to the death and destruction of racial others as something quintessentially white, perhaps even the essence of whiteness.

Ironically, this kind of historical understanding is itself racist on two levels: first and foremost, because it erases the nonwhite perspective, and secondly, because it implies that the white perspective is *only* that of racism. In other words, it suggests that to be white is to be racist inherently, almost biologically perhaps, and to foreclose the possibility of turning against racism. More than that, the argument even suggests that to be white is, by definition, to be a willing accomplice to genocide, and to have no choice in the matter, no human agency to go in a different direction. The argument of the apologist, for this reason, denigrates whites as well. Is it any wonder that with such a stunted understanding of what it means (or can mean) to be a person of European descent, that so few whites think antiracism our struggle? Is it any wonder that whites who have never been exposed to antiracist white history can't then see any alternative to going along with the system as we've inherited it, all the while making excuses about how "that's just how our people have always thought"?

But of course there *is* another history, and however much white antiracism has been trumped quantitatively by white supremacy, it is still vital to learn of this history, so as to put an end to the excuse making for those who chose to oppress others, as well as to point to a different set of role models whose vision young whites might choose to follow.

We could begin with Bartolomé de Las Casas, a priest who traveled with Columbus, and after witnessing the cruelty meted out against the Taino (Arawak) Indians by the "peerless" explorer (who we are still taught to venerate in this culture), turned against the genocidal activities of the Spanish crown and spoke and wrote eloquently in opposition to them. That we know of Columbus but that most have never heard of Las Casas is because of a choice we have made to highlight the one and ignore the other. That Las Casas existed gives the lie to the argument that Columbus can be excused based on the standards of his day.

We could follow up then with the group of whites in the Georgia territory, who, in 1738, petitioned the king of England to disallow the introduction of slavery there because they considered it morally repugnant and "shocking" to the conscience. The existence of these whites gives the lie to the argument that slavers in the eighteenth century can be excused based on the standards of their day.

Or going back even before the 1700s, we could discuss the ways in which colonial elites actually passed laws to punish whites for running away and joining Indian communities: a move they felt compelled to take only because this kind of emigration from whiteness happened so often that it was perceived as a threat. In other words, it can hardly be claimed that anti-Indian sentiment was "just the way everyone felt," if indeed many whites ran away to live among Indians, and had to then be compelled to stop on pain of imprisonment or even the death penalty in some colonies.

Likewise, the lack of antiblack racism among most of the white working class in the 1600s, and the recognition on the part of working class, landless white peasants that they had more in common with black slaves than European elites, led those elites to pass laws specifically designed to divide and conquer the class-based coalitions that were beginning to emerge. Why would that have been necessary, if antiblack racism was already a universally accepted ideology to which all whites adhered, and for which whites like Jefferson should be excused?

Or what of iconic USAmerican heroes like Thomas Paine, the famous pamphleteer and author of *Common Sense*, who (as Robert Jensen points out in his book, *The Heart of Whiteness*) was an ardent abolitionist, and who condemned so-called Christians for their support of the slave system? Or what of Alexander Hamilton, who freed the slaves that became his after marriage and started the New York Manumission Society? Surely Jefferson and Washington were familiar with Hamilton, to put it mildly, and his example gives the lie to the argument that they can be excused because of the standards of their day, which, after all, was his day too.

Or what of William Shreve Bailey of Kentucky, who advocated for the total and immediate abolition of slavery, and who was harassed in the mid-1800s for his opposition to the Fugitive Slave Act, and for operating an abolitionist paper in the heart of a slave state? That Bailey existed gives the lie to the notion that Southern slave owners and defenders of slavery can be excused, because, after all, "that's just how everyone felt back then."

What of Ohio politician Charles Anderson, who spoke out against what he called the "myth of Anglo-Saxon supremacy," as well as the material manifestations of that myth, including slavery and the conquest of much of Mexico in the 1840s?

What of John Fee (also a Kentuckian, as with Bailey), the radical abolitionist preacher, dismissed from his pastor's position by the Presbyterian Synod for refusing to minister to slaveholders, and who helped to found interracial Berea College in 1858?

Or what of celebrated writer Helen Hunt Jackson, who railed against Indian genocide and the repeated violation of treaties made with Indian nations by the U.S. government?

Or Robert Flournoy, a Mississippi planter who quit the Confederate army and encouraged blacks to flee to Union soldiers: an act for which he was arrested. Flournoy, whose name is known by almost no one, also published a newspaper called *Equal Rights*, and pushed for school desegregation at the University of Mississippi a century before it would finally happen.

Or George Cable, born to a wealthy family, who became one of the nation's most celebrated writers at one time, and whose classic, *The Silent South*, inveighed against the reestablishment of white supremacy in the wake of emancipation.

Or George Henry Evans, leader of the Workingmen's Party, who published a newspaper defending Nat Turner's rebellion at a time when most whites viewed Turner's insurrection as among the most vile acts imaginable. That Evans existed gives the lie to the notion that whites can be forgiven for their racism at that time, and in that place.

Or for that matter, poets like James Russell Lowell, or intellectuals like Henry David Thoreau and Ralph Waldo Emerson, or William Lloyd Garrison, or the Grimké sisters. The list, however much longer it should be, is far longer than most probably realize. And every single one of them gives the lie to the position of the apologist, that somehow the morals of the day excuse the racist acts of people like Andrew Jackson.

To be sure, not every one of these persons was free of racist sentiment, and not all of them opposed both slavery and Indian genocide (some, like Las Casas especially, chose to focus their ire on one or the other), but all of them suggest that there was not only one way of thinking about either of those subjects, even among whites, to say nothing of Indians or African Americans, of course. To accept the idea that the nation's founders should only be judged by the moral standards of their own time is to ignore that there has been no single set of morals accepted by all, at any point in history.

The victims of human cruelty have always known that what was being done to them was wrong, and have resisted oppression with all their might. As well, some among the class of perpetrators have seen clearly to this fundamental truth. And their lives and perspectives give the lie to the arguments of those who would rather excuse murderers than praise and emulate true heroes.

SEPTEMBER 2005

DEFLECTION

Passing the Buck and Missing the Point:

Don Imus, White Denial, and Racism in America

Let us dispense with the easy stuff, shall we?

First, the free speech rights of radio personality Don Imus have not been even remotely violated as a result of his recent firing, either by MSNBC or CBS Radio. The First Amendment protects us against state oppression or legal sanction for our words. It does not entitle everyone with an opinion to a talk show, let alone on a particular network. To believe or to demand otherwise would be to say that Imus's free speech rights outweigh the rights of his employers to determine what messages they will send out on their dime.

Secondly, those who are telling black folks to "get over it" when it comes to racial slurs, such as those offered up by Imus, are missing an important point: The slurs are not the real issue. The issue is that these slurs (be they of the "nappy-headed ho" variety or the semipsychotic string of vitriol spewed by comedian Michael Richards a few months ago) take place against a backdrop of systemic and institutional racism. And that backdrop—of housing and job discrimination, racial profiling, unequal health care access, and a media that regularly presents blacks in the worst possible light (think the persistent and inaccurate reports of murder and rape by African Americans in New Orleans during the Katrina tragedy)—makes verbal slights, even if relatively minor, take on a magnitude well beyond the moment of their issuance.

Those who so easily let slip dismissive clichés, such as "sticks and stones," have rarely themselves been the ones for whom slurs signaled a pending or extant campaign of oppression. So, for those whites who seek to change the subject to slurs used occasionally against *us*, like honky or cracker, please note, it is precisely the lack of any potent, institutional force to back up those words that makes them so much easier to shrug off. But people of color are well aware that the slurs used against them by whites are often the tip of a much larger and more destructive iceberg, beneath which lies an edifice capable of shattering opportunities, of damaging and even destroying lives. In truth, even the words themselves can injure, especially the young, for whom an insistence on the development of thick skin seems especially heartless.

Third, and please make note of it, this is not the first time Imus had done something like this. In the past he's referred to black journalist Gwen Ifill as "the cleaning lady," a Jewish reporter as a "boner-nosed, beanie-wearing Jewboy," and Arabs as "ragheads." Furthermore, he handpicked a sidekick who called Palestinians "animals" on the air and suggested that Venus and Serena Williams would make fine centerfold models for *National Geographic*. Imus is a serial offender, and his contrition now, while perhaps genuine, has been long overdue.

So, a quick review: Imus is a racist, words can wound, and his employers had both the right and responsibility to fire him. But such is hardly the stuff of which meaningful commentary is made. So now, let us consider a few other matters as they relate to the Imus affair: matters that have been largely underexplored amid the coverage of this story in recent weeks.

White Hypocrisy, Personal Responsibility, and Shifting the Blame to Black Folks

One thing has been made clear by the Imus incident: White folks are incapable of blaming other whites for white racism and racist behavior. Despite all the demands by whites that blacks take "personal responsibility" for their lives, their behaviors, and the problems that often beset their communities—and especially that they stop blaming whites for their station in life—the fact is, *we* can't wait to blame someone else when we, or one of ours, screws up. So please note, from virtually every corner of the white media (and from black conservatives who are quick to let whites off the hook no matter what we do), the conversation has shifted from Imus's racism to a full-scale assault on rap music and hip-hop. In other words, it's those black people's fault when one of ours calls them a name. After all, they do it themselves, and Imus can't be expected not to say "ho" if Ice Cube has done it. At this point, I'm halfway expecting to hear Bill O'Reilly say that white folks wouldn't have even *heard* words like "nigger" if it weren't for 50 Cent.

But this kind of argument is not only absurd on the face of it, even more, it's a complete affront to the concept of "personal responsibility." It ranks right up there with telling your mom that "Billy did it too," back when you were ten, playing ball outside, and broke your neighbor's window. As I recall, mom didn't much care, and responded by saying something about Billy, a bridge, and whether his desire to jump off like a damned fool would inspire similar stupidity on your part.

By seeking to shift blame for Imus's comments, or those of Michael Richards, or whomever onto black folks, white America has shown duplicity to be something over which we have no shame. Of course, we've been doing it a long time. Witness the way that whites are quick to point out, whenever the issue of slavery is raised, that "blacks in Africa sold other blacks into bondage," as if that would make blacks every bit as culpable as the folks whose wealth was built by the slave system; as if Europeans had only come to Africa for the weather, and had to be coerced into the transatlantic slave trade. Or consider the way that whites blame indigenous people for the mass death they experienced after the invasion of the Americas, by saying, with no sense of misgiving, "Well, it wasn't *our* fault, I mean, they mostly died of disease," as if Native folk would have contracted these diseases short of the desire by whites to conquer the planet for our own aggrandizement. Or consider the way that whites seek to rationalize racial profiling, by arguing that since blacks have higher crime rates, individual and perfectly innocent blacks really can't complain when cops target them, and should instead blame their own for the way blacks get viewed and treated. And it's the same thing with Arabs and terrorism; it's their fault, in other words, personal responsibility be damned.

Rap has been an especially useful scapegoat, such that whenever whites act out in a racist way we seem quick to blame the musical genre. When whites throw "ghetto" parties on college campuses, which denigrate the humanity of persons living in this nation's poorest and most marginalized communities, they routinely claim to be merely mimicking what they've seen on MTV. Snoop Dogg made 'em do it, see? Or perhaps it was Jay-Z, or Biggie, or 'Pac. Odd how the Sopranos never get blamed when white folks kill someone, nor do the *Saw* movies, nor for that matter (since we're on the subject of music) does Johnny Cash, who sang about shooting a man in Reno "just to watch him die." Hell, Johnny even sang that song *in a prison* to a bunch of inmates, with no apparent concern for inciting violence on their part.

And speaking of Cash, the rush to blame rap is especially intriguing given the history of violent themes in country music, a genre that is never blamed whenever some white NASCAR lover commits murder. Consider country legend Porter Wagoner, whose song "Cold Hard Facts of Life," tells of a man who kills his wife for cheating on him. Or better still, "The First Mrs. Jones," in which Wagoner's protagonist, speaking to his new wife (who has just left him) tells her how he stalked and murdered his former betrothed, after which killing he buried her body parts in the woods. In other words, unless the "second Mrs. Jones" comes back to him, she's going to join the first one, pushing up daisies in the forest. If Young Buck dropped a song like this, white America would be screaming about how he was encouraging violence against women. But for Wagoner, a revered and recently passed member of the Country Music Hall of Fame, no such concern attaches. He's just "telling a story."

Then there's Johnny Paycheck's classic, "Pardon Me, I've Got Someone to Kill," or Jimmy Rodgers, who sang, "If you don't want to smell my smoke, don't monkey with my gun," or several of the violent ditties recorded by Spade Cooley in the 1950s, a man who didn't just sing of violence, but practiced what he preached by beating his wife to death in front of their teenage daughter in 1961. That rap is viewed so much more negatively than any other genre of music, so many of which have had their fair share of disturbing, violent, and sexist imagery, attests to the racialized way in which danger has come to be understood. Only a fool could think race wasn't the primary reason for the double standard. In fact, research has found that when lyrics with violent themes are presented to whites in a focus group as being rap lyrics, the participants respond far more negatively than when the same lyrics are presented as the lyrics they actually are: from a folk song, sung by whites.

But blaming rap is not only conveniently opportunistic and intellectually dishonest, given all the pandering about personal responsibility. It also ignores the reasons why rap music sometimes (though not as uniformly as some seem to believe) peddles images of violence, or lyrics that are sexist. After all, if whites make 80 percent of all rap music purchases (and that is the conventional wisdom), then white consumers must be responding via their purchases to an already held impression of black people. Without such a preexisting mental schema firmly in place, the images of blacks as gangstas, pimps, dealers, and "hos" wouldn't resonate nearly so much as to make possible billions of dollars of sales annually. In other words, perhaps whites need to consider the possibility that the thug image has been marketable, and thus created a financial incentive for black artists to play to that trope because these images comport with the negative things that much of white America believes about blacks in the first place. Things that they believed, it should be noted, long before Cool Herc threw his first house party in the Bronx.

If white folks were interested in buying CDs by rap artists who sang about radical social transformation and community uplift (and yes there are many, many such artists out there), that's the music that would be churned out in larger numbers. But white consumers aren't by and large looking to buy songs about overthrowing the system from which we benefit. White boys in the stale and lifeless 'burbs would rather listen to songs about guns and drugs, and being a thug, through which music they can live a more exciting life, if only in their fantasies. So in the ultimate irony, it is white buyers who make that kind of rap profitable, but instead of asking for any responsibility from *them*, we blame the artists for doing what they're supposed to do in a capitalist system, which is respond to market demand, no matter the social consequences. Naturally, of course, it isn't capitalism that gets the blame—itself a thoroughly European creation that has brought misery to millions, as did state socialism (another issue from the womb of Europe)—but rather, the black folks who have taken the bait offered by the market system. Even better is to read Cal Thomas's column from this week, in which he blamed liberal values and permissiveness for the coarseness of rap music, rather than the values trumpeted by the right, like profit-making.

Sticking Our "Buts" in Where They Don't Belong

In addition to trying to shift the blame for white racism onto black folks, we whites seem to be almost congenitally incapable of simply condemning racism, and after such condemnation, ending the sentence with a period. No indeed, after each condemnation it appears as though we are compelled to offer a comma, followed by a semi-exculpatory clause, which minimizes or outright nullifies the force of the condemnation itself.

As in "Yes, what Imus said was horrible and mean-spirited" (and sometimes we'll even admit that it was racist, although several were unable to verbalize this word), "but he does wonderful charity work," or "runs a camp for kids with cancer."

As in "Yes, what Michael Richards said was awful and racist, but he was heckled and just lost control." (Actually, witnesses say he started in on black audience members before they had said anything to him, so this excuse is not only flimsy, in any event, it's also a lie.)

As in "Yes, Mel Gibson was wrong to say those things, but he'd been drinking."

As in "Yes, those white officers who shot Amadou Diallo were wrong, but it's tough being a cop in a dangerous neighborhood."

As in "Yes, the founding fathers mostly owned slaves and were racists, but they were just products of their time and can't be judged by the standards of today"—an argument that is thoroughly offensive, since admonitions against theft and murder (both of which were implicated in the slave system) have been around for thousands of years. Not to mention, the idea that "everyone felt that way back then" is false: The slaves certainly didn't, and neither did white abolitionists.

Or, my favorite, as regards the Imus matter: "Yeah, Imus was wrong to say what he said, but the people criticizing him, like Jesse Jackson and Al Sharpton, are even worse." One has to wonder what white folks would do if Jackson and Sharpton weren't around? Who would we have to divert attention from our own biases? Attacking these two is the default position of white America whenever one of ours does something wrong: "Well what about Jackson? What about Sharpton?" This is then followed by a reminder of the former's "Hymietown" statement, and the latter's involvement in the Tawana Brawley affair.

But even if one accepts the standard white critique of Jackson and Sharpton, the argument nonetheless amounts to a colossal failure to apply "personal responsibility" logic to oneself and one's community. It is yet another attempt by whites to change the subject. Not to mention, both men's past foibles exacted a price from them as well, from which it took several years to recover. It's not as if they received a free pass, and to be sure, had either man had a radio show at the time, there is no doubt that they too would have been canned by their employers for making racist or anti-Semitic comments. Twenty-three years later, Jackson's comments about New York still haunt him, and no doubt had an impact on his political career, for example. As with Jackson and Sharpton, Imus should be able to redeem himself over time, to be sure. But as with both men, he shouldn't expect redemption to happen immediately and without first paying a price.

And truthfully, to say that Sharpton and Jackson are more offensive than Imus is almost incomprehensible. On the one hand, you have two men who have spent their entire adult lives in the struggle for equal rights. On the other, you have a talk show host whose career has been about offending people and pushing the boundaries of good taste, a man who told *60 Minutes* in 1998 that he hired his cohost specifically to tell "nigger jokes," a man who calls tennis star Amelie Mauresmo a "big lesbo" on air, a man whose contribution to the world amounts to shocking people in morning drive time. These things are hardly comparable to registering voters, fighting for civil rights, running empowerment organizations that seek to build community unity, or any of the other endeavors in which Jackson and Sharpton have been involved.

But here's the bigger truth: If white folks are tired of seeing Jackson and Sharpton out front whenever white racism rears its ugly head, there's an easy way to solve that problem. Namely, all we have to do is do the work ourselves! If whites were willing to stand up and unapologetically, and without equivocation, condemn the racism in our community, following the lead of grassroots folks of color with names far less known than the two men in question, perhaps Jackson and Sharpton wouldn't have to be the ones leading the rallies. Maybe they could take a break. Maybe they could get a much-needed and earned vacation. But that's the problem: Most whites do *nothing* in the face of racism. Most of us *don't* speak up, *don't* talk back, and *don't* challenge family, friends, colleagues, or anyone else when they engage in racist actions or merely tell racist jokes. We sit back and remain largely silent, or condemn but only with caveats included. No wonder black leaders like Jackson and Sharpton end up being the visible faces of resistance: We aren't showing up at all, so what are they supposed to do?

At the end of the day, it is white silence and collaboration that has always made racism, whether of the personal or institutional type, possible. If whites had, in larger numbers, joined with folks of color to challenge white supremacy, there is no way that such a system could have been maintained. There is no way that racist persons would be able to spew their venom without fear of reprisal. They would know that such verbiage or racist actions would be met forcefully, and that those engaging in such things would be ostracized. But white silence and inaction have given strength to the racists, whether on radio or in corporate offices, or government positions, or police uniforms; it has emboldened them to act out, since they have long had little reason to believe anything would happen. Slave owners would have been powerless had the whites who didn't own slaves stood up to them and challenged their evil; so too with segregationists, those who lynched thousands of blacks from the late 1800s to the early 1960s, and those who engage in discrimination today. The silent and passive collaborators with injustice are just as bad as those who do the deed, and have always been such; and too often, those folks have been us.

Only when whites decide to connect with the alternative tradition of resistance, as opposed to collaboration, will things change. Only when we choose to take our place in the line, however much longer it should be, of antiracist white allies, will we be in a position to lecture folks of color on how *they* come at the issue. And even then, we'll have far more to learn than to teach in that regard. But until that time, and for however long white folks decide to remain on the sidelines in this struggle, our entitlement to say much of anything sideways to the Jacksons or Sharptons of the world will remain virtually nonexistent.

And Yet, the Bigger Issue: Missing the Systemic Forest for the Individual Trees

But perhaps the biggest problem with the coverage of this one man's racism, is the way in which the media rushes to cover individual acts of bigotry, à la Imus or Michael Richards, while largely ignoring the larger issue, and evidence of widespread systemic racism in health care, criminal justice, education, or employment.

So by now, pretty much everyone knows what Imus said, which is fine, so far as it goes. But why has there been no news coverage of the recent report that complaints of housing discrimination, including race-based complaints, are at an all-time high, and where is the outrage?

Why no coverage of the new report from the United Church of Christ, indicating persons of color are far more likely to live in neighborhoods where hazardous waste sites are placed, and that the typical host neighborhood for such sites has twice as many people of color as the typical neighborhood without such a site? And where is the outrage over this kind of environmental racism?

Where is the coverage of the recent study, which found that less access to high-quality health care is the primary reason for higher prostate cancer death rates for black men, relative to white men? And how many have heard that according to research published in the *American Journal of Public Health*, nearly nine hundred thousand blacks died from 1991 to 2000 who wouldn't have died had they had access to health care that was equal to that received by the average white person: roughly ninety thousand African Americans each year? And where is the outrage over racial disparity in health care?

Where is the media fanfare about the recently updated research from Melvin Oliver and Thomas Shapiro, to the effect that the racial wealth gap between whites and blacks has remained huge, even as income gaps have fallen? Oliver and Shapiro report that even among college-educated black couples with middle class incomes, their wealth disadvantage relative to similar whites remains massive: On average, these African American couples have less than one-fourth the net worth of their white counterparts. In large measure, the wealth gap can be traced to policies that historically restricted black asset accumulation and gave whites significant head starts in the same area, yet their findings have been reported in virtually no white-owned media outlets.

Or what about the research from Vanderbilt University, which finds that light-skinned immigrants to the United States have incomes that are significantly higher than those of immigrants who are otherwise similar in terms of experience, education, and skill levels, but who have darker skin? According to the research, which adds to a long line of data suggesting the role of colorism in the playing out of white supremacy, being one shade lighter than another immigrant is as beneficial to a person's income as an entire additional year of schooling. But where has the coverage been on this issue, and where is the outrage?

In other words, perhaps the biggest problem with the Imus coverage is the way that even liberal commentary on the subject has tended to reinforce the notion that racism is a one-on-one kind of thing, an interpersonal problem, or a character flaw, for which the easy solution is banishment from the airwaves, or perhaps several sessions of counseling.

So long as the bigger problem of institutional injustice remains off the radar screens of the media, however, even victories against personal bias will remain largely irrelevant. And this is so because it is that larger racial inequity that so often contributes to personal bias in the first place, by giving the impression to weak-minded individuals that those on the bottom of the social and economic structure must have something wrong with them, or else they'd be doing better. That is what our society encourages us to believe, after all. Until we get a handle on racism as a social phenomenon, we'll be unlikely to make lasting progress on ending it as a personal one, whether for Imus or anyone else.

APRIL 2007

Situational Ethics, Conservative Style

Conservatives never cease to amaze me.

On the one hand, they accuse "liberals" and those of us on the left of basing our politics on emotion, while theirs, they insist, is rooted in logic. Yet they regularly stake out positions that are utterly devoid of anything resembling reason.

So, for example, hardly a day goes by that I don't receive an e-mail castigating me for "harping" on racism or economic injustice in the United States, since, as my detractors insist, "If you think it's bad here, you should try living in Bosnia" (or the Sudan, or wherever). Irrespective of the nation chosen for comparison, the idea is that folks in the United States—blacks for example, or poor folks—have nothing to complain about, since they'd be worse off elsewhere.

Sometimes this argument gets made in a way that barely disguises the writer's racial animosity (not to mention his or her ignorance about colonialism), as in "Blacks are better off here than they'd be in Africa." Other times it comes from persons who feign liberality, as with a recent writer who said the poverty he'd seen while working in the Peace Corps had convinced him that everyone had it good in the United States, and they should remember that whenever they complained about injustice here.

That anyone could find such positions convincing speaks to the urgent need for schools to require introductory courses in logic. After all, these kinds of arguments give new meaning to the concept of a non sequitur.

To begin with, an injustice in one place cannot be dismissed or rendered unworthy of rectification just because there is another injustice of equal or even greater magnitude happening elsewhere. So, for example, one could not argue that Holocaust survivors have nothing to complain about, since after all, they could have been one of the many millions slaughtered by Stalin. To argue that one injustice cancels out the moral claim of victims of other injustices makes no sense, and does intellectual violence to the very notion of rational thought.

Extending this logic to its ultimate conclusion would lead to some especially appalling positions: among them, one could say that even under Jim Crow segregation, African Americans probably had it better than, say, black folks in the Belgian Congo, and therefore, instead of trying to end apartheid here, black folks should have just sucked it up and thanked the Lord for their good fortune. Indeed, following the trajectory of this mindset, one could argue that the United States could even reinstate segregation, and so long as the system remained somewhat less vicious than conditions in some other society, there would be no great injustice in doing so, or at least none worth protesting.

The kind of thinking in evidence here is similar to that which the right uses to excuse the actions, however depraved, of the United States abroad. So, for example, we have the attempts by many to excuse the mistreatment of Iraqis at Abu Ghraib prison, because at least we didn't behead anyone, as has happened to Nick Berg and Paul Johnson; it's the kind of thinking that excused U.S. support for dictators and death squads in Central America in the 1980s because of the crimes of the Soviets and their puppet regimes; it's the kind of thinking that we are told excuses any level of U.S. violence in Afghanistan or Iraq because of 9/11.

It is, in short, the logic of passing the buck, of refusing to take personal responsibility for one's own actions and the actions of one's nation: ironic, given the extent to which conservatives love to pose as the prophets of personal responsibility.

Of course, that conservatives are hypocrites should hardly surprise anyone. After all, the standard they would impose on others—stop your bellyaching, because things are better here than in any other country—is a logic they would never apply to their own whining. For example, these are folks who constantly moan about high taxes. Yet, if they lived in just about any other advanced industrial democracy, their tax burden would be far higher than it is here, seeing as how those places have much more extensive government social services paid from general tax revenue. So next time a conservative says that people of color or poor folks ought to shut up and be thankful they don't live in some other land, tell him, "Back at ya, jackass: Stop cryin' about taxes and be thankful you don't live in Sweden." Or the next time some evangelical Christian complains about the so-called anti-Christian bias of American elites, schools, and media, tell him to stuff it, and to be glad he isn't in the considerably less religious and less Christian-dominated nations of Europe, or Japan, or pretty much anywhere else on earth.

Fact is, the legitimacy of a nation's tax burden cannot be determined merely by looking at similar burdens elsewhere, nor can the degree of religious freedom or lack thereof be ascertained by simply comparing one nation to many others: In this regard, the right would be correct to reject the dismissals of their arguments above on such grounds. But so too must their own usage of similar arguments fall when applied to the persons whose complaining about injustice they seek to silence.

Like must be compared with like. African Americans are Americans, for example, and so their measure of opportunity must be viewed relative to other Americans, just as the Irish who came to this nation had every right to be treated equally to other Americans, and not constantly told to be glad they weren't still starving back home. If people have a right to be treated equitably once they are in a nation, the fact that they might be treated worse somewhere else becomes utterly irrelevant, and every day they are oppressed relative to others in a given place is a day they are artificially held back and others artificially advanced: a condition that cries out for reparation and recompense if justice is to have any meaning at all. At least for the Irish, Italians, Jews, or other European immigrants, we had the ability to "become white" over time and gain access to the perks of dominant group status. People of color have at no point enjoyed this option.

The measure of American goodness, let alone that much-heralded greatness we're always told to praise, can never be determined on a sliding scale that shifts and morphs to fit a particular circumstance. For a right wing that constantly denounces situational ethics, their tendency to brush off injustice at home by conjuring up injustices abroad surely smacks of the thing they claim to despise. But then again, consistency was never their strong suit, and like I said, conservatives never cease to amaze me.

JUNE 2004

Personal Responsibility Is a Two-Way Street:

Bill Cosby and the Pathology of Passing the Buck

Perhaps Bill Cosby should have known better.

After all, just because you're a black man loved by millions of white folks doesn't mean you can actually count on those whites to receive your words in the spirit you say you intended.

Such a lesson became obvious in late May 2004, when word spread about Cosby's remarks at the NAACP's 50th Anniversary Commemoration of the *Brown v. Board of Education* decision, striking down school segregation.

Instead of taking the opportunity to discuss the ongoing struggles for educational equity, or to address the remaining barriers of unequal funding, racially disparate tracking and discipline, and other obstacles to meaningful parity in our nation's schools, Cosby spent his time bashing the black poor, ridiculing them for the clothes they wear, the way they speak, even the names they give their children. It was a truly classist diatribe littered with inaccurate stereotypes, all of which proved that Cosby hasn't known many poor black folks for a very long time. After all, contrary to the imagery conjured in his rant, only a small percentage of low-income African Americans commit crime, most actually place a high value on education, and only a small percentage get pregnant as minors. But putting aside the inaccuracy of Cosby's statements that night, what was most disturbing was the way much of white America took them.

Although Cosby, to his credit, never said that racism was a thing of the past (and indeed such is not his position), and although he said nothing to the effect that white folks no longer had any responsibilities to address discrimination or racism, that's what a lot of whites, and pretty much all white conservatives, apparently heard. Though obnoxious in form and content, Cosby was merely calling for "personal responsibility" among poor blacks: an idea that is (contrary to what most whites seem to think) quite common in African American communities, and which exists side by side with a keen awareness of the need for continued vigilance against various forms of racism and exclusion.

But what whites often misunderstand is that if personal responsibility is good for the black goose, it must also be good for the white gander. Thus, not only do Cosby's words not let whites off the hook, the spirit of his comments actually requires us to be even *more* deliberate about taking responsibility for that over which we have some control: namely, white racism, and the discrimination that takes place in white-dominated institutions every day.

I remember the first time I had this argument with a black conservative, radio talk show host Ken Hamblin, on a nationally-syndicated TV show. He was carrying on much like Cosby about blacks taking responsibility for their own lives. Rather than argue with him about his views of the black community, I simply said, "Fine, if you want black folks to take responsibility for themselves, that's great. But meanwhile, what are whites supposed to take personal responsibility for? The St. Patty's Day parade? Oktoberfest?"

In other words, whites too often use "personal responsibility" as a bludgeon against others, when we no longer want to deal with the crap *we* put out there, whether it's discrimination in lending by white banks, racial profiling by cops, or moving away from a neighborhood when too many of "those" people move in. After all, how can black folks take responsibility for the fact that even when they have the same level of education and experience, they still are paid less than their white counterparts, and are more likely to be unable to find a job? How can black folks take responsibility for the fact that black men are, depending on the year, two to three times more likely than white men to have their cars stopped and searched for drugs, even though whites are anywhere from two to four times more likely to have drugs on us when we're stopped, according to Justice Department research?

Black and brown poor folks are doing self-help all the time, contrary to the common media imagery. They know they have little choice, having had enough experience with white institutions to know that such institutions have never done much to improve their situation, and nothing at all unless it was demanded and unless they were mobilized collectively to make it happen. But I see very little self-help or even self-reflection in the white community. Rarely do we spend time dealing with our own internalized racial biases and fears, or the discrimination that continues to plague people of color, and which only *we* have any control over, since the folks doing the discriminating are white like us.

Not only do we not reflect on it, we get angry when someone brings it up, which is why whites breathe a collective sigh of relief when someone like Cosby comes along and allows us to think our jobs are over. But our jobs are not over. And if we expect people of color to take personal responsibility, irrespective of racism's existence and impact on their lives, then surely we must apply the same logic to ourselves, and take personal responsibility, irrespective of how we think black folks are behaving, or how dysfunctional we may (falsely) perceive them to be. If *they* aren't allowed to pass the buck then neither can *we* be allowed to do so. For whites to point fingers at black and brown folks and tell *them* to do better is not taking personal responsibility; rather, it's lecturing others about *their* need to do so.

Even worse, many whites actually blame others for our own racial biases. So, for example, whites will often acknowledge negative perceptions of blacks as lazy, less intelligent, or violent, but then blame black folks for feeding that perception by their own actions. Talk about not taking personal responsibility! So because of the actions of a small, unrepresentative sample of the African American community (the 3 percent or so who commit a violent crime annually, for example), whites feel justified in thinking negative things about blacks as a group. And then, in what can only be viewed as the epitome of silliness, these same whites want everyone to believe that racism is no longer an obstacle for blacks, even though they have admitted to holding negative views about the entire community in question! So we are to believe that persons holding these biases would be able to fairly evaluate black job applicants, or potential tenants, or loan applicants; that somehow the stereotypes to which they confess would play no role in their evaluations of such persons in the real world. Just listen to the logic here: "Racism isn't holding blacks back; it's their own laziness!" If one cannot see the irony in this comment, go back and read it again; read it three or four times until you get it. If anything, statements like this are their own negation; they serve to disprove their own claim, even before someone has the chance to respond to them.

As for Cosby, white America's favorite black man (for now), perhaps we should ask how most whites felt about his comment several years ago that AIDS may well have been created by the U.S. government as a plot to destroy certain communities, or the statement of his wife, Camille, when their son was murdered, in which she noted that America had taught her son's Russian killer to hate blacks. As I recall, most whites either said nothing in response to these claims or went ballistic, accusing the Cosbys of "playing the race card."

See, white folks don't like the race card, unless it's the one that helps our own hand. Whites, by and large, never listen to black people, unless they're saying what we already want to hear. That's how desperate we are to avoid taking personal responsibility for the mess that racism has made of this nation, a mess in which we are more than a little implicated, historically speaking and still.

JUNE 2004

Selling the Police:

Reflections on Heroism and Hype

An e-mail arrives in my inbox, recommending a website that seeks to explain (one might say rationalize) the various killings of black men by Cincinnati police over the past few years. Its sender takes issue with some of my previous commentaries, wherein I cast a critical eye upon a number of these incidents, at least four of which occurred under highly suspicious circumstances, where evidence of imminent danger to the officers appears to have been nonexistent. To my detractor, since I wasn't there, I couldn't possibly know whether or not the killings were justified. That he too wasn't there, and therefore also has no firsthand knowledge of the incidents, naturally never enters his mind.

A few days later, another e-mail comes in, this time encouraging me to check out an article that "proves" the validity of racial profiling. Its sender insists police are heroes in the war on crime, and refers to the heroism of the NYPD in rescue efforts on 9/11.

Then a few nights before Christmas, my best friend, a professor in Los Angeles, gives me (as a joke, mind you) the hot new Christmas gift for California consumers: a handsome, well-crafted doll, modeled after a member of the LAPD—some white guy named "Officer West." The muscular, chiseled man-toy is "fully poseable" and comes with toy pepper spray, handcuffs, a flashlight, an automatic pistol, and a baton: the latter for beating up toy versions of Rodney King, I suppose. Officer West dolls are endorsed by the Los Angeles police union and made in China, another nation that places a premium on efficient law enforcement.

And finally, a few days after Christmas, I read about the opening of the Police Museum in New York City. A thoroughly uncritical celebration of the city's officers, the museum ignores such embarrassments as the Amadou Diallo and Abner Louima incidents, as well as a litany of corruption scandals involving drug dealing, payoffs, and bribes. Nor is there an exhibit to memorialize Operation Pressure Point: a drug sting in which police arrested street dealers of color by the dozens, while merely telling white buyers from the suburbs to turn their cars around and go home. Nor do the docents discuss the NYPD's sexist attempt to maintain their six-foot height requirement for officers: a move that prompted women to sue, since such a requirement was clearly a way to keep the department virtually all-male. Instead, visitors to the museum are led through a simulator, where they are challenged to "shoot or hold fire" on a make-believe criminal, displayed in a video. On the screen, you experience yourself sneaking up on a guy who spins around and pulls his wallet out of his back pocket, and most of the time you shoot him, fearing he had a gun. Then you realize your mistake, and more to the point, you realize how gosh-darned tough it is to be a cop.

Come to think of it, maybe that *is* the Amadou Diallo portion of the tour. Of course, police have been trained not to react in such a clumsy fashion, while average folks haven't. As such, the failure of civilians to make the right call can hardly explain, let alone excuse, similar screw-ups by law enforcement.

With so much pro-police sentiment flooding the nation, I guess throwing cold water on the positive mood won't be greeted favorably by most. But the fact is, there are any number of problems with the resurrection of the "heroic cop" image in the public imagination.

First, if we define heroism by the extent to which people put their life on the line in the course of their work, there is nothing all that heroic about policing. According to the Department of Labor, the on-the-job fatality rate for police is lower than that for gardeners, electricians, truck drivers, garbage collectors, construction workers, airline pilots, timber cutters, and commercial fishermen. In fact, fishermen have an occupational fatality rate that is fifteen times higher than that for cops, but rarely do we hear those who provide us with an endless supply of mahi-mahi described as heroes. An average of sixty-six police officers per year were killed feloniously during the '90s, with the number falling to only forty-two in 1999 (and remaining around fifty per year throughout the last several years). That's fewer than the number of cops who died from accidents, such as motor vehicle crashes and drowning.

Secondly, there is nothing inherently noble about police work. After all, would most Americans think highly of law enforcement officers in North Korea or Iraq? Of course not. What makes policing noble is only the validity of the system for which officers are working. And while I am hardly analogizing the U.S. justice system to that of any authoritarian nation, the point is still valid. If the system is rife with inequality and injustice, then those whose job it is to uphold that system are part of the problem, just as much as they may be part of the solution to something like crime.

By presenting police officers as inherently special and vital bulwarks against chaos, pro-cop ideologues paper over ongoing injustices in the system, making it more difficult to see and ultimately fix those problems. And these problems are more than a minor concern for millions of people. Despite what many on the right say about racial profiling, for example—that somehow it's justified because of the generally higher crime rates among African Americans—such claims are little more than rationalizations for racism. Racial profiling cannot be justified on the basis of general crime rate data showing that blacks commit a disproportionate amount of certain crimes, relative to their numbers in the population. I will explain why below, but first, let's make sure we understand what racial profiling means.

Racial profiling means one of two things: first, the overapplication of an incident-specific criminal description in a way that results in the stopping and harassment of people based on skin color. An example of this would be the decision by police in one upstate New York college town a few years ago to question every black male in the local university after an elderly white woman claimed to have been raped by a black man (turns out he was white). So while there is nothing wrong with stopping black men who are 6'2," 200 pounds, driving Ford Escorts, if the perp in a particular local crime is known to be 6'2," 200 pounds, and driving a Ford Escort, when that description is used to randomly stop black men, even those who aren't 6'2," aren't close to 200 pounds, and who are driving totally different cars, then that becomes a problem.

The second and more common form of racial profiling is the disproportionate stopping, searching, frisking, and harassment of people of color in the hopes of uncovering a crime, even when there is no crime already in evidence for which a particular description might be available. In other words, stopping black folks or Latinos on highways, surface streets, or in airports, and searching for drugs. Not only is this racist, it's also bad law enforcement, because whites are equally or more likely to use and possess drugs than blacks and Latinos, according to the National Institutes on Drug Abuse, the Centers for Disease Control, and several private studies. Blacks are about 13 percent of drug users (roughly the same as their share of the population), while non-Hispanic whites are over 70 percent of all drug users (slightly more than our share of the population). So to stop blacks for drug suspicion is to be wrong most often, and to ignore those who are the most likely drug possessors.

According to the February 2001 Justice Department report *Contacts Between Police and the Public*, blacks are more likely than whites to be stopped by police, and much more likely to be searched on suspicion of possessing illegal drugs, guns, or other contraband. This, despite the fact that searches of white vehicles, conducted less than half as often, were more than twice as likely to turn up evidence of criminality than those conducted on vehicles driven by blacks! (More recent reports suggest the disparity is even higher, with blacks being three times more likely to be stopped and searched, even while whites are four times more likely to be found with contraband in our vehicles.) Likewise, a few years ago it was reported that black women were nine times more likely to be stopped and searched at airport customs checkpoints, but white women were twice as likely to be carrying illegal contraband.

This is why general crime rates, which due to economic factors are higher for blacks, are irrelevant to the profiling issue. Police generally don't randomly stop and search people in the hopes of turning up last night's convenience store holdup man. They tend to have specific information to go on in those cases. As such, the fact that blacks commit a higher share of some crimes (robbery, murder, rape, assault) than their population numbers is of no consequence to the issue of whether profiling them is legitimate. The crime for which people of color are being profiled is drug possession; and in that case, the numbers suggest it is whites, not blacks, who are the problem.

Even for the other crimes, to profile blacks is absurd. After all, if cops stop blacks in the hopes of finding a violent criminal in the bunch, they will almost always be wrong, since less than 3 percent of the black population over the age of twelve (the cutoff for collecting crime data) will commit a violent crime in a given year. If they're looking for rapists, for example, roughly two-thirds of the time the perp will be white. So since profiles are based on the typical offender in a category, the profile of a rapist should be of a white person, and the same is true for assault, which is the most common violent crime. Evidence from New York City is instructive. From 1997–1998, even after controlling for the higher weapons possession and violent crime rates among African Americans, the NYPD was two to three times more likely to stop and search blacks on suspicion of weapons or violent crime violations. What's more, this disproportion was evidenced despite the fact that searches of whites were more likely to turn up evidence of criminal wrongdoing.

Despite the public's enhanced veneration of police in the wake of 9/11, the evidence indicates that there is plenty reason to withhold effusive praise. Policing is still not carried out in a fair and equitable manner. There are still far too many innocent and/or unarmed people being killed in questionable circumstances by law enforcement officers, and the culture of policing is still one that lends itself to a militaristic, good guy/bad guy mentality: one that almost inherently perpetuates not only brutality and misconduct but also the wall of silence that protects both.

Police don't deserve hero treatment based on the risks they take, which aren't nearly as daunting as they might like us to think. Rather, they will be deserving of such support only when they root out profiling, testosterone-soaked machismo, and the God complexes that allow so many of them to conclude that they *are* the law, instead of public servants and employees, whose employers are, ultimately, the very citizens they seek to control.

FEBRUARY 2002

Racism, Free Speech, and the College Campus

As has been the case every year for as long as I can recall, an American college campus is once again embroiled in controversy over the expression of racism in its hallowed halls and what it may seek to do in response.

This time the place is Bellarmine University, a Catholic college in Louisville, Kentucky, where, for the past several months, freshman Andrei Chira has been sporting an armband for "Blood and Honour"—a British-based neo-Nazi and skinhead-affiliated musical movement, that calls for "white pride" and white power. Created originally as a magazine by Ian Stuart of the Hitler-friendly and openly fascist band Skrewdriver, the Blood and Honour "movement" promotes bands that sing about racial cleansing and the deportation, if not extermination, of blacks and Jews. Blood and Honour's symbol, similar to the Nazi swastika, is that of the South African white supremacist movement, and is featured prominently on Chira's armband.

Chira, for his part, seems more confused than dangerous. All in the same breath he insists he is not a Nazi or neo-Nazi, but that he is a National Socialist (the term for which Nazi is shorthand). He insists he is not a white supremacist, a racist, or anti-Jewish, yet claims to be a supporter of the American National Socialist Movement (NSM), which calls for citizenship to be limited to those who are non-Jewish, heterosexual whites, and which group praises Hitler on its website.

All of which raises the larger question, which is not so much whether or not Chira should have the freedom to be an ignorant lout, but rather, how did someone so incapable of evincing even a modicum of intelligible (or merely internally consistent) thought get admitted to a good college like Bellarmine in the first place? Are there no standards anymore?

Naturally, the debate has now begun to turn on the issue of free speech: Does the university have the right to sanction Chira or force him to remove the armband, or do his First Amendment rights trump concerns about the feelings of students of color, Jews (yes, there are some at the Catholic school, both students and professors), and others who are made to feel unsafe by a neo-Nazi symbol? It's a tug-of-war that has divided American higher education for years, with some schools passing restrictive codes limiting language or symbols that express open racial or religious hostility, and others taking a more hands-off approach. Bellarmine has remained uncommitted to any particular course of action. The university president has spoken in defense of Chira's free speech rights (and of the principle, more broadly), and has called for a committee to study the issue and determine what kind of policy the school should adopt to deal with hate speech.

Buzz around campus has been split between free speech absolutists on the one hand (who seem to predominate), and those concerned about the way in which racist symbols might intimidate and further marginalize already isolated students, faculty, and staff of color, on the other. Faculty have sniped at one another from both sides of the issue, as have students, and a group of about a dozen students recently launched a sit-in outside the office of the vice-president for Student Affairs, to insist on the inviolability of free speech rights.

As students prepare to return for the spring semester, there is little doubt but that the issue will dominate time and energy on the Bellarmine campus in months to come, and that how the school resolves the issue will come to inform other colleges with regard to their own hate speech policies. Having spoken recently at Bellarmine, and having met dozens of conscientious students and faculty there, concerned about addressing racism, I would like to take this opportunity to chime in, both regarding the existing free speech debate and the larger (and I think more important) issue, which is how best to respond to racism, whether at a college or in society more broadly.

To be honest, I have never found the main arguments of either the free speech absolutists or those who support hate speech restrictions to be particularly persuasive.

On the one hand, the free speech folks ignore several examples of speech limitations that we live with everyday, and that most all would think legitimate. So, we are not free to slander others, to print libelous information about others, to engage in false advertising, to harass others, to print and disseminate personal information about others (such as their confidential medical or financial records), to engage in speech that seeks to further a criminal conspiracy, to speak in a way that creates a hostile work environment (as with sexual harassment), to engage in plagiarized speech, or to lie under oath by way of dishonest speech. In other words, First Amendment absolutism is not only inconsistent with constitutional jurisprudence; it is also a moral and practical absurdity, as these and other legitimate limitations make fairly apparent.

Secondly, the free speech rights of racists, by definition, must be balanced against the equal protection rights of those targeted by said speech. If people have the right to be educated or employed in nonhostile environments (and the courts and common sense both suggest they do), and if these rights extend to both public and private institutions (and they do), then to favor the free speech rights of racists, over and above the right to equal protection for their targets, is to trample the latter for the sake of the former. In other words, there is always a balance that must be struck, and an argument can be made that certain kinds of racist speech create such a hostile and intimidating environment that certain limits would be not only acceptable, but required, as a prerequisite for equal protection of the laws, and equal opportunity.

So, for example, face-to-face racist invective could be restricted, as could racist speech that carries with it the implied threat of violence. Whether or not a neo-Nazi symbol of a movement that celebrates Adolf Hitler qualifies in that regard is the issue to be resolved; but certainly it should not be simply assumed that all speech is protected, just because of the right to free speech in the abstract. Not to mention, does anyone honestly believe that Bellarmine, a Catholic school, would allow (or that most of the free speech absolutists would insist that they should allow) students to attend class with T-shirts that read HEY POPE BENEDICT: KISS MY PRO-CHOICE CATHOLIC ASS! or MY PRIEST MOLESTED ME AND ALL I GOT FROM MY DIOCESE WAS THIS LOUSY T-SHIRT? No doubt such garments would be seen as disruptive, and precisely because they do not truly express a viewpoint or any substantive content, but rather, simply toss rhetorical grenades for the sake of shock value (likely part of Chira's motivation too).

Chira's armband, in that regard, is quite different from a research paper, dissertation, or even a speech given on a soapbox, or an article written for his own newspaper, if he had one: Unlike these things, the armband is not a rebuttable argument, nor does it put forth a cogent position to which "more speech" can be the obvious solution. It provokes an emotional response only, and little else.

At the same time, the arguments of those who would move to ban hate speech have also typically fallen short of the mark, at least in my estimation. To begin with, speech codes have always seemed the easy way out: the least costly, most self-righteous, but ultimately least effective way to address racism. First, such codes only target, by necessity, the most blatant forms of racism—the overtly hateful, bigoted, and hostile forms of speech embodied in slurs or perhaps neo-Nazi symbolism—while leaving in place, also by necessity, the legality of more-nuanced, high-minded, and ultimately more dangerous forms of racism. So racist books like *The Bell Curve*, which argues that blacks are genetically inferior to whites and Asians, obviously would not be banned under hate speech codes (nor should they be), but those racists who were too stupid to couch their biases in big words and footnotes would be singled out for attention, in which case, we'd be punishing not racism per se, or even racist speech, but merely the inarticulate expression of the same.

In turn, this kind of policy would then create a false sense of security, as institutions came to believe they had really done something important, even as slicker forms of racism remained popular and unaddressed. Furthermore, such policies would also reinforce the false and dangerous notion that racism is limited to the blatant forms being circumscribed by statute, or that racists are all obvious and open advocates of fascism, rather than the oftentimes professional, respectable, and destructive leaders of our institutions: politicians, cops, and bosses, among others.

Secondly, hate speech codes reinforce the common tendency to view racism on the purely individual level as a personality problem in need of adjustment, or at least censure, rather than an institutional arrangement, whereby colleges, workplaces, and society at large manifest racial inequity of treatment and opportunity, often without any bigotry whatsoever. So, for example, racial inequity in the job market is perpetuated not only, or even mostly, by overt racism—though that too is still far too common—but rather by way of "old boys' networks," whereby mostly white, middle class and above, and male networks of friends, neighbors, and associates pass along information about job openings to one another. And this they do not because they seek to deliberately keep others out, but simply because those are the people they know, live around, and consider their friends. The result, of course, is that people of color and women of all colors remain locked out of full opportunity.

Likewise, students seeking to get into college are given standardized tests (bearing little relationship to academic ability), which are then used to determine in large measure where (or even if) they will go to college; this, despite the fact that these students have received profoundly unstandardized educations, have been exposed to unstandardized resources, unstandardized curricula, and have come from unstandardized and dramatically unequal backgrounds. As such, lower-income students and students of color, who disproportionately come out on the short end of the resource stick, are prevented from obtaining true educational equity with their white and more affluent peers. And again, this would have nothing to do with overt bias, let alone the presence of neo-Nazis at the Educational Testing Service or in the admissions offices of any given school.

In other words, by focusing on the overt and obvious forms of racism, hate speech codes distract us from the structural and institutional changes necessary to truly address racism and white supremacy as larger social phenomena. And while we could, in theory, both limit racist speech and respond to institutional racism, doing the former almost by definition takes so much energy (if for no other reason than the time it takes to defend the effort from constitutional challenges), that getting around to the latter never seems to follow in practice. Not to mention, by passing hate speech codes, the dialogue about racism inevitably (as at Bellarmine) gets transformed into a discussion about free speech and censorship, thereby fundamentally altering the focus of our attentions, and making it all the less likely that our emphasis will be shifted back to the harder and more thoroughgoing work of addressing structural racial inequity.

Perhaps most importantly, even to the extent we seek to focus on the overt manifestations of racism, putting our emphasis on ways to limit speech implies that there aren't other ways to respond to overt bias that might be more effective and more creative, and that might engage members of the institution in a more important discussion about individual responsibilities to challenge bigotry. So instead of banning racist armbands, how much better might it be to see hundreds of Bellarmine students donning their own come spring: armbands saying things like FUCK NAZISM, FUCK RACISM, or, for that matter, FUCK YOU, ANDREI (hey, free speech is free speech, after all).

That a lot of folks would be more offended by the word "fuck," both in this article and on an armband, than by the political message of Chira's wardrobe accessory, of course, says a lot about what's wrong in this culture, but that's a different column for a different day. The point here is that such messages would be a good way to test how committed people at Bellarmine really are to free speech, and would also send a strong message that racism will be met and challenged en masse, and not just via anonymous e-mails. In other words, if Chira is free to make people of color uncomfortable, then others are free to do the same to him and others like him. Otherwise, freedom of speech becomes solely a shield for members of majority groups to hide behind, every time they seek to bash others.

Instead of banning hate speech, how much better might it be if everyone at Bellarmine who insists that they don't agree with Chira, but only support his rights to free speech, isolated and ostracized him, refusing to speak to him, refusing to sit near him, refusing to associate with him in any way, shape, or form. That too would be exercising free speech, after all, since free speech also means the freedom *not* to speak, in this case, to a jackass like Andrei Chira.

Instead of banning hate speech, how much better might it be for Bellarmine University to institutionalize practices and policies intended to screen out fascist bottom-feeders like Chira in the first place? After all, Bellarmine, like any college, can establish any number of requirements for students seeking to gain admission, or staff seeking to work at the school, or faculty desiring a teaching gig. In addition to scholarly credentials, why not require applicants, whether for student slots or jobs, to explain how they intend to further the cause of racial diversity and equity at Bellarmine?

And before I'm accused of advocating the larding up of the school's mission with politically correct platitudes, perhaps it would be worth noting that these values are already part of Bellarmine's mission and vision statements to begin with. To wit, the school's mission statement, which reads:

Bellarmine University is an independent, Catholic university in the public interest, serving the region, the nation and the world by providing an educational environment of academic excellence and respect for the intrinsic value and dignity of each person. We foster international awareness in undergraduate and graduate programs in the liberal arts and professional studies where talented, diverse persons of all faiths and many ages, nations and cultures develop the intellectual, moral and professional competencies for lifelong learning, leadership, service to others, careers, and responsible, values-based, caring lives.

And this, from the school's vision statement:

Bellarmine University aspires to be the innovative, premier independent Catholic liberal arts university in Kentucky and the region for preparing diverse persons to become dynamic leaders to serve, live and work in a changing, global community.

In other words, the school's entire purpose is consistent with the search for diversity and equity, and entirely inconsistent with the racism and Nazism of persons like Chira. So why shouldn't the school seek to ensure that only persons who adhere to the school's mission, and are prepared to further the purpose of the institution itself, are admitted or hired to work there? Once there, individuals may indeed have free speech rights that protect even their most obnoxious of views, but that says nothing about the ability of the school to take steps that will make it much harder for such individuals to enter the institution to begin with.

Making a proven commitment to antiracist values a prerequisite for entry and requiring some form of training in these issues or antiracist service project in order to graduate or receive tenure or promotion would go far toward operationalizing the college's lofty (but thus far mostly impotent) mission, and would make controversies such as the present one far less frequent or relevant. If Bellarmine is serious about stamping out racism, it is this kind of institutional change—which would both limit the presence of racists and increase the numbers of people of color and white antiracist allies, by definition—that they should adopt. No more platitudes, no more promises, and no more unnecessary debates about free speech. Create an antiracist culture from the start by expanding affirmative action, diversifying the curricula, and using admissions and hiring criteria that send a clear signal: namely, you may have free speech, but so do we, and we are exercising ours to tell you that you are not welcome here.

Sadly, perhaps the most important missing ingredient in the struggle to uproot racism is white outrage. So notice how the free speech supporters wax eloquent about the importance of upholding Chira's right to be a racist prick, but they evince almost no hostility toward him and his message, beyond the obligatory throwaway line "I completely reject his views, but will fight for his right to express them." In other words, they are far more worked up about the possibility, however slim, that the administration may sanction the Nazi than they are about the fact that there is a Nazi on their campus in the first place. Which begs the question as to just how much Nazism really bothers them. One wonders, indeed, whether these students may have confused the valid concept of free speech with the completely invalid notion that one shouldn't even condemn racists out of some misplaced fealty to their rights (which notion of course relinquishes one's own right to speak back, and forcefully, to assholes like Chira).

I long for the day when whites will get as angry at one of our number supporting bigotry and genocidal political movements as we do at those who denounce the bigots and suggest that the right of students of color to be educated in a nonhostile environment is just as important as the right to spout putrid inanities. What's more, I long for the day when whites stage sit-ins to demand a more diverse and equitable college environment for students of color (which currently is threatened by rollbacks of affirmative action, for example), just as quickly as we stage them to defend free speech for fascists, which, at Bellarmine at least, shows no signs of being endangered, so quick has the administration been to defend Chira's liberties.

When whites take it upon ourselves to make racists and Nazis like Chira feel unwelcome at our colleges and in our workplaces, by virtue of making clear our own views in opposition to them, all talk of hate speech codes will become superfluous. Where antiracists are consistent, persistent, and uncompromising, and where antiracist principles are woven into the fabric of our institutions, there will be no need to worry about people like Chira any longer.

DECEMBER 2005

Of Immigrants and "Real" Amurkans:

Reflections on the Rage of the Ridiculous

According to a recent survey, more Americans can name the characters from *The Simpsons* than can recall the rights protected by the First Amendment to the U.S. Constitution. In fact, while roughly one in five Americans could name the *Simpsons* characters, only one in a thousand could name all five freedoms protected by the First Amendment. Only one in four could name more than one of the protected rights therein, and more people could name the three *American Idol* judges than could name three First Amendment rights. Even freedom of religion—one of the better-known freedoms guaranteed at the outset of the Bill of Rights—was only recognized by 24 percent, just slightly higher than the percentage who could name Homer, Bart, and the rest of the gang. Even more embarrassing, one in five actually believed that the "right to own a pet" was part of the First Amendment.

In and of itself this survey may not be of much interest, seeing as how it serves as just one more in a litany of such studies that demonstrate the woeful ignorance of the American public on all kinds of important matters: science, geography, you name it, and the odds are that we'll get it wrong. After all, in a society that values its people more as consumers of products than as civic-minded citizens, the fact that the masses have been kept in a state of suspended intellectual animation is hardly surprising. Mission accomplished, as some are fond of saying.

But what makes this kind of thing truly fascinating is to consider it within the context of the currently raging debates over immigration. After all, from the anti-immigrant camp one regularly hears yelps and screams about how Mexicans in particular (and especially undocumented migrants) refuse to learn "our ways" or assimilate to "our culture." We are bombarded with hateful vitriol about their contempt for USAmerican folkways and the English language, and warned that if immigration continues at current levels, the culture of our nation will be forever changed.

To which one can only ask, given how intellectually bankrupt that culture is at present, so the hell what? If being a good American means having a deep appreciation for the institutions of the United States (and assuming that one recognizes the Constitution as such an institution, over and above Nick at Nite, Nancy Grace, or MTV), then it's pretty clear that those currently residing here fail the test of good citizenship. How many times do we have to watch Jay Leno go out on the streets of New York and ask "real Americans" to identify the attorney general, or secretary of defense (which of course, they routinely cannot do) before we stop all the silliness about how outsiders are bringing the country down?

Are these the persons to whom undocumented migrants are being compared unfavorably? Are these the persons to whom we would rather entrust our nation's future, just because they were born here? Are you kidding me? These are folks for whom the test administered to persons seeking to become citizens legally, through the naturalization process, would prove far too difficult. Most couldn't answer half the questions put to persons seeking to join us, yet we deign to critique others as not being sufficiently committed to Americanism, whatever that means?

Well, if Americanism means not being able to identify members of the highest court in your land, or knowing how many amendments to the Constitution there are, let alone what they say, or knowing who becomes president in the event of the death of both the president and vice-president, then perhaps we need less Americanism, and more of whatever might replace it. If being an American means knowing who won each season of *Survivor*, or who the host of *Fear Factor* is, but not knowing what the Federal Reserve Board does, then we should do away with Americanism, and quickly.

Hell, an influx of immigrants could only improve the extent to which the U.S. public knew U.S. history, since those elsewhere almost always seem to know more about it than we do. Surely they would be smarter (or at least less gullible) than the 85 percent of American soldiers who, according to a Zogby International Poll in February 2006, still believe they are in Iraq to "avenge Saddam Hussein's role in the 9/11 attacks." And surely they could be of no worse character than the deceptive and duplicitous "Real Amurkans" who sent those soldiers there under false pretenses in the first place.

In fact, when it comes to character and behavioral tendencies, Mexicans often look quite a bit better than the rest of us. According to numerous studies, immigrants from Mexico and other points south actually have lower crime rates than their U.S.-born counterparts, and are more likely to abuse illegal narcotics the longer they stay in the United States—which is to say the more they become like us. If anything, then, it is "Americanism" that is the problem.

And as for "learning to speak English," really now, who are we to lecture others? In a nation where citizens have made a comedic superstar out of Larry the Cable Guy—whose tag line, "Git 'er done," suggests a fan base with a command of the mother tongue leaving more than a bit to be desired—demanding that others learn to speak proper English seems a bit silly. In a land where the president regularly mangles simple sentences in ways that would make a third-grade-grammar teacher palpitate, can we really do worse by having several million Mexicans join us?

Hell, "real Amurkans" don't even know what it means to be a member of their little club in the first place. So consider a recent survey, conducted by researchers at Purdue University, in which 54 percent said that one needed to be a Christian in order to be a real American (with four in ten believing this strongly), and nearly 80 percent said that military service is what makes one "truly American." This latter requirement, if taken seriously, would of course exclude most males and virtually all women in the country from being able to consider themselves Americans. With such an ignorant conception of national citizenship, why should anyone listen to the views of such persons when it comes to who should and should not be able to enter the nation and gain membership on equal terms with others?

To make the point even clearer, my great-grandfather was one of those who came to this country legally, though the fine upstanding "real Amurkans" of his time certainly didn't make it easy. In fact, at first, they turned him away and sent him home. Just so happens, the ship he was on entered New York harbor in 1901, shortly after President McKinley had been assassinated. Unluckily for him, McKinley's killer was the son of Eastern European immigrants, and being on a ship filled with Russians, he and his fellow passengers were deemed undesirable by officials and made, at least for the moment, illegal. After being forced back to Russia, it would take him several more years before he would be able to save the money to make the journey again. That "real Amurkans" felt they knew best who should and shouldn't be allowed into the United States—and that he didn't qualify, irrespective of his personal character, about which they could have known nothing at the time—tells me all I need to know about this bunch: those who insist that they and they alone are the best arbiters of who should be allowed into their country. Their judgment in this regard has always been lousy. It was lousy when they turned that boat around over a century ago, it was lousy when they passed Asian exclusion laws that remained in effect for roughly eighty years, and it is lousy today.

And yes, I know, these real Amurkans, however uninformed they may be about the culture they seek to "defend" from others, will insist they are only asking for adherence to the rule of law: one institution that they insist must be respected above all others. It's not that they dislike Mexicans. Goodness no! It's just that so many of them are coming illegally, and we are a law-abiding people who believe in playing fairly, and by the rules. Somewhere, the spirit of an Arapaho mother is laughing her ghostly ass off at that one, joined in her chorus of amusement by tens of millions more: Narragansett, Pequot, Lakota, you name it, all pissing themselves at the irony right about now.

There is, as the saying has long held, honor among thieves, be they bank robbers or those who steal whole continents; like the descendants of those who confiscated North America, and who now, without any sense of misgiving or just plain old-fashioned embarrassment, think nothing of saying how *their* ancestors came here legally, and that this is what makes them different, and one assumes, better, than those who come now from Mexico without adequate papers. Of course, those who insist their ancestors came to America legally ignore a crucial point: that if one was of European descent, there were no real limitations on immigrating to the United States blocking your way. In other words, all white folks could come legally, and in keeping with the terms of the Naturalization Act of 1790, become citizens within one year of entry, making the need for illegal subterfuge remote. To say that one's great-great-whatever followed the law when in truth there was no law to follow (or to break) is more than a bit disingenuous.

To be honest, the entire argument about the illegality of many migrants coming across the border is absurd. After all, 40 percent of those in the country illegally didn't come that way, but rather entered in full accordance with the nation's laws and simply over-stayed work or educational visas. Those in the anti-immigration movement who claim their only concern is for those breaking the law pay almost no attention to this group, for reasons that can only be ones of convenience (in other words, the border is a more visible target for garnering publicity), or racism, since large numbers of visa violators are European or Canadian and, frankly, aren't seen as a threat to the so-called "American way of life," the way brown-skinned, non-English-speaking folks are. That racism motivates much of the backlash should be obvious. Certainly no one can truly believe that the Minutemen would be camped out on the Canadian border if the bulk of illegal immigration were coming from the North, or that undocumented migrants from Nova Scotia would be met with the kind of hostility being meted out to those from Oaxaca.

If it were only illegality that bothered the anti-immigration crowd, they could just advocate for a streamlining of the process by which one can become a U.S. citizen in the first place. That, after all, would most certainly reduce the flow of "illegals" entering the country, by definition. But they will never advocate for such a thing, as they don't want Mexicans and others from the global south entering the United States, whether by the letter of the law or not.

The law isn't the point, and everyone knows it. After all, just because something is illegal doesn't mean it should be. Likewise, just because something is given cover of law doesn't automatically indicate its legitimacy. Laws reflect the wishes of any society's ruling elite at a given time, since they are the ones who make them. To that extent, laws are neither just nor unjust, in and of themselves. The law has, over time, enshrined slavery, theft of indigenous land, segregation, male-only voting and property owning, internment of Japanese Americans, and immigration restrictions based on race and nationality. That certain among those migrating to the United States break the law in order to do so is a matter of irrelevance, morally speaking, unless one starts with the absurd proposition that laws are legitimate simply because they exist.

To complain about the illegality of many current migrants is to beg the ultimate question: What makes someone illegal? Is it something essential to them as human beings, or does it have more to do with the decisions made by policy makers in the nation to which they migrate? To ask the question is to answer it, and yet to hear the nativists tell it, those who come to the United States illegally are by definition of bad character, precisely because of their decision to break the law: the law, in this case, of a country whose laws (until they get here) they are not bound to follow in the first place.

Others will insist that their opposition to an influx of low-wage, semi- and low-skilled labor is purely economic. In other words, it's nothing personal, but to have such a flood of folks enter the nation will drag down the wage base of all working people, especially those in the lower tier of the labor force. But while it is true that "illegals" likely do bid down labor costs, at least in some industries, this is hardly their fault, and it surely can't be remedied by immigration crackdowns. After all, so long as trade agreements allow and even encourage companies to flee to other nations to take advantage of low wage labor, the mere existence of such persons on the planet, as breathing, working humans, will bid down the costs of labor. The answer, of course, is to regulate wages globally and ensure the right of all working people, in whatever nation, to organize collectively within labor unions, protected in this right by international law. Only by doing so can the comparative advantage gained by the superexploitation of workers be eliminated or significantly undermined.

To the extent "real Amurkans" would prefer to limit the entry of low-wage workers into "our" nation rather than to limit high-profit companies from fleeing to theirs, we reveal our racial and ethnic chauvinism, and make it hard to believe that all the rancor over immigration is merely about declining wages and job opportunities. After all, the only reason Mexicans are willing to work for such low wages is that we have supported and helped to maintain a global economic system predicated on the lowest possible wages per unit of productivity—in other words, because we have sanctified as if it were holy the notion of free market capitalism. If, having done so, we come to realize that the fruits of this tree are considerably less tasty than we imagined and were led to believe by the supporters of such a system, it hardly makes sense to blame those who pick the fruit. Rather, the blame lies with those who planted the trees and who profit from their cultivation.

Bottom line, so long as capital is free to cross borders in search of the highest return on investment, and goods are free to cross borders in search of the highest price, to chain labor to its country of origin is to inherently tilt the economic game in favor of the haves and to the detriment of workers everywhere. It is not workers who hurt other workers, in this regard, but capital that does so. Restricting the prerogatives of capital and capitalists is the only way to boost the well-being of workers in the long run. But few if any of the voices in the anti-immigrant movement are saying anything about *that*. They are so busy pushing their white nationalist vision of the United States that they can't be bothered with examining the ways in which it is corporate citizens who are damaging the well-being of America: folks who share their skin color and legal status, if not their bank account size. Unless and until working people in the United States come to see workers of color in the global south as their brothers and sisters in a common struggle for economic justice and human dignity, and the owners of capital as their implacable economic enemies, nothing will change, or at least, not for the better.

In other words, until and unless "real Amurkans" start reflecting on the rich white folks who are truly to blame for their immiseration and insecurity, and stop scapegoating poor brown folks for the same, the pockets of white, black, and brown alike will continue to be picked by a hand that, though "invisible," is all too real.

MAY 2006

COMPETING VICTIMIZATION

On White Pride and Other Delusions

> The price the white American paid for his ticket was to become white
> . . . This incredibly limited, not to say dimwitted ambition has choked
> many a human being to death here: and this, I contend, is because the
> white American has never accepted the real reasons for his journey. I
> know very well that my ancestors had no desire to come to this place:
> but neither did the ancestors of the people who became white and who
> require of my captivity a song. They require of me a song less to cel-
> ebrate my captivity than to justify their own.
> —James Baldwin, "The Price of the Ticket," 1985

It seems like every week I get an e-mail from someone demanding to know why there's no White History Month, or White
Entertainment Television, or why whites aren't allowed to have
organizations to defend "our" interests, the way people of color are,
without being thought of as racists. One of these internet missives,
which has been making the rounds lately on MySpace and other
popular networking sites, implies that whites are somehow oppressed
because we can't get away with calling people of color any number
of racial slurs (a litany of which the author then proceeds to recite,
almost gleefully), while persons of color presumably call us names
like "cracker," "honky," or "hillbilly" all the time.

The e-mail goes on to express anger over, among other
things, Martin Luther King Day and Yom HaShoah (Holocaust

Remembrance Day in Israel), as if these were holidays that discriminated against whites. It then laments that white pride is seen as racist, but for people of color to feel and show pride in their group is seen as normal, natural, and even healthy.

The Reverse Racism Ruse (Or How to Ignore Power, History, and Logic)

That so many people find this kind of argumentation persuasive would be humorous were it not so dangerous, and so indicative of the way in which our nation has yet to come to grips with its racist history. Had we honestly confronted racism as an issue, past and present, it is unlikely that such positions would make sense to anyone. After all, *every* month has been white history month even if they weren't called that. White history has been made the normative history, the default position, and when your narrative is taken as the norm—indeed, when it gets to be viewed as synonymous with *American* history—the need to racially designate its origins is obviously a less pressing concern. White folks' contributions have never been ignored, diminished, or overlooked. As such, to now demand special time to teach about the people we've already learned about from the start seems a bit preposterous.

As for racial slurs, while it is certainly fair to point out that their use is always inappropriate, no matter whom they're directed against, to think that a term like hillbilly is truly equivalent to those used against people of color, like "nigger," "spic," "raghead," or "chink," requires one to exhibit a profound ignorance of history. These and other slurs against people of color not only sound more hateful, they have operated in a more hateful manner by forming the linguistic cornerstone of systematic oppression and institutionalized racial supremacy. Hundreds of thousands were enslaved and millions have died at the hands of those who thought of their victims as "niggers," "spics," "ragheads," and "chinks," and used those terms as they went about their murderous ways. America, in terms of its historic treatment of persons of color, has been nothing so much as an intergenerational hate crime, which didn't begin to end, even in theory, until the 1960s. On the other hand, antiwhite terms are typically the end of the line when it comes to antiwhite racism. People of color control no institutions that are capable of discriminating systematically against whites. They cannot keep whites from having jobs or getting a loan. Nor can black cops get away with racially profiling whites, even when whites actually do lead the pack in one or another form of criminal behavior (serial killing, corporate fraud, or drunk driving, for example). So no, the terms are not the same, even as all are inappropriate and offensive.

And the idea that whites working for white empowerment or "white rights" is no different than people of color working for the empowerment of their group (through such mechanisms as the NAACP, or the Congressional Black Caucus, for instance), also makes sense only if one takes a fundamentally dishonest glimpse at the nation's past. After all, groups representing persons of color were created to address the unique disempowerment experienced by those groups' members. Blacks, Latinos, Asians, and Native Americans have been systematically denied opportunities in the United States solely *because* of their group membership. Their "race" was the basis for housing discrimination, restrictions on educational opportunities, exclusion from jobs, and other forms of mistreatment. Whites have never been the targets of institutional oppression in the United States *as whites*, such that organizing as whites would have made sense. Sure, whites have been marginalized on the basis of ethnicity—the Irish, for example, or Italians, or Jews—and have long organized around ethnicity as a support system for job networking, educational benefits, or other purposes. But as whites, persons of European descent have been the dominant group. So to organize on that basis would be to come together for the purpose of providing collective support for one's existing domination and hegemony. It would be like corporate management forming a union to protect its interests from workers, or like the upper caste in India forming a Brahman support group to protect itself from the Dalits at the other end of the caste spectrum. Such a contingency would be redundant in the extreme.

To have a White Student Union would be absurd for this reason. To have a Congressional White Caucus, given the way in which white elites dominate the government, would be even worse. To have a White Entertainment Television would ignore that whites already predominate on most all existing networks, and that shows pegged to people of color are few and far between, and usually limited to a handful of smaller networks and cable outlets.

Though many argue that affirmative action has made whites the victims of massive "reverse discrimination," and thus necessitated the rise of a white rights movement to secure white collective interests, the evidence simply doesn't support such a view. Although individual whites have likely experienced instances of discrimination—and anecdotal data suggests this is true, though far less often than the occasions when people of color experience it—there is nothing to indicate that such incidents are a widespread social phenomenon against which whites now require organizations to protect them.

So, for instance, according to the Federal Glass Ceiling Commission, whites hold over 90 percent of all the management-level jobs in this country, receive about 94 percent of government contract dollars, and hold 90 percent of tenured faculty positions on college campuses. Contrary to popular belief, and in spite of affirmative action programs, whites are more likely than members of any other racial group to be admitted to their college of first choice, according to data from the American Council on Education. Furthermore, data from the Department of Labor indicates that white men with only a high school diploma are more likely to have a job than black and Latino men with college degrees, and even when they have a criminal record, white men are more likely than black men without one to receive a callback for a job interview, even when all their credentials are the same, as discovered by Princeton professor Devah Pager, and chronicled in her recent book *Marked: Race, Crime, and Finding Work in an Era of Mass Incarceration.* Despite comparable rates of school rule infractions, research from fourteen separate studies confirms that white students are only half to one-third as likely as blacks and Latino youth to be suspended or expelled, and despite higher rates of drug use, white youth are far less likely to be arrested, prosecuted, or incarcerated for a drug offense than are youth of color. So when it comes to jobs, education, housing, contracting, or anything else, people of color are the ones facing discrimination and restricted opportunities while whites remain on top, making the idea of organizing for our collective interests little more than piling dominance on top of dominance. Such collective organizing would not be to ensure a place at the table, but rather to secure the table itself and to control who gets to be seated around it, for now and always.

It is for this reason that white pride is more objectionable than "black pride" or "Latino pride." In the case of the latter two, those exhibiting pride are not doing so as a celebration of their presumed superiority or dominance over others. If anything, they are celebrating the perseverance of their people against great obstacles, such as those placed in their way by discrimination, conquest, and enslavement. In the case of white pride, whites as whites have not overcome obstacles in the same fashion because we have always been the dominant group. Although Irish pride or Italian pride may make sense given the way in which persons of those ethnicities have faced real oppression in the past (and even today, in the case of Italians, who sometimes face negative stereotypes), white pride, given the historic meaning of whiteness, can mean little but pride in presumed superiority.

White Bonding as a Dangerous Distraction

But especially ironic is that by seeking to bond on the basis of whiteness, those who espouse white pride ignore the way in which white identity has actually harmed persons of European descent by causing most of us to ignore our real interests all for the sake of phony racial bonding. To understand why this is so, it might help to have some historical perspective on how the notion of whiteness came into being in the first place, and for what purpose.

Contrary to popular belief, the white race is a quite modern creation, which only emerged as a term and concept to describe Europeans as a group in the late 1600s and after, specifically in the colonies of what would become the United States. Prior to that time, "whites" had been a collection of peoples from different nation-states who had little in common, and who often had long histories of conflict, bloodshed, and conquest of one another's lands. The English, for example, did not consider themselves to be of the same group as the Irish, Germans, Italians, or French. While most Europeans by that time may have thought of themselves as Christians, there is no evidence that they conceived of themselves as a race with a common heritage or destiny.

But the notion of the white race found traction in the North American colonies, not because it described a clear scientific concept or some true historical bond between persons of European descent, but rather because the elites of the colonies (who were small in number but controlled the vast majority of colonial wealth) needed a way to secure their power. At the time, wealthy landowners feared rebellions in which poor European peasants might join with African slaves to overthrow aristocratic governance; after all, these poor Europeans were barely above the level of slaves themselves, especially if they worked as indentured servants.

In 1676, for example, Bacon's Rebellion prompted a new round of colonial laws to extend rights and privileges to despised poor Europeans so as to divide them from those slaves with whom they had much in common, economically speaking. By allowing the lowest of Europeans to be placed legally above all Africans and by encouraging (or even requiring) them to serve on slave patrols, the elite gave poor "whites" a stake in the system that had harmed them. Giving poor Europeans the right to own land (and even rewarding them with fifty acres of land upon release from bondage), ending indentured servitude altogether in the early 1700s, and in some cases allowing them to vote were all measures implemented to convince lower-caste Europeans that their interests were closer to those of the rich than to those of blacks. It was within this context that the term "white" to describe Europeans en masse was born, as an umbrella term to capture the new pan-Euro unity needed to defend the system of African slavery and Indian genocide going on in the Americas. And the trick worked marvelously, dampening down the push for rebellion by poor whites on the basis of class interest, and encouraging them to cast their lot with the elite, if only in aspirational terms.

This divide-and-conquer tactic would be extended and refined in future generations as well. Indeed, the very first law passed by the newly established Congress of the United States was the Naturalization Act of 1790, which extended citizenship to all "free white persons," and *only* free white persons, including newly arrived immigrants, so long as the latter would make their homes in the United States for a year. Despite long-standing animosities between persons of European descent, all blood feuds were put aside for the purpose of extending pan-Euro or white hegemony over the United States.

During the Civil War, the process of using "whiteness" to further divide working people from one another continued. So, for example, Southern elites made it clear that their reason for secession from the Union was the desire to maintain and extend the institutions of slavery and white supremacy, which institutions they felt were threatened by the rise of Lincoln and the Republican Party. One might think that seceding and going to war to defend slavery would hardly meet with the approval of poor white folks who didn't own slaves. After all, if slaves can be made to work for free, any working class white person who must charge for his or her labor will be undercut by slave labor and find it harder to make ends meet. Yet by convincing poor whites that their interests were racial, rather than economic, and that whites in the South had to band together to defend "their way of life," elites in the South conned these same lower-caste Europeans into joining a destructive war effort that cost hundreds of thousands of lives.

Then, during the growth of the labor union movement, white union workers barred blacks from apprenticeship programs and unions because of racism, encouraged in this by owners and bosses who would use workers of color to break white labor strikes for better wages and working conditions. By bringing in blacks and others of color to break strikes, bosses counted on white workers turning on those replacing them, rather than turning on the bosses themselves. And indeed, this is what happened time and again, further elevating whiteness above class interest in the minds of European Americans. The effectiveness of racist propaganda to unite whites around race, even if it meant overlooking economic interests, was stunning. Nowhere was this phenomena better summed up than in the words of one white Texas fireman— recounted in the magisterial volume *Who Built America?* edited by historian Herbert Gutman—who responded to the suggestion that the ranks of railroaders should be opened up to blacks by saying, "We would rather be absolute slaves of capital than to take the Negro into our lodges as an equal and brother."

White Bonding and the Continued Conning of the Working Class

Today, whiteness continues to serve as a distraction to working class persons of European descent. So in the debate over immigration, it is often claimed that immigrants of color are driving down the wages of white workers, and that sealing the border is necessary to secure jobs and decent incomes for the working class. But such an argument presumes that the only thing keeping employers from giving white workers a raise (or black workers for that matter) is the presence of easily exploited foreign labor; as if closing the border would suddenly convince them to open up their wallets and give working people a better deal. In truth, however, were companies unable to exploit immigrant labor, they would simply move their entire operations to Mexico, or elsewhere, to take advantage of low-wage labor or nonexistent regulations on their activities. And if they were the kind of companies that couldn't move their operations abroad (such as construction firms, for example), they would likely shift to more contingent, part-time, and temp labor, which would mean that whoever ended up with those jobs would still have little or no benefits, and insecure wages. This is hardly the recipe for real improvement in the conditions of working people.

White workers would be far better off joining up with workers of color, including the undocumented, to push for higher wages and better working conditions, and they would surely be better off if those coming from Mexico were made legal and organized into unions. But thinking as whites has made this kind of cross-racial solidarity virtually unthinkable. Instead of focusing on the trade agreements that allow companies to move wherever they can get the best return on investment—agreements that have, even by the government's admission, resulted in the loss of hundreds of thousands of good-paying jobs—white workers are encouraged by racism and white bonding to focus their ire on the workers themselves. After all, the workers are brown, while the owners are almost all white, which is to say that the latter are the ones with whom the white working class has been convinced to identify.

For an especially painful example of how destructive white racial thinking can be, consider St. Bernard Parish in Louisiana, right next door to New Orleans. In the aftermath of Hurricane Katrina, St. Bernard was among the hardest-hit communities. Next to the 94 percent black Lower Ninth Ward, in New Orleans, 94 percent white St. Bernard was probably the most devastated part of the region. Though racially different, the communities are both predominantly working class and populated by families with moderate income; and when the federal government, via the

Corps of Engineers failed to ensure the proper construction of the levees, or when the local levee board diverted levee repair funds to build interstate off-ramps for the area's casinos, both the Lower Ninth and St. Bernard saw their communities utterly destroyed. But despite the common interests of the two community's residents, if you had asked most any white person in St. Bernard about the folks who lived in the Lower Ninth, prior to the storm (or for that matter today), you would have been treated (or still would be) to an uninterrupted string of racist invective. To whites in "da parish," as it's known, blacks from New Orleans are the source of all the region's problems. This is why, in 1991, more than seven in ten whites from St. Bernard voted for neo-Nazi David Duke when he ran for governor of Louisiana. This is why the very first thing that Parish government did upon returning home after the storm, and starting to rebuild, was to pass a blood relative law for renters. In other words, you couldn't rent in St. Bernard unless you were a blood relative of the person who was to be your landlord. It was a clear attempt to block people of color from moving in, and once legal action was threatened the Parish backed down, as they could offer no nonracist reason for passing such a law.

And yet, what has the racialized thinking of whites in St. Bernard gotten them? It didn't keep them safe from busted levees. Indeed, had they been less racist and less given to thinking with their color, they might have noticed how much they had in common with their Ninth Ward neighbors. But instead of joining hands with blacks in New Orleans, and marching alongside them in Washington DC or Baton Rouge, and demanding that their joint concerns be addressed, whites in places like Chalmette have been content to sit around talking about the "niggahs," and how lucky they were not to have to live side by side with them.

In a final irony, when students from historically black Howard University went to the New Orleans area to do relief work earlier this year, they were assigned to work in St. Bernard, rebuilding homes—homes that, were it up to Parish leaders, they wouldn't have been able to live in. When one busload of students arrived at the site to which they had been sent that day, locals promptly called police, because after all, a bunch of black people in the neighborhood must be a sign of trouble. So much for solidarity.

Conclusion: White Solidarity Illogical and Hurtful for All

It is perhaps understandable that young whites, uninformed about the history of racism in America, might fall prey to the lure of "white rights" thinking. After all, without a full understanding of the way in which whites have been elevated above people of color, and continue to be favored in employment, housing, criminal justice and education, it would make sense for whites to wonder why things like affirmative action or Black History Month were necessary, or why groups that advocate for the interests of persons of color were still needed. If you start from the assumption that the United States is a level playing field, then these kinds of things might seem odd, even racially preferential. But given the historical context, not to mention the vital information regarding ongoing discrimination in the present, the importance and legitimacy of these initiatives and organizations becomes evident to all but the most unreasonable.

What is most important for white folks to understand is that our interests do not lie with the racial bonding we are being asked to embrace. Indeed, the very concept of the white race was invented by the wealthy to trick poor and working class European Americans into accepting an economic system that exploited them, even as it elevated them in relative terms over persons of color. As such, for whites to organize on the basis of whiteness is to codify as legitimate a category that was always and forever about domination and privilege relative to those who couldn't qualify for membership in the club.

Finally, to organize as whites in a white-dominated society, where whites have eleven times the average net worth of blacks and eight times the average net worth of Latinos, have unemployment rates half that of blacks, poverty rates one-third as high as that for blacks and Latinos, and where whites run virtually every major institution in the nation, is by definition to organize for the continuation of that domination and supremacy. It is to seek to enshrine one's head start; it is to seek the perpetuation of hegemony established in a system of formal apartheid, as if to say that that system were perfectly legitimate and worthy of survival. It is fundamentally different than for a minority group to organize collectively so as to secure their interests, since the interests and opportunities of minorities cannot be assumed or taken for granted, thanks to their lesser power, while those of the majority typically can.

And to organize on the basis of whiteness is to cast one's lot with the elite, who desperately wish for working class people to believe their enemies are each other, rather than the bosses who cut their wages, raid their pension funds, and limit their health care coverage. The more that white working people fight working people who are black and brown, the less they'll be likely to take aim at those who pick their pockets every day they show up for work: the employers who pay them only a fraction of the value of the products and services they provide, all in the name of profits that they have no intention of truly sharing with their employees. Whiteness is a trick, but sadly one that has worked for nearly three and a half centuries. Only when white folks wise up and realize that whiteness itself is our problem will we ever stand a chance of true liberation. Until then, our whiteness will provide us privileges and advantages, but only in relation to those at the bottom of the racial caste structure. It will provide a psychological wage, as W. E. B. Dubois put it, as an alternative to real wages. Not a bad deal, until you're struggling to feed your family and keep a roof over their heads. For in times like that, real currency works a bit better.

MAY 2007

A Particularly Cheap White Whine:

Racism, Scholarships, and the Manufacturing of White Victimhood

Consider a few things that have happened in the past month and a half, in no particular order: First, comedian Michael Richards goes on a racist tirade at an L.A. comedy club, screaming the n-word at two black audience members, over and again for several minutes. Then, white students at four entirely different colleges dress up in black-face or throw "ghetto" parties, at which they mock low-income African Americans. Next, a group of Muslim clerics are thrown off a plane because passengers got nervous after seeing them engaged in evening prayers prior to boarding their flight, and finally, New York police fire fifty shots at a group of unarmed black men, for no apparent reason, killing one who was due to be married the next day.

Oh, and then there is this: In spite of the above-mentioned events, the president of the College Republicans at Boston University announces that race-based scholarships for people of color are the "worst form of bigotry confronting America today," demonstrating the desperate need for BU to require a course in "Getting Some Perspective 101," for all incoming first-year students.

In response to this most horrible of racist practices, the campus GOP has announced its plans to offer a "Caucasian Achievement and Recognition Scholarship" for deserving white students. According to the head of the group, the scholarship is not being offered to help whites, per se, but rather, to point out the unfairness and immorality of "racial preferences" in American society. Merit, rather than race, should determine scholarships, they insist. Yet upon close examination it becomes apparent that the arguments made against race-based scholarships, whether at BU or elsewhere, fail to demonstrate even the most rudimentary flirtation with intellectual honesty.

To begin with, and to place things in some perspective before getting into a larger philosophical discourse about race-based scholarships on principle, a few things should be noted. First, although white students often think that so-called minority scholarships are a substantial drain on financial aid resources that would otherwise be available to them, nothing could be further from the truth. According to a national study by the General Accounting Office, less than 4 percent of scholarship money in the United States is represented by awards that consider race as a factor at all, while only 0.25 percent (that's one-quarter of 1 percent for the math-challenged) of all undergrad scholarship dollars come from awards that are restricted to persons of color alone. In other words, whites are fully capable of competing for and receiving any of the other monies—roughly 99.75 percent of all the bucks out there for college. But apparently, that's just not good enough for the likes of the BU Republicans. To them, one-quarter of 1 percent of all scholarship money is the "worst form of bigotry confronting America today." The suggestion would be laughable were it not so sad, so indicative of a fundamental break with the ability to think critically and logically about the world.

What's more, the idea that large numbers of students of color receive the benefits of race-based scholarships—something that is often supposed, usually with an unhealthy dose of white racial resentment—is also lunacy of the highest order. In truth, only 3.5 percent of college students of color receive *any* scholarship even partly based on race, suggesting that such programs remain a pathetically small piece of the financial aid picture in this country, irrespective of what a gaggle of reactionary white folks might believe.

The Myth of Meritocracy and the Reality of White Privilege

Additionally, to suggest that race-based scholarships are some unique and illegitimate break with an otherwise meritocratic system is preposterous. Fact is, there are plenty of scholarships that have nothing to do with merit per se, but about which conservatives say nothing: scholarships for people who are left-handed, or kids whose parents sell Tupperware; or the children of horse-breeders; or descendants of the signers of the Declaration of Independence, among many thousands of such awards. Apparently, it's OK to ensure opportunity for members of these groups, despite the fact that none of them have faced systemic oppression before, but it's the height of immorality to do the same for students of color, who have indeed faced explicitly racial obstacles in their lives.

Interestingly, even the scholarship considered by most to be the very model of merit-based reward is rigged in a way that subverts pure meritocracy. The National Merit Scholarship, which is awarded to fifteen thousand students each year, based on pre-SAT (or PSAT) score, is distributed proportionately to representatives of each state, so that each state has the same number of winners as they have a percentage of the nation's overall high school graduates. Because the quality of schools varies dramatically across states, average scores on the PSAT will also vary wildly, but students in Mississippi will always get their "fair share" even though many of them wouldn't have qualified had they attended school in a state like Massachusetts. Yet never have conservative defenders of the merit system complained about this arrangement: After all, most of the winners are white, and it helps out folks in the red states whose school systems lag far behind those in the blue states, so what's not to like?

Of course, on an even more basic level, to complain about so-called unfair preferences for students of color, be it in terms of scholarships or affirmative action policies in admissions, is to ignore the many ways in which the nation's educational system provides unfair advantages to whites, from beginning to end. It ignores data from the Department of Education and the Harvard Civil Rights Project, which indicates that the average white student in the United States attends school with half as many poor kids as the average black or Latino student, which in turn has a direct effect on performance, since attending a low-poverty school generally means having more resources available for direct instruction. Indeed, schools with high concentrations of students of color are eleven to fifteen times more likely than mostly white schools to have high concentrations of student poverty. It ignores the fact that white students are twice as likely as their African American or Latino counterparts to be taught by the most highly qualified teachers, and half as likely to have the least qualified instructors in class. This too directly benefits whites, as research suggests being taught by highly qualified teachers is one of the most important factors in school achievement. It ignores the fact that whites are twice as likely to be placed in honors or advanced placement classes, relative to black students, and that even when academic performance would justify lower placement for whites and higher placement for blacks, it is the African American students who are disproportionately tracked low, and whites who are tracked higher. Indeed, according to the Harvard Civil Rights Project, schools serving mostly white students have three times as many honors or AP classes offered, per capita, as those serving mostly students of color.

To ignore this background context, and to award scholarships based solely on so-called merit, is to miss the ways in which the academic success and accomplishments of white students have been structured by unequal and preferential opportunity, and the ways in which students of color have been systematically denied the same opportunity to achieve. It is to compound the original injury and to extend white privilege at the point of admissions or financial aid awards beyond the level to which it has already been operating in the lives of white students. In other words, to award scholarships on the basis of so-called merit, when merit itself has been accumulated due to an unfair head start, is to perpetuate a profound injustice. On the other hand, to offer scholarship monies to capable and high-achieving students of color, who through no fault of their own have been restricted in their ability to accumulate "merit" to the same degree, is to ensure as equitable and fair a competition as possible, and to do justice in an otherwise unjust system.

But Is It a Double Standard? And Is It Racist?

Despite the claim by the right that race-based scholarships amount to a double standard (since scholarships for folks of color are considered legitimate but white scholarships aren't), in truth, the standard is simple, straightforward, and singular: Persons belonging to groups that have been systematically marginalized in this society should have opportunities targeted to them, so as to allow for the development of their full potential, which otherwise might be restricted by said marginalization. Special efforts to provide access and opportunity to such persons should be made, not because they are black per se, or Latino, or whatever, but because to be a person of color has *meant* something in this country, and continues to mean something, in terms of one's access to full and equal opportunity.

In effect, these are not scholarships based on race, but rather scholarships based on a recognition of *racism* and how racism has shaped the opportunity structure in the United States. Because race has been the basis for oppression and continues to play such a large role in one's life chances, it is perfectly legitimate to then offer scholarships on the basis of that category which has triggered the oppression. If people of color have been denied opportunity because of their race, then why is it so hard to understand the validity of remedying that denial, and its modern-day effects, by also making reference to their race? After all, that was the source of the injury, so why shouldn't it also be the source of the solution?

As for whether race-based scholarships for persons of color are inherently racist, the claim is absurd on the face of it, as is the notion that such efforts amount to bigotry (the position put forward by the BU Republicans). Bigotry is defined as "intolerance," and the behavior or attitude of someone who holds "blindly and intolerantly to a particular creed or opinion." Surely scholarships for people of color are not predicated on intolerance for whites, nor are they based on some kind of blind contempt for whites as a group. Rather they are rooted in the quite reasonable belief that people of color have been singled out for mistreatment on the basis of race, and thus, special efforts should be made to provide full opportunity to them, by taking account of the thing that had prompted the mistreatment in the first place. Even if one chooses to disagree with the premise that those who have been victimized should have special efforts made on their behalf, it would still be dishonest to claim such a premise was "intolerant."

As for racism, it is typically defined in two ways, both as ideology and practice. In terms of ideology, racism is the belief in the inherent superiority/inferiority of one race to another, while institutionally it refers to policies, practices, or procedures that have the effect of perpetuating systemic inequalities between the races, and which deny persons of a particular race equal opportunity with those of other races. Clearly, race-based scholarships pegged to people of color are not based on notions of racial superiority or innate difference. They are predicated only on the notion that there have been real differences in opportunity on the basis of race, and that these opportunity gaps should be remedied to the greatest extent possible. Secondly, such efforts also fail the test of institutional racism. Student of color scholarships do not perpetuate racial inequity (if anything they would have the effect of reducing it), nor do they prevent whites from enjoying equal opportunity. Indeed, without affirmative action efforts, in admissions and scholarships (and for that matter employment and contracting), whites would enjoy *extra* and unearned opportunity relative to people of color, thanks to preexisting advantages to which we were never entitled in the first place. As such, to deny whites access to a minuscule percentage of financial aid awards is not to deny us access to anything to which we were morally entitled. We are "losing out," if you will, only on something to which we have no moral claim: namely, the ability to keep banking our privileges, and receiving the benefits (be they scholarships, college slots, or jobs) of a system that has been skewed in our favor.

Since scholarships would have been more equitably distributed between the races in a system without a history of institutionalized discrimination—and to doubt this is to assume that folks of color still wouldn't have qualified for them, which means that one would have to believe in inherent inferiority on their part, which belief is the textbook definition of racism—to now steer scholarships to such persons is only to create a situation closer to that which would have existed anyway, but for a legacy of racial oppression. Even if one disagrees with the philosophical argument here, to label such efforts racism makes no sense.

Race-Based Scholarships as a Vital Tool for Equity

If anything, American colleges and universities should be offering *more* assistance to students of color than is currently the case, including so-called race-based scholarships. And the reason is simple: Even persons of color from families with stable economic profiles face obstacles on the basis of race, and these obstacles deserve attention and consideration by institutions of higher education. According to all the available evidence, even when families of color have decent incomes and occupational statuses, their children typically attend much higher-poverty and lower-resourced schools, are more likely to be tracked into lower-track classes, even when compared to whites of more moderate income, and face substantial barriers to equal housing opportunity, all of which translates to diminished opportunities solely on the basis of race, and not merely economics. To provide increased financial assistance merely on the basis of need—even a measurement of need that closely aligns with race, like wealth and asset status—would be to overlook the uniquely racial burdens that persons of color continue to carry with them into the college environment.

However the College Republicans at Boston University may

seek to spin it, make no mistake, the effort to end affirmative action, whether in terms of admissions or scholarships, will have an undeniable impact: It will mean fewer opportunities for students of color, irrespective of their true abilities; it will mean that even highly capable students will be locked out of opportunities, due solely to the disadvantages they have inherited due to racism; and it will mean that colleges will become increasingly populated with white students whose SAT scores might be mightily impressive, but whose moral and ethical compasses, to say nothing of their understanding of the real world, leave something just as mighty to be desired.

DECEMBER 2006

Chocolate Cities and Vanilla Indignation:

Reflections on the Manufacturing of "Reverse" Racism

If you're looking to understand why discussions between blacks and whites about racism are often so difficult in this country, you need only know this: When the subject is race and racism, whites and blacks are often not talking about the same thing. To white folks, racism is seen mostly as individual and interpersonal, as with the uttering of a prejudicial remark or bigoted slur. For blacks, it is that too, but typically more: namely, it is manifested in the practices and policies of institutions, which practices and policies have the effect of perpetuating deeply embedded structural inequities between people on the basis of race. In other words, to blacks and most folks of color, racism is systemic, while to whites, it is most often seen as merely personal.

These differences in perception make sense, of course. After all, whites have not been the targets of systemic racism in this country, so it is much easier for us to view the matter in personal terms. If we have been targeted for mistreatment based on our race, it has been only on that individual, albeit regrettable, level. But for people of color, racism has long been experienced as an institutional phenomenon. It is the experience of systematized discrimination in housing, employment, schools, or the justice system. It is the knowledge that one's entire group is under suspicion, at risk of being treated negatively because of stereotypes held by persons with the power to act on the basis of those beliefs, and the incentive to do so, as a way to retain their own disproportionate share of that power and authority.

The differences in white and black perceptions of the issue were on full display recently, when whites accused New Orleans's Mayor Ray Nagin of racism for saying that New Orleans should be and would be a "chocolate city" again, after blacks dislocated by Katrina had a chance to return. To one commentator after the other—most of them white, but a few blacks as well—the remark was by definition racist, since it seemed to imply that whites weren't wanted, or at least not if it meant changing the demographics of the city from mostly African American (which it was before the storm) to mostly white, which it is now, pending the return of black folks. To prove how racist the comment was, critics offered an analogy. What would we call it, they asked, if a white politician announced that their town would or should be a "vanilla" city, meaning that it was going to retain its white majority? Since we would most certainly call such a remark racist in the case of the white politician, consistency requires that we call Nagin's remark racist as well. Seems logical enough, only it's not; and the reason it's not goes to the very heart of what racism is and what it isn't, and the way in which the different perceptions between whites and blacks on the matter continue to thwart rational conversations on the subject.

Before dealing with the white politician/vanilla city analogy, let's quickly examine a few simple reasons why Nagin's remarks fail the test of racism. First, there is nothing to suggest that his comment about New Orleans retaining its black majority portended a dislike of whites, let alone plans to keep them out. In fact, if we simply examine Nagin's own personal history—which since Katrina has been obscured by many on the right, who have tried to charge him with being a liberal black Democrat—we would immediately recognize the absurdity of the charge. Nagin owes his political career not to New Orleans's blacks, but New Orleans's white folks. It was whites who were responsible for his initial election as mayor, having voted for him at a rate of nearly 90 percent, while blacks only supported him at a rate of 42 percent, preferring instead the city's chief of police (which itself says something: black folks in a city with a history of police brutality preferring the *cop* to this guy). Nagin has always been, in the eyes of most black

New Orleanians, pretty vanilla. He was a corporate vice president, a supporter of President Bush, and a lifelong Republican prior to changing parties right before the mayoral race.

Secondly, given the ways in which displaced blacks especially have been struggling to return—getting the runaround with insurance payments, or dealing with landlords seeking to evict them (or jacking up rents to a point where they can't afford to return)—one can safely intuit that all Nagin was doing was trying to reassure folks that they were wanted back and wouldn't be prevented from reentering the city.

And finally, Nagin's remarks were less about demography per se than an attempt to speak to the cultural heritage of the town, and the desire to retain the African and Afro-Caribbean flavor of one of the world's most celebrated cities. Fact is, culturally speaking, New Orleans is what New Orleans *is* because of the chocolate to which Nagin referred. True enough, many others have contributed to the unique gumbo that is New Orleans, but can anyone seriously doubt that the predominant flavor in that gumbo has been inspired by the city's black community? If the city loses its black cultural core (which is not out of the question if the black majority is unable to return), then indeed New Orleans itself will cease to exist, as we know it. That is surely what Nagin was saying, and it is simply impossible to think that mentioning the black cultural core of the city and demanding that it will and should be retained is racist: Doing so fits no definition of racism anywhere, in any dictionary on the planet.

As for the analogy with a white leader demanding the retention of a vanilla majority in his town, the two scenarios are not even remotely similar, precisely because of how racism has operated, historically and today, to determine who lives where and who doesn't. For a white politician to demand that his or her city was going to remain white would be quite different, and far worse than what Nagin said. After all, when cities, suburbs, or towns are overwhelmingly white, there are reasons for it (both historic and contemporary) having to do with discrimination and unequal access for people of color. Restrictive covenants, redlining by banks, racially restrictive homesteading rights, and even policies prohibiting people of color from living in an area altogether—four things that whites have never experienced anywhere in this nation *as whites*—were commonly deployed against black and brown folks throughout our history. James Loewen's newest book, *Sundown Towns*, tells the story of hundreds of these efforts in communities across the nation, and makes clear that vanilla suburbs and towns have become so deliberately.

On the other hand, chocolate cities have not developed because whites have been barred or even discouraged from entry—indeed, cities often bend over backward to encourage whites to move to the cities in the name of economic revival—but rather, because whites long ago fled in order to get away from black people. In fact, this white flight was directly subsidized by the government, which spent billions of dollars on highway construction (which helped whites get from work in the cities to homes in the 'burbs) and low-cost loans, essentially available only to whites in those newly developing residential spaces. The blackness of the cities increased as a direct result of the institutionally racist policies of the government, in concert with private sector discrimination, which kept folks of color locked in crowded urban spaces, even as whites could come and go as they pleased.

So for a politician to suggest that a previously brown city should remain majority "chocolate" is merely to demand that those who had always been willing to stay and make the town their home should be able to remain there and not be run off in the name of gentrification, commercial development, or urban renewal. It is to demand the eradication of barriers for those blacks who otherwise might have a hard time returning, not to call for the erection of barriers to whites—barriers that have never existed in the first place, and which there would be no power to impose in any event, quite unlike the barriers that have been set up to block access for the black and brown. In short, to call for a vanilla majority is to call for the perpetuation of obstacles to persons of color, while to call for a chocolate majority in a place such as New Orleans is to call merely for the continuation of access and the opportunity for black folks to live there. Is that too much to ask?

Funny how Nagin's comments simply calling for the retention of a chocolate New Orleans have brought down calls of racism upon his head, while the very real and active planning of the city's white elite to actually change it to a majority *white* town in the wake of Katrina—which plans were all but admitted to by some of those elites in the pages of the *New York Times* and *Wall Street Journal*—elicited no attention or condemnation whatsoever from white folks. In other words, talking about blacks coming back and making up the majority is racist, while planning to practice (or actually *engaging* in) ethnic cleansing by demolishing black neighborhoods like the Lower Ninth Ward, as many want to do, is seen as legitimate economic development policy.

It's also interesting that whites chose the "chocolate city" part of Nagin's speech, delivered on MLK Day, as the portion deserving condemnation as racist, rather than the next part, in which Nagin said that Katrina was God's wrath, brought on by the sinful ways of black folks, what with their crime rates, out-of-wedlock childbirths, and general wickedness. In other words, if Nagin casts aspersions upon blacks as a group—which is really the textbook definition of racism—whites have no problem with *that*. Hell, most whites agree with those kinds of antiblack views, according to polling and survey data. But if Nagin suggests that those same blacks, including, presumably, the "wicked" ones, be allowed to come back and live in New Orleans, thereby maintaining a black majority, *that* becomes the problem for whites, for reasons that are as self-evident as they are (and will remain) undiscussed.

Until white folks get as upset about racism actually limiting the life choices and chances of people of color as we do about black folks hurting our feelings, it's unlikely things will get much better.

In the end, it's hard to take seriously those who fume against this so-called reverse racism, so petty is the complaint, and so thin the ivory skin of those who issue it.

JANUARY 2006

When Blacks Attack!

*Reflections on White Victimology
and the Ironies of Institutional Racism*

"Everything you said in there was so insulting to me."

The words came harsh and unexpected. I had just given a speech on racism and white privilege at an upstate New York college and was nearing the end of an after-event reception, when the young woman, who had been seething with anger, waiting to confront me, finally stepped forward.

"You don't *know* me," she continued. "How dare you say that I have privilege just because I'm white. My family had nothing; we lived in neighborhoods where we were the only white people around, and I got called a white bitch by black girls every day, and got beat up regularly by black kids on my block. How dare you say that I had advantages being white. That's bullshit!"

It's never easy to know the right words at a moment such as this. On the one hand, I knew that the young woman had horribly misinterpreted my comments that night, and those in my book *White Like Me*, which she and her first-year classmates had been asked to read last fall. On the other hand, you can't just tell someone who is obviously in pain that she missed the point. To do so would be cruel. So instead, I tried a different approach.

First, I told her how sorry I was that those things had happened to her. There is no excuse for anyone to treat another person that way, and I have never suggested otherwise. Those who had abused her and called her names were assholes, and nothing they had experienced in life could justify their lashing out at her. Nothing.

Then I tried to explain, as best I could, what my point had been. And I sought to make it very clear that my comments hadn't really been directed at her in the least.

"My book is a memoir," I noted. "So, by definition it's about my experience. All I'm asking people to do is to reflect on those experiences to see how many of them hold true in their own lives as well. Some will, others won't, and that's fine."

She still wasn't buying it. "Yes, but you said that all whites have privilege, not just you."

"In some ways, yes," I noted. "Being white means having advantages in employment, education, the justice system, and housing, for example. I provided statistical support for those claims in my speech, and if you have data to the contrary, by all means share it with me. Otherwise, I'm not sure what the argument is, or how to respond to your concerns. I never said that all whites have easy lives. It's just that as a general rule, to be white confers advantage, just like being rich, or male, or straight, or able-bodied does, relative to those who are poor, women, LGBT, or disabled."

Having no data to contradict anything I had offered in the talk, she changed her line of attack.

"Well, it's just that you spent all your time talking about 'whites this' and 'whites that,' and I just feel you should have talked about other types of racism too, not just white racism and white privilege. What about people like me, who have been attacked for being white? Why don't you spend the same amount of time talking about *that*?"

It was a fair enough question; indeed, it was one I've gotten many times before. First, I noted that as a white person it just makes sense that I must deal with my piece of the problem—my two nickels in the quarter so to speak—since it is white racism and privilege over which I, as a white person, have the most direct control. "I can't control what black folks think of me, or how they treat me," I explained. "But a system that gives me unfair advantages and opportunities is something I can take responsibility for."

"Yeah," she replied. "I get that, but it just seems you should be more balanced."

"Well, think of it this way," I responded. "If data indicates [and it does, surprisingly] that every year there are maybe a few dozen attacks on heterosexuals by LGBT folks, which are apparently motivated by bias against straight people, does that make anti-straight bias the functional equivalent of homophobia and gay-bashing? And should people who speak about gay-bashing and discrimination against LGBT folks feel compelled to give equal time to 'straight-bashing' and 'heterophobia'?"

"No," she answered.

"Okay then," I replied. "So, in other words, even if we acknowledge that sometimes the less powerful group in a society does something bad to the more powerful group, and even if we suggest that sometimes members of the more powerful group suffer injustices, the larger institutional patterns can remain in place, right?"

Though she seemed to understand what I was getting at, her anger was far from spent. The tension between us continued to mount, ultimately tapering off into an exchange that probably was less productive than either of us would have liked.

Because I feel a responsibility to explain my views in a way that is clear and convincing to others, I struggled for the next few days, wondering what I could have done differently in our conversation. What could I have said that would have allowed the young woman to hear me? What could I have said that might have allowed us to connect with one another, share perspectives, and reach some kind of synthesis, even if we ultimately ended up agreeing to disagree?

Though I hadn't thought of it that evening, a few days later, still pondering our confrontation, I finally came to realize perhaps the most important thing about her experiences as a child, growing up white in an almost all-black neighborhood: namely, that experience itself was a symptom of institutional racism—the kind that creates racially isolating environments to begin with. In other words, the abuse she had suffered didn't disprove my position; rather, it confirmed it in a most visceral way. The young woman's abuse was made more likely by virtue of her extreme racial isolation. After all, people feel more emboldened to abuse others who are different when they have the power in numbers to back them up. The young woman's isolation, which had so emboldened her abusers in this instance, was the result of social forces that have allowed neighborhoods to become so racially separated in the first place: forces such as institutional racism and white privilege.

Were it not for the history of racism, which has kept black folks concentrated in low-income and mostly black spaces thanks to housing bias, there would be no (or at least very few) neighborhoods like the one in which that young woman grew up and faced abuse. In fact, one study by the Urban Institute found that if where people lived were solely a matter of their ability to pay (in other words, if factors like racism didn't play an independent role, above and beyond mere finances), fewer than 1 percent of African Americans would live in communities where they were the majority. As such, we can safely estimate that in the absence of race-based obstacles to equal housing opportunity, there would be no spaces where blacks would be such a majority and whites such a minority that the latter might become a target for the former, seeking to take advantage of their numerical power.

If equal opportunity were the norm—in other words, were white privilege and institutional racism uprooted—there would be few if any spaces left where one group would be able to view itself as the norm and thereby objectify others as abnormal, for the purpose of picking on them or abusing them. If white kids and kids of color grew up together, shared neighborhoods and schools, and socialized on a plane of equity from the beginning, the odds of such race-based abuse manifesting would be greatly diminished if not eradicated. There would still be occasional fights, to be sure, but there would be little reason to expect these conflicts to take on a uniquely racial angle. As such, the ability of racial resentments to develop, in either direction, or for racial stereotypes to persist over time would diminish as well.

In other words, the conditions under which she (and her

abusers) grew up stemmed from a system of racial inequity, and could not likely have persisted in its absence. And although most whites are able to escape the downside of that system by way of having access to greener pastures, "better" neighborhoods, and spaces in which they (we) will be the norm, some, as with her family, were not. So ironically, she ended up reaping the consequences of a system that, although it was set up for the benefit of persons like her, occasionally leaves even some white folks out in the cold. She ended up experiencing the blowback of a system of privilege that occasionally fails even those for whom it was intended as a system of support. But the fact of that system's imperfections—the fact that occasionally some whites fall through the cracks anyway—neither minimizes the extent to which the system is in place, nor the extent to which whites as a group benefit from it, nor the extent to which whites such as the young woman that evening should continue to interrogate that system and ultimately seek to change it for their own benefit, and not merely out of the goodness of their hearts.

To some, this analysis may appear to let the perpetrators of the abuse off the hook. Perhaps it sounds like excuse making, or like blaming the system for the actions of individuals. In this case, perhaps some will think that I'm blaming whites (or at least white racism) for the bigoted acts of black people. But trying to locate the source of a behavior, or a particular set of incidents, does not equate to excusing the behavior; nor does it suggest that the incidents in question are not serious; nor does it imply that those who perpetrate such abuse should be let off without punishment. Let me be clear: Those who physically or verbally assault others should be punished, and all such persons should bear the burden of repairing the damage they have done.

But that's the easy part; in much the same way that advocating the locking up of rapists and armed robbers is easy but stops neither rape nor armed robbery in the long run. I, for one, am interested not merely in getting tough with criminals and abusers, but on reducing criminal victimization and abuse, which is a decidedly different thing. Understanding a phenomenon, whether rape, drug abuse, child molestation, terrorism, or racial intimidation and hate, does not require the coddling of those who engage in these things. I want to understand what motivated the Columbine shooters, or the 9/11 hijackers, or any number of serial killers, not to excuse their deeds, but so I might gain some insight into how to prevent such things from happening again.

To write off such behavior and criminality to mere "evil," perpetrated by people who are just plain "bad" (which appears the operative and sophomoric response of conservatives to pretty much everything nowadays), is to leave society with very few tools to diminish such behavior. It's about as helpful as saying that the cause for all the world's woes is Satan. After a while, these kinds of answers are not merely evidence of an ignorance so detached from reason as to boggle the imagination; worse, they become formulas for continued suffering, seeing as how they hold out almost no hope for betterment other than prayer, exorcism, mass incarceration, or perhaps the dropping of bombs to eradicate evildoers. Never has such a pessimistic set of choices been seen as satisfactory among an otherwise moderately intelligent population.

Like it or not, moral lectures won't stop kids from abusing those like the young woman that evening. If we wish to keep others from experiencing what she experienced (whether those kids are white, black, or anything else), the best thing we could do is break up hypersegregated, racially concentrated communities (be they in the cities or the suburbs) with more enforcement of fair housing laws, crackdowns on predatory lending, low-interest loans to encourage integration, and equitable community development, replete with racial equity "impact statements" to gauge the effects of gentrification, commercial projects of various sorts, and the availability of affordable housing.

To be sure, such efforts would need to be carefully crafted lest they displace more people of color from urban spaces than there would become space available for them in less-exclusively black and brown communities. Some type of "no net loss" policy when it comes to housing for folks of color might mitigate the potentially negative consequences of a large influx of whites into previously black and brown space. And without doubt, any economic "redevelopment" in urban spaces that have long been home to folks of color should require direct input and approval from those who had been there prior to the influx of newcomers. Small-d democratic accountability needs to accompany "new urbanism" or integration efforts lest they devolve into a form of colonialism. But however we might create more mixed space in practice, there can be little doubt that only by creating a broader and more equitable mix of residents and students in an area will we likely prevent any one group from feeling so empowered by its sheer numbers as to take advantage of those in the minority. Such efforts would almost certainly reduce the tendency toward *us* vs. *them* thinking so common today, given the extreme racial isolation and separation to which we are often subjected.

What we cannot afford to do is to allow the effects of institutional racism to torpedo the push for racial equity. We cannot allow our own occasional injury, as whites, to distract us from the real culprit in that experience: not merely the individuals who took advantage of or abused us, but also the systemic forces that made the abuse likely. It is white supremacy and privilege that set us against one another to begin with. It is white supremacy and privilege that continues to skew opportunities hundreds of years after they were set in place. It is only the eradication of white supremacy and privilege that can put an end to it, *all* of it, once and for all.

JANUARY 2008

On the Making of Undeserving Martyrs:

Fact and Fiction in the Duke Lacrosse Case

"So now what do you have to say, smart-ass?"

I can think of better ways to be greeted in the morning, but sadly, this was how my day began a few weeks ago, upon opening my e-mail browser and piecing through the messages that had accumulated overnight. The author of the above missive was wanting to know, as the rest of his love note would amply reveal, my feelings about the recent dismissal of all criminal charges against the three Duke University lacrosse players, who, for the past year, had been facing possible prosecution for rape.

He went on to declare their ordeal a prime case of "reverse racism," since the accuser was black and the accused were white, and insisted that folks like me, who write about racism, would never speak out about the injustice done to these "fine young men," because we only care about black victims. We were hypocrites (and worse) to hear him tell it, since we had all rushed to judgment in this case, prepared to "lynch" the Duke 3, simply because they were white, and rich, and jocks—three groups "despised by leftists and liberals."

Before weighing in on the issues of so-called reverse racism and the rush to presume guilt in this case—not to mention a few important things to remember about these "fine young men"—let me note that I never previously wrote one word about this case, nor gave one speech in which I discussed the guilt or innocence of the accused, nor even speculated on the matter. So whatever others may or may not have said, or may or may not have believed, I kept my opinions to myself, awaiting the evidence, as I try to do in all cases of alleged criminality.

Let me also note, so as to acquit at least myself of the charge of being antisports, that I am an avid sports fan, and was a very accomplished baseball player in my youth. While it is true that competitive, for-profit athletics often engenders dysfunctional social priorities among young people, and adults for that matter, I would venture to guess that it does this no more so than is true in profit-based publishing, entertainment, filmmaking, or any other endeavor of life. It is not sports that are the problem, but rather the way in which sporting events are organized in a market-driven economy that often distorts the players, the coaches, the fans, and the games being played.

Finally, let me be clear that the allegations against the Duke lacrosse players were, so far as I can tell from the available evidence, horribly unjustified. The accuser was wrong to allege rape, the accused were innocent of that offense, and they have every right to be bitter about the way in which the spectacle played out in the press, and within the Durham, North Carolina, district attorney's office. With all of that said, however, the arguments put forward by my electronic pen pal about this case couldn't be much weaker and more absurd.

The Difference Between the Duke Case and Racial Persecution

To claim that the allegations against the lacrosse players amounted to "reverse racism," as many have done, does violence to the English language and utterly ignores the way in which racism truly operates. To begin with, the term "reverse racism" implies equivalence with old-fashioned racism (the white-on-black kind) that simply doesn't exist. With old-fashioned racism (and in truth, there's nothing that old about it) several of the things we saw transpire in the Duke case wouldn't likely have happened. The accused wouldn't have been in a position to hire high-priced attorneys to defend them against even the most bogus of charges. Not having such attorneys, black defendants accused of raping a white woman would have likely been appointed a public defender who would have pressured them to accept a plea to a lesser charge, in return for a lighter sentence. The public wouldn't have been nearly as inclined to rush to the defense of a black defendant, or several, had the accusations been reversed in terms of racial identity. And certainly with old-fashioned racism, the odds that the charges would have been dropped before trial would have been far more remote. Throughout our nation's history there have been literally thousands of blacks murdered by white mobs, and/or the state, for allegedly raping white women in cases where the charges were completely without merit. The Duke lacrosse players were not murdered, not lynched, not incarcerated without bail, and not even brought to trial. There is simply no equivalence here, however horrible the experience of being falsely accused surely must have been for them.

Indeed, had the racial shoes been on the other feet, so to speak, what we might well have seen is what we in fact *did* see in the case of Darryl Hunt, whose name is unknown to most, and whose story has provoked nowhere near the sympathy from conservative whites, angered by the persecution of innocent people, as has the case of the Duke 3. But Hunt, unlike the Duke 3, *was* tried for the crime of which he was accused: the rape and murder of a white woman in Winston-Salem, North Carolina, in 1984. Like the Duke players, he was falsely accused (identified as the killer by a former KKK member), and like the wealthy white men at Duke, there was no physical evidence to indicate his guilt. Also, as with the Duke boys, Hunt was pursued by an overzealous prosecutor who disregarded all exculpatory evidence in his case. But very much unlike the lacrosse players, Hunt was convicted (as it turns out, by an all-white jury) and sentenced to life in prison. Ten years later, DNA evidence proved beyond any question that Hunt was innocent, but the courts refused to exonerate or release him for an additional decade. Hunt, unlike, say, Reade Seligmann, spent nearly two decades in prison for a crime he didn't commit. It's also worth noting that the persons who prosecuted Hunt have never been threatened with professional ethics charges or disbarment. For that matter, they haven't even been criticized that harshly, unlike DA

Nifong in Raleigh, in the wake of the Duke scandal, whose career has been ended.

Presumptions of Guilt or Innocence: An All-Too-Common Malady

As for civil rights leaders and activists who supposedly "rushed to judgment" in this case, a few important points should be made. First, the statement signed by the Duke faculty members known as the "Group of 88" nowhere passed judgment on the three accused men. That many have read their comments to do so suggests an inability on their part to comprehend words on a page. Instead, the statement made reference to larger issues of race and gender, and the climate for women as women, and people of color on the Duke campus. By giving voice to those who have long felt marginalized despite very real concerns about racial and sexual harassment and abuse at Duke, the statement provided an opportunity to air those grievances now that the community's attention had been riveted to the larger subject matter because of the allegations against the lacrosse players.

Secondly, the idea that a rush to judgment on the part of some in the black community (or among those of us in the white community who do antiracism work) was a unique break with the otherwise sacrosanct presumption of innocence is laughable. Honestly, how many of the persons blasting those who presumed the lacrosse players guilty actually keep an open mind when they hear about someone in an inner-city community who's been arrested for a crime? How many of them, watching the news and seeing coverage of a young black or Latino male being arrested and led to booking, honestly consider the alleged perp in such a case innocent? How many of the conservative whites condemning black activists in the Duke case presumed Kobe Bryant was guilty of the charges brought against him, which were ultimately dropped as well? How many had decided that O.J. Simpson was guilty of double murder even before they had heard any of the evidence in the case?

Sadly, the rush to presume guilt in criminal cases is all too common for most of us, myself included; and the crimes for which we rush to presume guilt probably say something about our political and ideological orientations. For those on the right, the black or Latino suspect in a carjacking, drug crime, or drive-by shooting is likely to be presumed guilty because these individuals fit the reactionary image of danger and deviance. For those of us on the left, it's likely the case that we rush to judgment, ahead of the evidence, in cases involving corporate misconduct. I will admit that I was convinced of the guilt of Ken Lay, or the Savings and Loan bandits, even before truly looking at the evidence in their respective cases. The point is, to criticize some in the black community of Durham, or to blast national commentators for presuming the guilt of the suspects in the Duke case, is to miss how readily we all tend to violate the maxim of the presumption of innocence when looking at criminal suspects.

Indeed, for whites to lecture black folks about rushing to presume guilt in the Duke case takes nerve, especially given how quick those same whites are to believe the negative stereotypes of black folks as deviant and criminal. According to academic research stretching back several years, large percentages of whites view blacks as violent and dangerous. What's more, adherence to these stereotypes is, in turn, highly correlated with a tendency to presume guilt, evidence notwithstanding, whenever the person who adheres to those views is confronted with a crime that fits their mental schema regarding black criminals. Ironically, this time around the defendants who fell prey to the mentality of presumed guilt happened to be quite different from the more "traditional" criminal defendant. But make no mistake, this kind of presumption is an everyday occurrence among the white public, for whom blacks in custody are seen as almost surely guilty.

And let us not forget, the rush to presume guilt has been given license by top political officials, as with former attorney general Ed Meese, who famously noted that "People who have been arrested aren't innocent." Or, for that matter, what can we call the detentions of suspects at Guantanamo Bay who have been accused of no actual crimes, if not the institutionalization of a presumption of guilt in public policy?

...And a Few Words About Those "Fine Upstanding Young Men"

And although even the most repulsive of persons doesn't deserve to be falsely accused of a crime, especially one as serious as rape, it might do us well to step back a bit from all the acrimony and gnashing of teeth over the damaged reputations of Messrs. Seligmann, Finnerty, and Evans to remember one important detail: Had these men and their teammates not set out that evening to sexually objectify women by hiring strippers to entertain them, none of this would have ever happened.

In other words, and not to put too fine a point on it, the Duke 3, though not rapists, are hardly the choirboys some would suggest, and as the media has all but insisted they are since the charges were dropped. This team consists of a bunch of men who view women as sex objects to be ogled and used for their sexual titillation. They drink to excess underage, in violation of the law and the Duke student conduct code. At least some of them called the women "niggers" when they left the house that evening, according to all accounts, and denied by no one, and one of them, within two hours of the party that night, sent a violent e-mail in which he fantasized about raping and murdering women in his dorm room. These are not the actions of upstanding young men who should be seen as bearing no responsibility for the drama into which they were thrown this past year. If we demand that Nifong and the accuser, Crystal Mangum, take responsibility for their actions (as they should), then so too must we expect some responsibility to be taken by these men, whose names and characters would never have been sullied had they been content to just have a regular keg party that night, without strippers. Had they viewed women as their equals, and not as beings put on earth to entertain them sexually, they would have gotten to play lacrosse last year, and no one would have ever wondered, even for a second, about whether or not they were rapists.

And please note, I bring the issue of the men's culpability up not simply as a way to bash Seligmann, Finnerty, and Evans. Indeed, all of us who are men need to demand more from ourselves. After all, it is the rare heterosexual man who hasn't indulged and projected some objectifying fantasy onto the flesh of women, either through pornography, or at some strip club, or during some testosterone-soaked bachelor party.

In other words, there are no angels in this tragedy, and no unique devils either. The lacrosse players are no better, and sadly not much worse than most of us who are men; the DA is every bit as voracious and political as every DA in the country who regularly panders to the public's desire for toughness; and the accuser is not much different from anyone else with a lot of problems, who in a moment of weakness and intoxication does something stupid, even tragic, and then finds it difficult to extricate herself from the mess she's made. Only our ability to see ourselves in the shoes of each of these characters, and to see how easily we could be them, *any* of them, given the right set of circumstances, will allow us to minimize the likelihood of such things happening in the future. If, on the other hand, we make Mangum into a pariah, while letting the boys get away with their push for public beatification, we will miss the lessons of this case, which are principally these: We must all be responsible for the things we do, and for the things we put out there in the world, and at the end of the day, we all have a lot of issues to work on, with regard to our criminal justice system and our own tendencies to presume the guilt of criminal suspects.

And one more thing, despite the facts in this case, let us above all else remember that rape is a real and all-too-frequent crime in this society, and that for every false accusation there are literally thousands of tragically real ones. It should be our goal to stand strong against that culture of sexual abuse, and never allow a case like that at Duke to lessen our willingness to listen to those women who have been real victims and survivors of such horrors.

MAY 2007

Of Bigots and Broken Records:

Reflections on the Psychopathology of Racist Thinking

Sometimes it seems as if there are people who sit around almost hoping for awful things to happen, just so they can use these incidents, however tragic, to make some kind of political point. So consider the evangelical preachers who responded to Hurricane Katrina by claiming that the tragic inundation of New Orleans occurred because God was mad at the city for its decadent ways; or even worse, consider Christian fascist Fred Phelps, who argues that soldiers get killed in Iraq because God is punishing America for having "tolerated" homosexuality.

Then there are the right-wing radio hosts who seemingly relish terrorist attacks around the world, as these attacks feed their fevered demands for an all-out war on Islam, or who pounce on every crime committed by an undocumented migrant as evidence that we need to seal the border with Mexico. One has to wonder how folks like this would make their case were it not for the occasional drunk driver who crossed the Mexican border without proper paperwork and then killed someone; or how they would hold the attention of their sheeplike followers if al-Qaeda were to take a break from their terrorist proclivities for a few years.

Lately, however, it has been white supremacists who have taken the cake when it comes to exploiting tragedy to further their agenda.

Shameless but Predictable: Racializing Tragedy at Virginia Tech

So, for instance, in the wake of the mass shooting at Virginia Tech, which was carried out by a young Korean American, racists were using the catastrophe as evidence of why America needed to be an all-white nation. On the public comments section of

American Renaissance—the nation's leading "highbrow" white supremacist website, which prides itself on its academic and pseudoscholarly tone—one could read any number of racist comments in the wake of the shootings. Among them, one writer noted, "This sad incident goes to prove that non-whites, whether they be Asians, blacks, Arabs, Polynesians or Mexicans are completely unfit for life in white societies and all should be deported forthwith." Another, basing his comments on the early (and inaccurate) reports that the shooter may have been romantically involved with the first female victim, proclaimed that the entire incident was yet another example of a "multiracial relationship ending in violence and death." Another, echoing that theme (and ignoring the fact that over 90 percent of white women who are murdered are murdered by white men), noted that the incident proved whites should only date members of their own race because they are "much less likely to carry their emotions to extremes."

Others called for tight restrictions or even outright bans on immigration in the wake of the killings, with one proclaiming of Asians, "They are not white and they do not add any major positives by being here; they need to go, just like all the others!" Another took advantage of the tragedy to proclaim her disdain for Korean dry cleaners, grocery store operators, and landlords, for presumably overcharging or refusing to rent to whites.

Ignoring that the shooter had been in the United States for almost his entire life, one commentator, apparently unself-conscious about his own redundancy, exhorted: "The murderous foreigner who murdered all those helpless people is just another example of foreign invaders murdering our people and trashing our sovereignty." Yet another proclaimed these crimes to be proof of the "third world's war of immigration" on the United States—strange, considering that South Korea is not a so-called third world country—and insisted that criminality is genetically "innate" in "black and brown races."

One especially bizarre comment on the AR site, from someone

seeking to condemn gun control measures, noted that murderers like the young man at Virginia Tech could always find compliant victims in pacifistic Amish country should they desire to kill a bunch of people: ironic, considering that just recently it was a *white* man who went into an Amish school and massacred over a half-dozen young girls. Still others essentially blamed the victims of the shooting for having chosen to attend a multiracial school in the first place.

Exploiting a Double Murder: Racists Allege Media Ignores Black-on-White Killings

But if a story about a Korean American mass murderer is good for stoking racist hysteria, it pales in comparison to a good black-folks-raping-and-killing-whites tale. Nothing beefs up white rage and paranoia better than that, and sadly, such a story recently came to light: a truly awful crime in Knoxville, Tennessee, which occurred in early January.

According to the charges in the criminal indictment, three black men in Knoxville carjacked and kidnapped Christopher Newsom and his girlfriend, Channon Christian, and were then joined by a female suspect at the home of one of the perpetrators. Once there, the four raped both victims over several days before murdering them. Clearly, this was a horrible crime, and all thinking people can agree that the perpetrators should face harsh punishment.

Unfortunately, for the professional racists, like those who populate the message boards at American Renaissance or Stormfront.org, this crime has become the stuff of a crusade: so much so that they have actually sought to fabricate certain details of the crimes, which the victims' families and the county medical examiner, as well as law enforcement, indicate are false. So, for example, neo-Nazi groups have claimed that Newsom's penis was cut off, as were Christian's breasts: details that are utterly without merit, but which indicate the psychosexual hang-ups of the white supremacist types who have concocted them.

To the racists, the murders of Christian and Newsom prove that blacks are dangerous "animals" who pose a mortal threat to whites, and the only reason the crimes haven't received national media attention, to hear them tell it, is because the perpetrators were black and the victims white. Presumably, if the roles had been reversed, the crime would have been front-page news and the lead story on every network. As proof, they mention the way in which the national press covered the dragging death of James Byrd at the hands of white racists in Jasper, Texas, in 1998. Or even better, they note the coverage of the rape allegations at Duke University, in which case the media jumped all over a story that, in the end, wasn't even true. The reason? According to the white supremacists, it was because the alleged rapists were white and the alleged victim black.

Just yesterday I received an angry e-mail from yet another one of these folks who asked, regarding the Knoxville killings, "Where be the Revs Al and Jesse [*sic*]?" Answering his own question, he then insisted that the only reason they weren't providing counsel to the families of the victims was because the victims were white. Furthermore, the reason the NAACP and ACLU and *New York Times* hadn't called for an investigation into the event was because the victims were white; and the reason the FBI hasn't investigated the crime as a hate crime was for the same reason.

But although white supremacists may try to score political points from this horrible tragedy, thinking people shouldn't be taken in by their simplistic arguments. As for Jesse Jackson, Al Sharpton, or the NAACP being involved in the case, why would they be? These crimes were not, according to any available evidence, based on racial hatred against the victims. So they are not the purview of either man or the NAACP as a group, which deals with issues of racial discrimination. To be angry with them for not getting involved would be like asking "Where's Ralph Nader?" Or, for that matter, "Where's Ross Perot?" Jackson and Sharpton don't visit the families of most murder victims, of whatever race, because few murders involve the area of specific advocacy for which both men are known: the area of race-based discrimination or mistreatment.

As for investigations of the incident, the suspects are in custody, and the DA is gathering the necessary evidence for trial and presumably is capable of investigating all possible angles for these horrific crimes. There is nothing at all to suggest the crimes were motivated by racial hatred, but if they were, then surely the police department at the heart of the investigation will be able to determine that. And if such information came to light, there is little doubt but that the FBI would become involved. But until the state investigation and prosecution of the suspects is completed, it would be absurd to expect the FBI to rush in to investigate the possible prosecution of double murderers as hate criminals. It would be like having the feds rush in to prosecute a mafia don for embezzlement in the middle of a murder trial.

Does Media Ignore Black-on-White Crime? Uh, No, Not Really

With regard to the allegations of racially biased press coverage, to suggest that this case has failed to receive media attention because of the respective races of the perps and the victims is absurd. Research has found that local news (which is the source most of us rely on for crime information) overrepresents blacks as offenders, relative to their share of crimes committed, and overrepresents whites as victims, relative to the white share of actual crime victims. Furthermore, on both a local and national level, media tends to give more attention to violent crimes committed by blacks against whites than the reverse.

There are several reasons, besides racial bias, why a crime even as brutal as this might not receive national news coverage. To begin with, very few crimes, including the most gruesome homicides, make national news. There are typically between twelve and fifteen thousand homicides each year in the Unites States, and only a few become fodder for national coverage. Of these, about twelve to fourteen hundred or so are interracial, with only a few of these being apparently motivated by racial bias. Of the interracial homicides, anywhere from three hundred to four hundred of these involve white killers and black victims, according to homicide trend data from the FBI, but very few of these get national coverage, contrary to the claims of the racists. James Byrd is actually the exception, not the rule, so conjuring his case as evidence that the media cares more about black victims when victimized by whites than vice versa proves nothing. The year that Byrd was dragged to death, for example, there were 363 blacks killed by whites in America, and the other 362 of them have names that are known to virtually no one but their families.

Those murders that do receive national coverage normally have some unique news hook: the perpetrator is a serial killer, or the crime occurs in a public place, or involves a hostage situation, or involves a mass killing spree, or involves the violation of federal law and thus takes on national implications, or perhaps the crime has some kind of political overtone. If we look at some of the prominently covered national crime stories from recent years, for example, we find several involving black perpetrators and white victims; but in each case, some special circumstance attached to the incident, thereby making what otherwise would have been a story with only local implications into a national event.

Consider, as just a few examples, the Central Park Jogger rape in the 1980s; Colin Ferguson's shooting spree on the Long Island Railroad in 1993; the DC snipers in 2003; the beating of Reginald Denny by three African Americans during the L.A. riots in 1992; the shooting of a judge and police officer, among others, in Atlanta in 2005 by a black defendant headed to trial; and the shooting of a young girl in a Flint, Michigan, elementary school by a black child in the late '90s, not to mention the O.J. Simpson case. But what differentiates all of these cases from the case in Knoxville, and likely led to them receiving maximum coverage, is that each involved a special "news hook" that made the incident relevant to a national audience.

So, for instance, the rape in Central Park took place in a national landmark, where millions of people from around the world visit each year. Had it occurred in an alley in Greenwich Village, or somewhere in Akron, Ohio, for that matter, it wouldn't have received the same attention, even had the crime been every bit as brutal. Ferguson's mass murder shooting took place on a commuter rail train used daily by thousands of people heading to and from work. It also appeared to have a particular antiwhite racial motivation so that it fit within a special news frame that a typical shooting incident likely would not have. The DC snipers were shooting people randomly in the District of Columbia, Virginia, and Maryland, and were on the loose, making the relevance of the crimes to a large audience fairly obvious. Denny was beaten in the midst of the Los Angeles riots, which were a major news event at the time; not to mention, the beating was captured on video. The shooting in the Atlanta courthouse involved the murder of a state judge, a court reporter, a sheriff's deputy, and a federal agent (after the killer, Brian Nichols, fled), and the perp was on the loose for a time, thus major coverage was to be expected. The classroom shooting in Flint took place against the backdrop of a string of shootings that had taken place in schools across the country, and even though the specifics of the case were quite different from the others—it wasn't a mass shooting, and it didn't seem to be the result of a particularly premeditated or thought-out act on the part of the shooter—it nonetheless wasn't surprising to see any school-based incident such as this covered in the wake of several campus-based events of that nature. And O.J., well, is O.J.

As for coverage of the rape allegations against members of the Duke lacrosse team, this story became a national issue not because of the races of the various parties, but because the supposed crime was claimed to have taken place on one of America's most respected college campuses. Furthermore, the alleged perpetrators were elite lacrosse players, making the details of the supposed crime unique for any number of reasons. Had the crime been alleged at a community college in Durham, or anywhere else for that matter, it is unlikely that the nation would have heard about it at all. The economic status of the alleged perps is what likely mattered here, as with Robert Chambers, the so-called "preppy murderer" in 1987, or Alex Kelly, the rapist from upscale Darien, Connecticut, who took off to Europe and stayed on the run for years, rather than stand trial for his crimes.

And to suggest, as the racists do, that stories with white perpetrators and victims of color automatically receive national coverage is simply inaccurate. So, for instance, there have been several recent cases of white violence against persons of color, which received no national coverage. After just a half hour of research, I was able to discover the following examples for the past few months alone: In late April, three seventh-graders in Highland, California, placed a rope around the head of a biracial child and dragged him around the playground at their school, while yelling racial slurs, according to the local paper in San Bernardino; earlier that same month, in Palm Springs, a neo-Nazi stabbed a black couple outside of a Starbucks, in front of a crowd of two dozen people, in a crime that received coverage in the *L.A. Times*, but then gained no national traction whatsoever; in March, a black couple (one of whom was a pregnant woman) were beaten outside their home in Merrillville, Indiana, by two white men who yelled racial slurs during the attack and later sprayed the word "nigger" on their car. But that's not all: According to the *Sacramento Bee*, five whites in Elk Grove, California, attacked a black teen in March of 2007, with one of the white men running his car into the black youth while the latter was riding his bike. In February, two security guards in Stockton, California—one of whom is Asian American and the other black—were attacked by white teenagers who poured gasoline on the road, then lured the guards into the street and threw a Molotov cocktail at them in an attempt to light them on fire. That same month, in Tarpon Springs, Florida, a white man shot at two black men, hitting one of them while they walked down the road, according to the *St. Petersburg Times*. In January, a neo-Nazi in Newport Beach, California, attacked a black man in a wheelchair by pushing him into a lamppost. In Bellevue, Washington, in January, two white contractors attacked one of their black coworkers and tried to gouge out his eyes, and, in Knoxville, the same month as the murders of Christian and Newsom, a group of whites shoved a black student's face into a bus window while shouting racial slurs. None of these cases received attention nationally, nor could they be expected to (except perhaps the Starbucks stabbing), so the idea that white-on-black hate crimes automatically garner mass publicity is demonstrably absurd.

Hysteria and Hypocrisy: Using Tragedy to Condemn Entire Groups

But what is especially disturbing is how white supremacists and racists use any case of black-on-white crime to "prove" the criminal tendencies of African Americans. Websites like American Renaissance and neo-Nazis like David Duke regularly report on any such crime they learn of, anywhere in the country, even when there is no apparent racial motivation for the incident, as if to say "See, we told you so, these people are a threat to whites everywhere!" In other words, the criminal acts of a small handful of blacks come to represent blackness in the minds of weak-minded persons, the likes of whom are attracted to such sites and organizations. Lacking the ability to think critically, racists assume that the roughly seven thousand blacks who commit murder each year do so *because* they're black, which leaves one to wonder what it is about the other thirty-five million or so, also black, who don't.

What racists demonstrate by virtue of their reactions to horrible crimes like those at Virginia Tech, or the murders of Christian and Newsom in Knoxville, is that they have no scruples whatsoever. Anything that can be used to further stoke white racial resentment is good from their perspective. These are people who literally *need* whites to die at the hands of persons of color. Without such incidents to help whip the masses into a state of racist frenzy, their shtick would only grow more tired. David Duke *wants* to see white people victimized by people of color, as do the hate-addled denizens of American Renaissance. If such crimes never occurred they would have a much harder time convincing whites of the need to remake the United States into an all-white nation. White supremacists care nothing for the victims of these crimes, or for their families. They view both only through the distorted lens of their venal propaganda interests. They should be ashamed, but of course, they won't be. It's difficult, after all, to shame those for whom the word has no meaning.

MAY 2007

Confronting White Privilege

Even when whites are willing to acknowledge the existence and persistence of racism, and its consequences for people of color, it is still often the case that we fail to own up to the other end of the racism equation: namely, the reality of white privilege. When discussing racism, liberal whites, for example, may aver that racism continues to limit opportunity for persons of color, but refuse to note that for every "down" there is an "up," and for every act of discrimination there is not only someone whose life chances are diminished, but someone else whose opportunities are, by necessity, enhanced. So, if there are two million cases of housing discrimination against black and brown folks each year, that means millions of additional opportunities for whites looking to rent or purchase a place to live. If people of color are racially profiled and whites aren't, the result of such mistreatment isn't merely a type of "tax" on color, but a subsidy for whiteness. There is no down without an up and no under without an over—meaning that if there is an "underclass" or "underprivileged" group, there must be an "overclass" and "overprivileged" as well. The fact that such words fail to appear in the dictionary doesn't render the concepts they seek to describe inoperative or illusory.

The essays in this section seek to explore the workings of white privilege—what Paula Rothenberg has called "the other side of racism." First, the pieces explore the real material and psychological advantages that come from being white in a white-dominated culture and society; then I turn to the way in which the perspectives of whites—on matters of historic and contemporary reality itself—end up shaping the dominant discourse in the nation. This privilege—the privilege of "perspectivism," which allows the white narrative to become the predominant national narrative—empowers whites in any number of ways and makes it difficult to recognize the extent of the racism problem, since white reality (and the denial that defines it) is the privileged version of truth, in schools and mainstream discourse. Finally, in several commentaries, I explore the *costs* of white privilege, not only for people of color who do not possess it but even for whites who do. It is my contention, as I explain herein, that white privilege, though immensely beneficial in *relative* terms, vis-à-vis people of color, is actually detrimental in the long run to the economic, social, cultural, and community-related interests of whites as well. In other words, in these essays I seek to explain why whites should fight for an end to racism and privilege, not merely as an act of altruism toward others, but for our own sakes too.

THE REAL FACE OF RACIAL PREFERENCE

Whites Swim in Racial Preference

Ask a fish what water is and you'll get no answer, and not only because fish can't speak. Even if they were capable of vocalizing a reply, they wouldn't likely have one for such a question. When water surrounds you every minute of the day, explaining what it is becomes virtually impossible. It simply *is*. It's taken for granted.

So too with this thing we hear so much about called "racial preference." While many whites apparently are convinced that the notion originated with affirmative action programs, intended to expand opportunities for historically marginalized people of color, racial preference has actually had a long and very white history.

Affirmative action for whites was embodied in the abolition of European indentured servitude, which left black (and occasionally indigenous) slaves as the only unfree labor in the colonies that would become the United States. Affirmative action for whites was the essence of the 1790 Naturalization Act, which allowed any European immigrant to become a full citizen, even while blacks, Asians, and American Indians could not. Affirmative action for whites was the guiding principle of segregation, Asian exclusion, and the theft of half of Mexico for the fulfillment of Manifest Destiny.

In recent history, affirmative action for whites motivated racially restrictive housing policies that helped fifteen million white families procure homes with FHA loans from the 1930s to the '60s, while people of color were essentially excluded from the same programs. In other words, on balance, white America has been the biggest collective recipient of racial preference in history. Such preference has skewed our laws, misshaped our public policy, and helped create the glaring inequalities with which we still live.

White racial preference explains why white families, on average, have a net worth eleven times that of black families: a gap that remains substantial even when only comparing families of like size, composition, education, and income status; it also helps explain, at least in part, why a full-time black male worker in 2003 made less in real dollar terms than similar white men were earning in 1967. Such realities do not merely indicate the disadvantages faced by blacks, but indeed are evidence of the preferences afforded whites—preferences that are the necessary flip side of discrimination.

Indeed, the value of preferences to whites over the years has been so enormous that the baby boomer generation of whites is currently in the process of inheriting between $7–10 trillion in assets from their parents and grandparents, property handed down by those who were able to accumulate assets at a time when people of color couldn't. To place the enormity of this intergenerational wealth transfer in perspective, consider that this is an amount greater than all the outstanding mortgage debt, all the credit card debt, all the savings account assets, all the money in IRAs and 401(k) retirement plans, all the annual profits for U.S. manufacturers, and our entire merchandise trade deficit combined.

Yet few whites think of our position as resulting from racial preference. Indeed, we pride ourselves on our hard work and ambition, as if we invented the concepts, as if we have worked harder than the folks who were forced to pick cotton and build levees for free; harder than the Latino immigrants who spend ten hours a day in fields picking strawberries or tomatoes; harder than the (mostly) women of color who clean up messy hotel rooms or change bedpans in hospitals, or the (mostly) men of color who collect our garbage: a crucial service without which we would face not only unpleasant smells but the spread of disease.

We strike the pose of self-sufficiency while ignoring the advantages we have been afforded in every realm of activity: housing, education, employment, criminal justice, politics, and business. We ignore that at every turn, our hard work has been met with access to an opportunity structure to which millions of others have been denied similar access. Privilege, to us, is like water to the fish, invisible precisely because we cannot imagine life without it.

It is that context that best explains the duplicity of the president's critique of affirmative action at the University of Michigan, during the court battle over so-called racial preferences at that institution a few years ago. President Bush, himself a lifelong recipient of affirmative action—the kind that is set aside for the rich and mediocre—proclaimed that the school's policies were unfair. Yet in doing so he not only showed a profound ignorance of the Michigan policy, but also made clear the inability of yet another white person to grasp the magnitude of white privilege still in operation, an inability sadly ratified by the Supreme Court when it ruled in favor of the plaintiffs in the Michigan case, in June 2003.

To wit, the president, and ultimately the Supreme Court, attacked Michigan's policy of awarding 20 points on a 150-point evaluation scale to undergraduate applicants who were members of underrepresented minorities, which at Michigan meant blacks, Latinos, and American Indians. To many whites such a "preference" was blatantly discriminatory. Yet what Bush and the court failed to mention were the greater numbers of points awarded for other things, and which had the clear effect of preferencing whites to the exclusion of people of color.

For example, Michigan awarded twenty points to any student from a low-income background, regardless of race. Since those points could not be combined with those for minority status (in other words, poor blacks didn't get forty points), in effect this was a preference for poor whites. Then Michigan awarded sixteen points to students from the Upper Peninsula of the state: a rural and almost completely white area.

Of course both preferences were fair, based as they were on the recognition that economic status and geography, as with race, can have a profound effect on the quality of schooling that one receives, and that no one should be punished for such things that are beyond their control. But note that such preferences, though disproportionately awarded to whites, remained uncriticized throughout the litigation on this case, while preferences for people of color became the target for reactionary anger. Once again, white preference remained hidden because it wasn't *called* white preference, even if that was the effect.

But that's not all. Ten points were awarded under the Michigan plan to students who attended top high schools, and another eight points were given to students who took an especially demanding advanced placement (AP) and honors curriculum. As with points for those from the Upper Peninsula, these preferences may have been race-neutral in theory, but in practice they were anything but. Because of intense racial isolation—and Michigan's schools are the most segregated in America for blacks, according to research by the Harvard Civil Rights Project—students of color will rarely attend the "best" schools, and on average, schools serving mostly black and Latino students offer only a third as many AP and honors courses as schools serving mostly whites. So even truly talented students of color would have been unable to access those extra points simply because of where they live, their economic status, and ultimately their race, which is intertwined with both. Then up to twelve points were awarded for a student's SAT score, which is itself directly correlated with a student's socioeconomic status, which in turn is highly correlated with race in a way that favors whites and disadvantages most students of color. Four more points were awarded to students with a parent who attended the university: a kind of affirmative action with which the president is intimately familiar, and which almost exclusively goes to whites.

In other words, Michigan was offering twenty "extra" points to the typical black, Latino, or indigenous applicant, while offering various combinations worth up to *seventy* extra points for students who would be almost all white. But while the first of these were seen as examples of racial preferences, the second were not, hidden as they were behind the structure of social inequities that limit where people live, where they go to school, and the kinds of opportunities they have been afforded. White preferences, by being the result of the normal workings of a racist society, can remain out of sight and out of mind, while the power of the state is turned against the paltry preferences meant to offset them.

To recognize how readily whites ignore the workings of white privilege, one need only consider how often whites say things like "If I had only been black I would have gotten into my first-choice college." Such a statement not only ignores the fact that whites are more likely than members of any group, even with affirmative action, to get into their first-choice school but it also presumes that if whites had grown up black, everything else about their lives would have remained the same, and that it would have made no negative difference as to where they went to school, what their family income was, or anything else.

But this ability to believe that being black would have made no difference (other than a beneficial one when it came time for college), and that being white has paid no positive dividends, is rooted in privilege itself: the privilege of not having one's intelligence questioned by books like *The Bell Curve*, or one's culture attacked as dysfunctional by politicians and so-called scholars; it's the privilege of not having to worry about being viewed as "out of place" when driving, shopping, buying a home, or attending the University of Michigan, or the privilege of not being denied an interview for a job because your name sounds "too black," as a recent study discovered happens often to African American job seekers.

So long as those privileges remain firmly in place and the preferential treatment that flows from those privileges continues to work to the benefit of whites, all talk of ending affirmative action is not only premature but a slap in the face to those who have fought and died for equal opportunity.

AN EARLIER VERSION OF
THIS ESSAY WAS PUBLISHED IN MAY 2003

Default Position:

Reflections on the Brain-Rotting Properties of Privilege

To truly understand a nation, a culture, or its people, it helps to know what they take for granted. After all, sometimes the things that go unspoken are more powerful than the spoken word, if for no other reason than the tendency of unspoken assumptions to reinforce core ways of thinking, feeling, and acting, without ever having to be verbalized (and thus subjected to challenge) at all. What's more, when people take certain things for granted, anything that goes against the grain of what they perceive as "normal" will tend to stand out like a sore thumb, and invite a hostility that seems reasonable, at least to those dispensing it, precisely because their unspoken assumptions have gone uninterrogated for so long.

Thus, every February I encounter people who are apoplectic at the thought of Black History Month, and who insist with no sense of irony or misgiving that there should be no such thing, since, after all, there is no White History Month: a position to which they can only adhere because they have taken for granted that "American history" as told to them previously was comprehensive and accurate, as opposed to being largely the particular history of the dominant group. In other words, the normalcy of the white narrative, which has rendered every month since they popped out of their mama's womb White History Month, escapes them and makes the efforts of multiculturalists seem to be the unique break with an otherwise neutral color blindness.

Sorta like those who e-mail me on a semiregular basis to insist, as if they have just stumbled upon something of unparalleled profundity, that there should be an Ivory Magazine to balance out *Ebony*, or that we need a White Entertainment Television network to balance out BET, or an NAAWP to balance out the NAACP.

Again, these dear souls ignore what is obvious to virtually all persons of color but remains unseen by those whose reality gets to be viewed as the norm: namely, that there are already two Ivory Magazines, *Vogue* and *Cosmopolitan*; that there are several WETs, which just so happen to go by the names of CBS, NBC, and ABC; and that the Fortune 500, U.S. Congress, and Fraternal Orders of Police are all doing a pretty good job holding it down for white folks on the organizational front. Just because the norm is not racially named doesn't mean it isn't racialized.

Likewise the ongoing backlash against affirmative action by those who seem to believe that opportunity would truly be equal in the absence of these presumably unjust efforts to ensure access to jobs and higher education for persons of color. We are to believe that things were just fine before affirmative action, and that were such efforts abolished now, we could return to this utopian state of affairs: To hell with the persistent evidence that people of color continue to face discrimination in employment, housing, education, and all other institutional settings in the United States.

So if the University of Michigan gives applicants of color 20 points on a 150-point admission scale, so as to promote racial diversity and balance out the disadvantages to which such students are often subjected in their K–12 schooling experience, *that* is seen as unfair racial preference. But when the same school gives out sixteen points to kids from the lily-white Upper Peninsula, or four points for children of overwhelmingly white alumni, or ten points for students who went to the state's "top" schools (who will be mostly white to be sure), or eight points for those who took a full slate of Advanced Placement classes in high schools (which classes are far less available in schools serving students of color), this is seen as perfectly fair, and not at all racially preferential. What's more, the whites who received all those bonus points due to their racial and class position will not be thought of by anyone as having received unearned advantages, in spite of the almost entirely ascriptive nature of the categories into which they fell that qualified them for such bonuses. No matter their qualifications, it will be taken for granted that any white student at a college or university belongs there.

This is why Jennifer Gratz, the lead plaintiff in the successful "reverse discrimination" suit against Michigan's undergraduate affirmative action policy, found it a supreme injustice that a few dozen black, Latino, and American Indian students were admitted ahead of her, despite having lower SATs and grades; but she thought nothing of the fact that more than fourteen hundred other white students also were admitted ahead of her and her co-plaintiffs, despite having lower scores and grades. "Lesser-qualified" whites are acceptable, while "lesser-qualified" people of color must be eliminated from their unearned perches of opportunity.

This is the kind of logic that also explains the effort of whites at Roger Williams University, in Rhode Island, to start a "white scholarship fund" on the pretense that scholarships for students of color are unfair and place whites at a disadvantage. This, despite the unmentioned fact that over 90 percent of all college scholarship money goes to whites; despite the fact that students of color at elite and expensive colleges come from families with about half the average income of whites; despite the fact that there are scholarships for pretty much every kind of student under the sun, including children of Tupperware dealers, kids whose parents raise horses, kids who are left-handed, kids whose families descend from the founding fathers: You name it, and there's money available for it.

While there are plenty of whites unable to afford college, the fault for this unhappy reality lies not with minority scholarships, but rather with the decisions of almost exclusively white university elites who have raised the price of higher education into the stratosphere. But to place blame where it really belongs, on the rich white folks who have made the decisions to jack up tuition costs, would be illogical. After all, many folks take it for granted that one day we too might be wealthy, and we wouldn't want others to question our decisions and prerogatives come that day either. Better to blame the dark-skinned for our hardship, since we can take it for granted that they're powerless to do a damned thing about it.

Whites take a lot for granted in this country. We take it for granted that we won't be racially profiled even when members of our group engage in criminality at a disproportionate rate, whether the crime is corporate fraud, serial killing, child molestation, abortion clinic bombings, or drunk driving. And indeed we won't be.

We take it for granted that our terrorism won't result in whites as a group being viewed with generalized suspicion. So Tim McVeigh represents only Tim McVeigh, while Mohammed Atta gets to serve as a proxy for every other person who either has his name or follows a prophet of that name.

We take it for granted that we will never be viewed as a "special interest" group, precisely because whatever serves *our* interests is presumed universal. So, for example, while politicians who pursue the support of black, Latino, gay, or other "minority" voters are said to be pandering to special interests, those who bend over backward to secure the backing of NASCAR dads and soccer moms, whose racial composition is as self-evident as it is unmentioned, are said to be politically savvy and merely trying to connect with "normal folks."

We take it for granted that "classical music" is a perfectly legitimate term for what really amounts to one *particular* classical form (mostly European orchestral and piano concerto music), ignoring that there are classical forms of all musical styles, as well as their more contemporary versions.

We take it for granted that the only controversy regarding Jesus is whether or not he was killed by Jews or Romans, or whether the depiction of his execution by Mel Gibson in *The Passion of the Christ* is too violent for children, all the while ignoring a much larger issue, which is why Gibson (and for that matter every other white filmmaker or artist in the history of the faith) feels the need to make Jesus white: something he surely could not have been and was not, with all due apology to Michelangelo, Constantine, Pat Robertson, and the producers of *Jesus Christ Superstar*.

That the only physical descriptions of Jesus in the Bible indicate that he had feet the color of burnt brass, skin the color of jasper stones, and hair like wool poses a slight problem for Gibson and other followers of the white Jesus hanging in their churches, adorning their crucifixes (if Catholic), and gracing the Christmas cards they send each December. It is the same problem posed by the anthropological evidence concerning the physical appearance of first-century Jews from the so-called Middle East. Put simply, Jesus did not look like a longhaired version of my Eastern European great-grandfather in his prime. But to even bring this up is to send most white Christians (and sadly, even many of color) into fits, replete with assurances that "It doesn't matter what Jesus looked like; it only matters what he did." Which is all fine and good, until you realize that indeed it *must* matter to them what Jesus looked like; otherwise, they wouldn't be so averse to presenting him as the man of color he most assuredly was, a man dark enough to guarantee that were he to come back tomorrow and find himself on the wrong side of New York City at the wrong time of night, reaching for his keys or his wallet in the presence of the Street Crimes Unit, he'd be dispatched far more expeditiously than was done at Golgotha two thousands years ago.

But never fear, we needn't grapple with that because we can merely take it for granted that Jesus had to look like us, as did Adam and Eve, and as does God himself. And indeed, most whites apparently believe this to be true, as suggested by the images found in most every Bible story picture book for kids made by a white person, all of which present these figures in such a way. A good example is the classic and widely distributed Arthur Maxwell Bible Series for children, popularly known as the "blue books" that are found in pediatrician and ob-gyn offices around the country (and almost unanimously, it seems, in the South). In Volume One, readers learn (at least visually speaking) that the Garden of Eden was apparently in Oslo: a little-known fact that will stun Biblical scholars to be sure. It would all be quite funny were it not so incontestably insane, so pathological in terms of the scope of our nuttiness. What else, after all, can explain the fact that when a New Jersey theater company put on a passion play a few years ago with a black actor in the lead role, they received hundreds of hateful phone calls and even death threats for daring to portray Jesus as anything other than white?

What else but a tenuous grip on reality could explain the quickness with which white Americans ran around after 9/11 saying things like, "Now we know what it means to be attacked for who we are!" Now we know? Some folks *always* knew what that was like, though their pain and suffering never counted for much in the eyes of the majority.

What else but delusion on a scale necessitating medication could lead one to say, as I saw a thirtysomething white guy do in the wake of the O.J. Simpson "not guilty" verdict, that he now realized everything he had been told about the American justice system being fair was a lie? *Now* he realized it! See the theme here?

That's what privilege is, for those who constantly ask what I mean when I speak of white privilege. It's the ability to presume that your reality is *the* reality; that *your* experiences, if white, are universal, and not particular to your racial identity. It's the ability to assume that you belong and that others will presume that too, the ability to define reality for others, and expect that definition to stick because you have the power to ensure that it becomes the dominant narrative. And it's the ability to ignore all evidence to the contrary, claim that *you* are the victim, and get everyone from the president to the Supreme Court to the average white guy on the street to believe it.

It is Times New Roman font with one-inch margins all around. In other words, it is the default position on the computer of American life, and it has rendered vast numbers of its recipients utterly incapable of critical thought.

Only by rebelling against it, and pursuing freedom from the mental straitjacket into which we have been placed as whites by this system, can we hope to regain our full humanity, and be of any use as allies to people of color in their struggle against racism.

THIS ESSAY WAS PUBLISHED IN
APRIL 2004, UNDER THE TITLE "WHITE WHINE"

THE POWER OF PERSPECTIVISM

Of National Lies and Racial Amnesia:

Jeremiah Wright, Barack Obama, and the Audacity of Truth

For most white folks, indignation fits about as well as a cardigan sweater accidentally placed in the washer and dried on high heat. Sadly, having remained silent in the face of (and having even supported) so much injustice over the years in this country—including the genocide of indigenous persons, the enslavement of Africans, and a century of formal apartheid after abolition—we are just a bit late to get into the game of moral rectitude. And once we enter it, our efforts at righteousness tend to fail the test of sincerity.

Yet here we are, many of us at least, in 2008, fuming at the words of Pastor Jeremiah Wright, of Trinity United Church of Christ in Chicago—Barack Obama's former pastor, whom Obama credits with having brought him to Christianity—for merely reminding us of those evils about which we have remained so quiet and unconcerned. It is not the crime that bothers us, but the remembrance of it, the unwillingness to *let it go*: these last words being the first ones uttered by most whites whenever anyone, least of all an "angry black man" like Jeremiah Wright, foists upon us the bill of particulars for several centuries of white supremacy.

But our collective indignation, no matter how bombastically we may announce it, cannot drown out the truth. And as much as white America may not be able to hear it (and as much as politics may require Obama to condemn it), let us be clear: Jeremiah Wright fundamentally told the truth.

I know that for some such a comment will seem shocking. After all, didn't he say that America "got what it deserved" on 9/11? And didn't he say that black people should be singing "God Damn America" because of its treatment of the African American community throughout the years?

Well, actually, no he didn't.

Wright said not that the attacks of September 11 were justified, but that they were, in effect, *predictable*. Deploying the imagery of chickens coming home to roost is not to give thanks for the return of the poultry or to endorse such feathered homecoming as a positive good; rather, it is merely to note two things: first, that what goes around, indeed, comes around—a notion with long-standing theological grounding—and secondly, that the United States has indeed engaged in more than enough violence against innocent people to make it just a tad bit hypocritical for us to then evince shock and outrage about an attack on ourselves, as if the latter were unprecedented.

On this last point, Wright's scholarship is beyond dispute. In addition to the enslavement of Africans, this nation's leaders slaughtered millions of Indian folk, killed at least a half million in the Philippines (some say more than a million) at the turn of the last century in an attempt to crush the independence movement there, and helped overthrow democratic governments and replace them with vicious dictatorships that butchered and tortured hundreds of thousands in Iran (1953), Guatemala (1954), Indonesia (1965), and Chile (1973), among others. More recently, U.S. sanctions against Iraq after the first Gulf War led to the deaths of at least half a million children there—this, by the admission of former secretary of state Madeleine Albright, who famously claimed in a 1996 television interview that such an outcome was "worth it."

Indeed, the notion that our actions abroad are implicated in terrorist attacks against us is not something said only by the likes of

Wright. So, for instance, in Colin Powell's memoir, he makes it quite clear that the actions of the United States can and have precipitated terrorist atrocities. Referencing the attack on the U.S. Marine barracks in Lebanon in October 1983, in which 241 soldiers were killed, Powell noted that prior to the attack an American aircraft carrier had been "hurling 16-inch shells into the mountains above Beirut . . . as if we were softening up the beaches . . . prior to an invasion. What we tend to overlook in such situations is that other people will react much as we would." And according to the U.S. Department of Defense in its 1997 "Final Report from the Summer Study Task Force on DoD Responses to Transnational Threats," issued in October of that year by the Defense Science Board, "Historical data show a strong correlation between US involvement in international situations and an increase in terrorist attacks against the United States." In other words, Wright's argument about the "blowback" of American foreign policy is endorsed by the very government he was talking about.

Wright also noted that we killed far more people, far more innocent civilians in Hiroshima and Nagasaki than were killed on 9/11 and "never batted an eye." Once again, he is correct, first on the math, then on the innocence of the dead (neither city was a significant military target), and finally, on the lack of remorse about the act: Sixty-plus years later most Americans still believe those attacks were justified to end the war and "save American lives." And this remains true, even though there is ample evidence that the Japanese had signaled their willingness to surrender, and that this willingness was believed by most of our military commanders (including Douglas MacArthur and Dwight Eisenhower) to be genuine enough so as to make the dropping of atomic weapons unnecessary. Indeed, according to the United States Strategic Bombing Survey of 1946:

> Based on a detailed investigation of all the facts, and supported
> by the testimony of the surviving Japanese leaders involved, it

is the Survey's opinion that certainly prior to 31 December 1945, and in all probability prior to 1 November 1945, Japan would have surrendered even if the atomic bombs had not been dropped, even if Russia had not entered the war, and even if no invasion had been planned or contemplated.

So there you have it. But to simply mention these inconvenient facts of history, as Wright has done, is to make one a pariah. We far prefer the logic of George Bush the First, who once said that as president he would "never apologize for the United States of America. I don't care what the facts are."

And no, Wright didn't say that blacks should literally walk around singing "God Damn America." He was merely suggesting that blacks owe little moral allegiance to a nation that has treated so many of them for so long as undeserving of dignity and respect, and which even now locks up hundreds of thousands of nonviolent offenders (especially for drug possession), even while whites who do the same crimes (and according to the data, when it comes to drugs, more often in fact) are walking around free. His reference to God in that sermon was more about what God *will* do to such a nation than it was about what should or shouldn't happen. It was a comment derived from, and fully in keeping with, the black prophetic tradition, and although one can surely disagree with the theology (I do, actually, and don't believe that any God either blesses or condemns nation-states for their actions), the statement itself was no call for blacks to turn on America. If anything, it was a demand that America earn the respect of black people, something the evidence and history suggests it has yet to do.

Finally, although one can certainly disagree with Wright about his suggestion that the government created AIDS to get rid of black folks—and I do, for instance, having seen no evidence to indicate the accuracy of such a claim—it is worth pointing out that Wright isn't the only one who has said this. In fact, none other than Bill Cosby (perhaps white America's favorite black man) proffered his belief in the very same thing back in the early '90s in an interview on CNN, when he said that AIDS may well have been created to get rid of people whom the government deemed "undesirable," including gays and racial minorities. Given the history of government experimentation on black people—from the testing of unsterile surgical procedures on slave women in the mid-1800s to the Tuskegee experiment, which lasted from the '30s to the early '70s (during which time black men infected with syphilis were falsely told they were receiving treatment and then studied to determine the effects of the disease), to the forced sterilization of hundreds of thousands of black and indigenous women throughout the twentieth century—black suspicions about the willingness of elites to harm or kill them is far from mere paranoia. And given the CIA's publicly acknowledged MK ULTRA program of the 1950s and 1960s, during which the government released a virus in San Francisco Bay to determine its effectiveness as a weapon, exposed citizens in a Long Island suburb to a whooping cough epidemic for the same purpose, and gave unwitting hospital patients doses of LSD to gauge its effects on the human brain (all of this documented in congressional testimony and by former CIA officials dating back three decades), it shouldn't surprise anyone that some might believe the United States capable of such deviousness again.

While past misdeeds and conspiracies on the part of government elites certainly do not prove that old patterns are necessarily repeating themselves, so too is it absurd to think that such leopards have changed their spots simply because pages on the calendar have turned, the hands on the clock have moved, and thus, we are to presume an evolution to a more enlightened and less predatory state. Of course, those condemning Wright for his statements about AIDS have not, themselves, examined any of the evidence for or against the proposition that the government deliberately created the virus. They are, instead, merely demanding that such a thought is *incomprehensible*, as if the United States government is literally, because of some inherent goodness or moral calibration, *incapable* of such a thing: this, despite the historical evidence of what we've done in the recent past; in their own lifetimes, in fact.

So that's the truth of the matter: Wright made one comment that is highly arguable (the one about AIDS), but one that has also been voiced by none other than the guy who sells us Jell-O Pudding Pops and has been making us feel good these last few years by lecturing the black poor about their pathologies; another (the God Damn America reference) that was horribly misinterpreted and stripped of all context; and then another (regarding the killing of innocent people by the United States military and intelligence agencies) that was demonstrably accurate. And for this, he is made into a virtual enemy of the state; for this, Barack Obama may lose the support of just enough white folks to cost him the presidency; all of it because Jeremiah Wright, unlike most preachers, opted for truth. If he had been one of those "prosperity ministers" who says Jesus wants nothing so much as for you to be rich, that would have been fine. Had he been a retread bigot like Jerry Falwell was, or Pat Robertson is—and as for Robertson, let us remember, several years ago he suggested that exploding a nuclear device inside the State Department would be the answer to the nation's problems—he might have been criticized, but he would have remained in good standing and surely not have damaged a presidential candidate in this way. But unlike these characters, Jeremiah Wright refused to feed his parishioners lies.

What Jeremiah Wright knows, and told his flock (though they surely already knew it), is that 9/11 was neither the first nor the worst act of terrorism on American soil. The history of this nation for folks of color was, for generations, nothing less than an intergenerational hate crime, one in which 9/11s were woven into the fabric of everyday life: hundreds of thousands of the enslaved who died from the conditions of their bondage, thousands more who were lynched (as many as ten thousand in the first few years after the Civil War, according to testimony chronicled in that period's equivalent of the Congressional Record), millions of indigenous persons wiped off the face of the earth. No, to some, the horror of 9/11 was not new. To some it was not on *that* day that "everything changed." To some, everything changed four hundred years ago, when that first ship landed at what would become Jamestown. To some, everything changed when their ancestors were forced into the hulls of slave ships at Goree Island and brought to a strange land as chattel. To some, everything changed when their homes in Northern Mexico were swallowed up in a massive land grab, annexed into a newly engorged United States, thanks to a war of conquest initiated by the U.S. government. To some, being on the receiving end of terrorism has been a way of life. Until recently it was absolutely normal in fact.

But white folks have a hard time hearing these truths. We find it almost impossible to listen to an alternative version of reality. Indeed, what seems to bother white people more than anything, whether in the recent episode or at any other time, is being confronted with the recognition that black people do not, by and large, see the world like we do, that black people, by and large, do not view America as white people view it. We are, in fact, *shocked* that this should be so, having come to believe, apparently, that the falsehoods to which we cling like a kidney patient clings to a dialysis machine are equally shared by our darker-skinned compatriots.

This is what James Baldwin was talking about in his classic 1972 work, *No Name in the Street*, wherein he noted

> White children, in the main, and whether they are rich or poor, grow up with a grasp of reality so feeble that they can very accurately be described as deluded—about themselves and the world they live in. White people have managed to get through their entire lifetimes in this euphoric state, but black people have not been so lucky: a black man who sees the world the way John Wayne, for example, sees it would not be an eccentric patriot, but a raving maniac.

And so most whites were shocked in 1987, when Supreme Court Justice Thurgood Marshall declined to celebrate the bicentennial of the Constitution, because, as he noted, most of that history had been one of overt racism and injustice, and to his way of thinking, the only history worth celebrating had been that of the past two or three decades.

We were shocked to learn that black people actually believed that a white cop who was a documented racist might frame a black man, and we're shocked to learn that lots of black folks still perceive the United States as a racist nation. We're literally stunned that people who say they experience discrimination regularly and who have the social science research to back them up actually think that those experiences and that data might say something about the nation in which they reside. Imagine.

Most whites are easily shocked by what we see and hear from Pastor Wright and Trinity Church, because what we see and hear so thoroughly challenges our understanding of who we are as a nation. But black people have never, for the most part, believed in the imagery of the "shining city on a hill," for they have never had the option of looking at their nation and ignoring the mountain-sized warts still dotting its face when it comes to race. Black people do not, in the main, get misty-eyed at the sight of the flag the way most white people do—and this is true even for millions of black veterans—for they understand that the nation for whom that flag waves is still not fully committed to their own equality. They have a harder time singing those tunes that so many whites seem eager to belt out, like "God Bless America," for they know that whites sang those words loudly and proudly even as they were enforcing Jim Crow segregation, rioting against blacks who dared move into previously white neighborhoods, throwing rocks at Dr. King and then cheering, as so many did, when they heard the news that he had been assassinated.

Millions of whites refuse to remember (or perhaps have never learned) that which black folks cannot afford to forget. I've seen white people stunned to the point of paralysis when they learn the truth about lynchings in this country—when they discover that such events were not just a couple of good old boys with a truck and a rope hauling some black guy out to the tree, hanging him, and letting him swing there. They had never been told that lynchings were often community events, advertised in papers as "Negro Barbecues," involving hundreds or even thousands of whites, who would join in the fun, eat chicken salad, and drink sweet tea, all while the black victims of their depravity were being strung up, then shot, then burned, and then having their body parts cut off, to be handed out to onlookers. They are stunned to learn that postcards of the events were traded as souvenirs, and that very few whites, including members of their own families, did or said anything to stop it.

Rather than knowing about and confronting the ugliness of our past, whites take steps to excise the less flattering aspects of our history so that we need not be bothered with them. So, in Tulsa, Oklahoma, for example, site of an orgy of violence against the black community in 1921, city officials literally went into the town library and removed all reference to the mass killings in the Greenwood district from the papers with a razor blade: an excising of truth and an assault on memory that would remain unchanged for over seventy years.

Most white people desire, or perhaps even require, the propagation of lies when it comes to our history. Surely we prefer the lies to anything resembling, even remotely, the truth. Our version of history, of our national past, simply cannot allow for the intrusion of fact into a worldview so thoroughly identified with fiction. But that white version of America is not only extraordinarily incomplete, in that it so favors the white experience to the exclusion of others; it is more than that; it is actually a slap in the face to people of color, a reinjury, a reminder that they are essentially irrelevant, their concerns trivial, their lives unworthy of being taken seriously. In that sense, which few if any white Americans appear capable of grasping at present, classic television programs like *Leave It to Beaver* and *Father Knows Best* and *The Andy Griffith Show* portrayed an America so divorced from the reality of the times in which they were produced as to raise serious questions about the sanity of those who found them so moving, so accurate, so real. These iconographic representations of life in the United States are worse than selective, worse than false; they are assaults to the humanity and memory of black people, who were being savagely oppressed even as June Cleaver did housework in heels and laughed about the hilarious hijinks of Beaver and Larry Mondello.

These portraits of America are certifiable evidence of how disconnected white folks were—and to the extent we still love them and view them as representations of the "good old days" to which we wish we could return, still are—from those men and women of color with whom we have long shared a nation. Just two months before *Leave It to Beaver* debuted, proposed civil rights legislation was killed thanks to Strom Thurmond's twenty-four-hour filibuster speech on the floor of the U.S. Senate. One month prior, Arkansas Governor Orville Faubus called out the National Guard to block black students from entering Little Rock Central High, and nine days before America was introduced to the Cleavers, and the comforting image of national life they represented, those black students were finally allowed to enter, amid the screams of enraged, unhinged, viciously bigoted white people, who saw nothing wrong with calling children niggers in front of cameras. *That* was America of the 1950s: a brutal, racist reality for millions, not the sanitized version into which so many escape thanks to the miracle of syndication, which allows white people to relive a lie, year after year after year. It is the lie of national innocence: a condition delivered stillborn at the founding of the nation, but which the nation's white majority chose to believe was still breathing, despite all evidence to the contrary.

No, it is not the pastor who distorts history: Nick at Nite and your teenager's textbooks do that. It is not he who casts aspersions upon "this great country," as Barack Obama put it in his public denunciations of him; it is the historic leadership of the nation that has cast aspersions upon it; it is they who have cheapened it, who have made gaudy and vile the promise of American democracy by defiling it with lies. They engage in a patriotism that is pathological in its implications, that asks of those who adhere to it not merely a love of country but the turning of one's nation into an idol to be worshipped, if not literally, then at least in terms of consequence.

It is they—the flag-lapel-pin-wearing leaders of this land— who bring shame to the country with their nonsensical suggestions that we are always noble in warfare, always well-intentioned, and although we occasionally make mistakes, we are never the ones to blame for anything. Nothing that happens to us has anything to do with *us* at all. It is always about *them*. They are evil, crazy, fanatical, hate our freedoms, and are jealous of our prosperity. When individuals prattle on in this manner we diagnose them as narcissistic, as deluded. When nations do it—when our nation does—we celebrate it as though it were the very model of rational and informed citizenship.

So what can we say about a nation that values lies more than it loves truth? A place where adherence to sincerely believed and internalized fictions allows one to rise to the highest offices in the land, and to earn the respect of millions, while a willingness to challenge those fictions and offer a more accurate counternarrative earns one nothing but contempt, derision, indeed outright hatred? We can say this: Such a place is signing its own death warrant. We can say this too: Such a place is missing the only and last opportunity it may ever have to make things right, to live up to its professed ideals. And we *must* say this: Such a place can never move forward, because we have yet to fully address and come to terms with that which lies behind.

What can we say about a nation where white preachers can lie every week from their pulpits without so much as having to worry that their lies might be noticed by the shiny white faces in their pews, while black preachers who tell one after another essential truth are demonized, not only for the stridency of their tone—which needless to say scares white folks, who have long preferred a style of praise and worship resembling nothing so much as a coma—but for merely calling bullshit on those whose lies are swallowed whole?

And yes, I said it: White preachers lie. In fact, they lie with a skill, fluidity, and precision unparalleled in the history of either preaching *or* lying, both of which histories stretch back a ways and have often overlapped. They lie every Sunday, as they talk about a Savior they have chosen to represent dishonestly as a white man, in every picture to be found of him in their tabernacles, every children's storybook in their Sunday Schools, every Christmas card they'll send to relatives and friends this December. But to lie about Jesus, about the one they consider God—to bear false witness as to who this man was and what he looked like—is apparently no cause for concern.

Nor is it a problem for these preachers to teach and preach that those who don't believe as they believe are going to hell. Despite the fact that such a belief casts aspersions upon God that are so profound as to defy belief—after all, they imply that God is so fundamentally evil that he would burn nonbelievers in a lake of eternal fire—many of the folks who now condemn Jeremiah Wright welcome that theology of hate. Indeed, back when President Bush was the governor of Texas, he endorsed this kind of thinking, responding to a question about whether Jews were going to go to hell by saying that unless you accepted Jesus as your personal savior, the Bible made it pretty clear that indeed, hell was where you'd be heading.

So you can curse God in this way—and to imply such hate on God's part is surely to curse him—and in effect, curse those who aren't Christians, and no one says anything. That isn't considered bigoted. That isn't considered beyond the pale of polite society.

People are not disqualified from becoming president in the minds of millions because they go to a church that says that kind of thing every single week, or because they believe it themselves. And millions do believe it, and see nothing wrong with it whatsoever.

So white folks are mad at Jeremiah Wright because he challenges their views about their country. Meanwhile, those same white folks, and their ministers and priests, every week put forth a false image of the *God* Jeremiah Wright serves, and yet it is whites who feel *we* have the right to be offended.

Pardon me, but something is wrong here, and whatever it is, is not to be found at Trinity United Church of Christ.

MARCH 2008

Breaking the Cycle of White Dependence:

A Modest Call for Majority Self-Help

The experts call it projection, when someone subconsciously realizes that a particular trait applies to them, and then attempts to locate that trait in others, so as to alleviate the stigma or self-doubt engendered by the trait in question. It's a well-understood psychological concept, and explains much: like why men who are struggling with their sexuality are often the most outwardly homophobic; or the way whites during slavery typified black men as rapists, even though the primary rapists were the white slave owners themselves, taking liberties with their female property.

I got to thinking about projection recently, after receiving many an angry e-mail from folks who had read one or another of my previous commentaries, and felt the need to inform me that people of color are "looking for a handout," and are "dependent" on government, and of course, whites. Such claims are making the rounds these days, especially as debate heats up about issues like reparations for enslavement or affirmative action. And this critique is a prime example of projection, for in truth, no people have been as dependent on others throughout history as white folks.

We depended on laws to defend slavery and segregation to elevate us, politically, socially, and economically. We depended on the Naturalization Act of 1790 to make all European immigrants eligible for automatic citizenship, with rights above all persons of color. We depended on land giveaways like the Homestead Act, and housing subsidies that were essentially white-only for years, like FHA and VA loans. Even the GI Bill was, in practice, largely for whites only, and all of these government efforts were instrumental in creating the white middle class. But it goes deeper than that.

From the earliest days, whites were dependent on the land and resources of the Americas, Africa, and Asia. Since Europe offered no substantial riches from its soil, European economic advance was entirely reliant on the taking of other people's land by force, trickery, or coercion. Then these same Europeans relied on slave labor to build a new nation and to create wealth for themselves. That wealth, in turn, was instrumental to financing the American Revolution, as well as allowing the textile and tobacco industries to emerge as international powerhouses. From 1790 to 1860 alone, whites and the overall economy of the United States reaped the benefits of as much as $40 billion in unpaid black labor.

Though apologists for black oppression enjoy pointing out that Africans often sold Africans into slavery, this too indicates how dependent whites have been on blacks, having to pay and bribe Africans to catch their own and deliver them to us so as to fatten the profits of European elites. We couldn't even do that by ourselves.

Then whites were dependent on the indigenous peoples of the Americas to teach us farming skills, as our ineptitude in this realm left the earliest colonists starving to death and turning to cannibalism when the winters came in order to survive. We were dependent on Mexicans to teach us how to extract gold from riverbeds and quartz—a skill that was critical to the growth of the economy in the mid to late 1800s—and had we not taken over half their nation in an unprovoked war, the Pacific ports so vital to the modern U.S. economy would not have been ours, but rather Mexico's. Then we were dependent on still more Mexican labor in the mid-twentieth century under the bracero program, through which over five million Mexicans were brought into the country for agricultural work, and then sent back across the border. And we were dependent on Asian labor to build the railroads that made transcontinental commerce possible. Ninety percent of the laborers used to build the Central Pacific Railroad in the 1860s were Chinese, imported for the purpose, and exploited because the rail bosses felt they could better control them than white workers.

In fact, throughout U.S. labor history, whites have depended on the subordination of workers of color, on the marking of black and brown peoples as the bottom rung on the ladder, a rung below which they would not be allowed to fall. By virtue of this racialized class system, whites could receive the "psychological wage" of whiteness, even if their real wages left them destitute. That too is dependence, and a kind that has marked the experience of even the poorest whites.

The plantation owners in the South were surely dependent on blacks, and for more than field labor. They relied on black women to suckle and care for their children. They relied on blacks to build the levees that kept rivers like the Mississippi from their doorstep. They relied on blacks to do everything: cooking, cleaning, making white beds, polishing white shoes, chopping the wood to heat white homes, and nursing white folks back to health when they would fall ill. Whites prided ourselves on being (or aspiring to be) men and women of leisure, while black and brown folks did all the work. That, and a lot more, is dependence, yet we still insist *they* are the lazy ones. And Northern industrial capitalism relied on black labor too, especially to break the labor militancy of white ethnics by playing off one group of workers against the other. That too is dependence.

During the Civil War, the Confederacy relied on blacks to cook for the troops and make the implements of war they would use in battle. Likewise, the Union relied on nearly two hundred thousand black soldiers to ultimately win the war. That, too, is most assuredly dependence.

And white dependence on people of color continues to this day. Each year, African Americans spend over $700 billion with white-owned companies, money that goes mostly into the pockets of the white owners, white employees, white stockholders, and the white communities in which they live. And yet we say black people need *us*? We think *they* are the dependent ones, relying on the paltry scraps of an eviscerated welfare state? But who would be hurt more:

black folks if all welfare programs were shut down tomorrow, or white folks, if blacks decided they were through transferring three-quarters of a trillion dollars each year to white people and were going to keep their money in their own communities?

Or what about the ongoing dependence of white businesses on the exploitation of black labor? Each year, according to estimates from the Urban Institute, African Americans lose more than $120 billion in wages thanks to discrimination in labor markets. That's money that doesn't end up in the hands of the folks who earned it, but rather remains in the bank accounts of owners.

Our dependence on people of color even extends to our need to have them as spokespeople for our agendas: thus, we've seen the proliferation of high-profile conservatives of color who bash their own people *for* us, so we don't have to do it alone. Ken Hamblin, Clarence Thomas, Larry Elder, Walter Williams, and Linda Chavez: all of them walking, talking lawn jockeys, shining their lights for white supremacy. And oh yes, our need for them is most certainly a form of dependence.

Then, we rely on still more people of color to help further the agenda of white dominance: namely Asians, whom we proclaim to be "model minorities." "See how hard the Asians work," whites love to say, "Why can't blacks be more like *them*?" Of course, we fail to mention the staggering poverty among Southeast Asians, or the fact that the most successful Asian subgroups came to this country with business experience and usually college educations, or the fact that Asian Pacific Islanders still earn less than their white counterparts, even when their qualifications are equal. Never mind all that: The model minority myth has a power all its own, and is one more way in which those who are white have become dependent on those who are not.

Indeed, I'm beginning to think whites are so dependent on people of color that we wouldn't know what to do without them. If there were no black and brown folks around, whites would have no one to blame but ourselves for the crime that occurred, no one to blame but ourselves when we didn't get the jobs we wanted, no one to blame but ourselves when our lives turned out to be less than we'd expected. In short, we *need* people of color, especially in a subordinate role, as a way to build ourselves up and provide a sense of self-worth we otherwise lack.

To be sure, our very existence as whites depends on a negative. To be white has meaning only in terms of what it *doesn't* mean. To be white only has meaning in so far as it means *not* to be black or brown. Whiteness has no intrinsic meaning culturally. Can anyone even articulate what "white culture" means? Not our various European cultures mind you, which do have meaning but have been largely lost to us in the mad dash to accept whiteness and the perks that come with it, but white culture itself.

In workshops I have asked white folks and people of color what they like about being black, white, or whatever they in fact may be. For African Americans the answers always have to do with the pride they feel coming from families who have struggled against the odds, fought injustice, persevered, and maintained dignity in the face of great obstacles. In other words, to be black has meaning derived from the positive actions and experiences of black people themselves. Variations on the same theme tend to be expressed by Latinos, Asians, and indigenous peoples as well. But for whites, if we can come up with anything, it is typically something about how nice it is *not* to have to worry about being racially profiled by police, or how nice it is *not* to be presumed less competent by employers, or discriminated against when applying for a loan or looking for a home. In other words, for whites, our self-definition is wrapped up entirely in terms of what and who we *aren't*. What it means to be white is merely to not be "the other." And for that to have any meaning whatsoever there first must be an "other" against which to contrast oneself.

And that is the most significant dependence of all.

MAY 2001

Anywhere but Here:

Examining the Crimes of Thee, but Not of Me

Imagine that in Germany, public officials and teachers decided to develop a school curriculum about the horrors of racism and intolerance. Now imagine that this curriculum never mentioned the Holocaust of European Jewry, or Germany's persecution of homosexuals, Romany, persons with disabilities, or any of the other groups singled out by the Nazi regime. While avoiding these topics, so obviously pertinent to their national experience, let us instead imagine that this curriculum focused on racism and oppression in the United States: slavery, Indian removal, Asian exclusion, and Jim Crow laws, all of it presented in clear and convincing detail, but nary a mention of anything even remotely similar done by the German republic itself.

I suspect most would recognize the absurdity of such a thing. Yet apparently studying racism elsewhere, while resisting any mention of the same at home, is appropriate when the teachers and students are Americans. Then, it is acceptable to teach of the European Holocaust (and it alone) as evidence of man's inhumanity to man. At least this appears to be the case in Tennessee, where officials have developed new curricula for those seeking their high school equivalency degree, so as to foster an "appreciation for diversity," which takes the European Holocaust as its sole example of the opposite of such appreciation.

Please don't misunderstand. As a Jew, I can viscerally appreciate the importance of studying the European Holocaust, and I have no doubt about its ability to teach certain universal lessons about how simple prejudice can develop over time into persecution and even genocide. But these lessons can likewise be taught by discussing this nation's own crimes, all of which go unmentioned in the new course. So far as Tennessee is concerned (and other states that are apparently looking to copy the model), there is nothing to be learned from chattel slavery, nothing to be learned from the Trail of Tears, which began on the very land where the Holocaust will now be taught as if it were unique in human history. Indeed, the author of Indian removal, Andrew Jackson, made his home just a few minutes' drive from the offices of Tennessee's Department of Labor and Workforce Development, which supports the new curriculum because it will, in their words, "foster an appreciation for diversity, as more and more immigrants and refugees move to Tennessee."

Which begs the obvious, if yet unasked, question: How can learning about the mistreatment of Jews and other European sub-groups have any effect on the attitudes that people in Tennessee have toward those new immigrants, almost none of whom are European, but who are mostly Latino or Asian? After all, despite ongoing prejudice occasionally flung our way by hate groups, Jews are, for all intents and purposes (at least in the United States) seen as whites, accepted as part of the grand schema of European civilization, viewed as intelligent, hard-working, and successful, unlike people of color, who are still typified as lazy, unintelligent, prone to crime and all manner of social pathology. Getting students to acknowledge the humanity of a group of white people, however much this group may differ from most of them in terms of religion and certain cultural traditions, is a far cry from convincing them of the equal value of nonwhite immigrants, who may not look like them, who might not speak the same language, and who are routinely viewed as taking white jobs and soaking up welfare dollars.

Put simply, interethnic discrimination and oppression is different from racism. In the former, a common or similar skin tone allows all within that group to become convinced, if they were not already, of their common bond with others of that skin tone. But racism, by prioritizing certain outward characteristics as paramount to categorization, makes such recognition infinitely more difficult.

Indeed, what else but a fundamental racism against people of color, but which now exempts Jews, could explain the very different reaction to Holocaust Studies courses compared to attempts to teach about racism in the United States? When, after all, have mainstream conservatives derided learning about the Holocaust, which is actually quite common in schools, as "political correctness"? When have they suggested that teaching of the consequences of Hitlerism renders Jews permanent victims, or encourages anger and bitterness on our part? The answer is that such things are never said, though they are common when the discussion is about the oppression of people of color. There, any in-depth conversation about slavery or Indian genocide is viewed as inciting blacks or indigenous persons to hate white people, and to adopt a victim mentality that borders on paranoia. Some victims, it appears, are more worthy than others, and are able to learn about the depths of their oppression without resorting to negative and self-defeating cultural traits. Others can't be trusted with the knowledge of what has happened to their ancestors, because they are presumed irrational, quick to anger, and, God forbid, prone to payback.

As for the emerging Tennessee program, it is especially ironic to note that the students being subjected to this highly selective curriculum include a large number of immigrants learning English for the first time, and poor women coming off welfare. After all, those students could themselves teach a class on intolerance and discrimination, having been subjected to English-only legislation, anti-immigrant crackdowns, and welfare cuts thanks to widespread stereotypes and a steady drumbeat of rhetoric against the so-called underclass.

Those teaching the course say they want their students to think about how people could have stopped the Holocaust instead of passively collaborating with it through silent inaction. As one instructor explained, it was especially tragic that in the midst of the Holocaust, "less than half a percent of the population of Europe helped others" escape persecution.

Apparently, however, she doesn't find it equally tragic, or worthy of mention, that so few whites in this country (including most likely her own ancestors) ever raised a voice against slavery, lynching, the slaughter of American Indians, or segregation. In fact, if confronted with such unpleasant subject matter, she would probably say something akin to, "All that was in the past and has nothing to do with me," a rhetorical dodge quite commonly heard, I suspect, though in a different language, in the streets of Berlin, and which is equally grotesque in both instances.

Though it is too soon to determine whether or not this course will usher in a new era of tolerance among the good people of Tennessee, early evidence suggests the program is serving what is likely the real interest of its designers: to reinforce the notion of American exceptionalism. As one graduate of the program recently explained, the class had made her more grateful than ever to "live in the land of the free." A land that (and I'm guessing they skipped this part in Holocaust class) refused to provide refuge to Jews during Hitler's reign that would have saved them from destruction, and even turned boats away that were filled with Jewish refugees from Europe. A land whose corporate giants actually collaborated with the Nazi regime, and whose intelligence agencies helped over five thousand Nazi scientists and doctors find refuge in the United States after the war, including many who had been directly involved in atrocities. A land whose programs to sterilize "mental defectives" actually served as the blueprint for the Nazis' own eugenic programs in the 1930s, and whose sterilization programs existed both before and after the fall of the Third Reich.

A land whose students are now left to ponder how truly awful some of this planet's other inhabitants can behave. They are shocked, simply shocked, to learn of such a thing.

NOVEMBER 2003

Some Folks Never Felt Safe:

The Truth about National Unity

"United we stand!" Thus comes the proclamation from political leaders and national media. "Americans are pulling together like never before," say still others in the wake of the horrific attacks of September 11. American flags are popping up everywhere: on lapel pins, car antennae, hastily printed T-shirts, and as inserts in the newspaper, the latter for those who want to show their national pride but can't hustle it down to the local Target or Wal-Mart to pick up a fancier version.

And so it is amid this national outpouring of manufactured and marketed patriotism, this presumption of unity, that one might take note of the lingering signs that we are in fact anything but one nation. Osama bin Laden aside, and duly noting the ability of a common enemy to oftentimes paper over existing divisions for the time being, the simple truth is, fissures are everywhere. One such fault line emerged this past week, when Officer Stephen Roach, of the Cincinnati Police Department, was acquitted on all charges stemming from his April shooting of Timothy Thomas, the fifteenth black man killed by police there in the last few years.

Roach, who shot an unarmed Thomas after chasing him down an alley, was praised by the Judge in the case as having an "unblemished" record, as opposed to Thomas, who, the judge stressed, did not. Indeed, Thomas had fourteen outstanding citations, mostly for traffic violations. Apparently, in this unified nation, such misdemeanors are sufficient to justify being killed if you then run from police for fear of being either arrested or roughed up, as Cincinnati cops have been known to do from time to time.

Not only was the negligent homicide charge dismissed, so too was the charge that Roach had obstructed the ensuing police investigation by lying about the incident. Although there was no attempt to deny Roach had lied, first claiming Thomas had "reached for something in his waistband," and then saying he had been startled by Thomas coming around a corner, the Judge threw out the charge anyway, saying it had no significant effect on the investigation. That such light treatment of intentional police deception might set a bad precedent for future incidents was apparently of no concern to the judge.

Were such things extraordinarily rare, one might be inclined to chalk them up to aberration. But in fact, it is all too common for people of color to be on the receiving end of police brutality, even to the point of death. As the Stolen Lives Project has documented, there are thousands of cases in the last few years of persons killed by law enforcement, an overwhelming number of these unarmed, and black or brown; and it's the rare instance when even one of these results in anything more severe than administrative punishment for the offending cop. In fact, it is just as likely that the officers involved in such incidents will receive a raise and commendations as it is that they will ever serve a day in jail.

So despite the rhetoric of national unity, the deep divisions in our criminal justice system, especially regarding police misconduct toward people of color, rear their ugly head again, and remind us that unity is, after all, just a word. Or more to the point, unity is in the eye of the beholder, as are most things. Perspective is shaped by experience, and not just one experience like the World Trade Center attacks, but a multitude of experiences over a lifetime. Perspective grows directly from one's position, for it is from that position that one surveys the stuff of everyday existence. For those who are used to feeling safe and secure, the events of this past month will no doubt have had a particularly jarring effect. But for others, terrorism from abroad may only feel like a more extreme manifestation of life as usual.

Amid the horror of September 11, many a voice has been raised to exclaim that, "Now we Americans finally know what it's like" to be the targets of someone else's hatred. Yet, were it not for the resurgent hypernationalism that has characterized the past few weeks, perhaps we might have noticed that some Americans have long understood what it means to be targeted for who they were, to be terrorized, attacked, even killed. All the "we're all in this together" blather aside, there are millions of Americans who never felt safe or secure, and never assumed that their citizenship protected them from a thing, for indeed it never had before.

For too many people of color, poor folks of all colors, and gays and lesbians, there was no sense of security to shatter, no feeling of invincibility to which Osama bin Laden could even theoretically lay waste. For these Americans, the possibility of being victims of targeted violence or institutional neglect is all too real, and those they've learned to fear are hardly foreign. Whether the violence is done by individual thugs, organized hate groups, police, or lawmakers who turn the other way as poverty, infant mortality, and inadequate health care ravage entire communities, the result is the same: Injured is injured, and dead is most certainly dead. Dying as the result of a plane crash or crumbling building may indeed be more dramatic, and the thought of it is certainly more ghastly, but I doubt it is any more painful or final than any of the multitudinous ways that tens of thousands of our nation's least powerful have been dying for years now.

Of course, a nation that is proud of its selective memory, only remembering the parts of our past that flatter us while studiously avoiding mention of the rest, won't be able to see any of this. A nation whose dominant majority never heard of the Tulsa Race Riot of 1921 (which wasn't a riot so much as a white-led orgy of violence against the city's prosperous black business community) will naturally think terrorism on American soil is a recent phenomenon. A nation whose majority has no idea what happened in Rosewood, Florida, and that has forgotten the lynching parties known as "Negro Barbecues" that were a common occurrence in the South not long ago, will naturally be stunned at the barbarity of the Arab or Muslim "fanatic."

That white-on-black riots were a common thread linking North, South, East, and West for most of the first fifty years of the twentieth century, ultimately costing hundreds of lives and destroying millions of dollars of property remains unspoken, presumably irrelevant in our discussions of terrorism. So too the terroristic enterprise whose actions led to the founding and building of the United States in the first place: namely, the marauding bands of cavalry, assorted soldiers, and so-called pioneers who instigated vicious and depraved attacks on Indian peoples, not only to take their land but also to break down their resistance, instill fear, and force them to retreat against the advance of our collective vision. Truth be told, this is pretty much the textbook definition of terrorism.

I'm thinking here of Captain William Tucker, who in the 1600s took his soldiers to negotiate a peace treaty with the Powhatans, after which he persuaded them to drink a toast with poisoned wine. Two hundred died immediately and his soldiers killed fifty more, bringing back heads as souvenirs.

I'm thinking of Thomas Jefferson, who a century and a half later, unsatisfied with the pace at which Indians were dying, would write: "Nothing will reduce those wretches so soon as pushing the war into the heart of their country. But I would not stop there. I would never cease pursuing them with war while one remained on the face of the Earth."

I'm thinking of Andrew Jackson, who supervised the mutilation of over eight hundred Indian corpses after the Battle of Horseshoe Bend, at which time his men cut off noses and sliced strips of flesh from the bodies for use as bridle reins; or perhaps the Third Colorado Volunteer Cavalry, which massacred both Cheyenne and Arapaho noncombatants at Sand Creek, scalped the dead, severed testicles for use as tobacco pouches, and paraded in Denver with severed female genitals stretched over their hats.

Terrorism on American soil is anything but new, and while there are clear and important differences between the Taliban and al-Qaeda on the one hand, and this nation's founders, like

Jefferson, on the other, the fact remains, as mentioned previously, that dead is dead. To the victims of the latter, it hardly matters that in his better moments he might have waxed eloquent about representative democracy.

Just as the heinous destruction of thousands of lives at the hands of hijackers this month will be remembered forever, so too must these other acts of terror. That individually they may have involved lower body counts, and that we didn't get to see the damage done on live television, seems fairly irrelevant. Terrorism is not defined by the enormity of its death toll, after all.

So while the majority of Americans, especially whites, may see the recent attacks as sui generis in our nation's history, for Indian peoples, African Americans, and others who have been the victims of targeted, hate-inspired violence, the tragedy, while appalling, had the ring of the familiar to it. Even if it is only part of the collective memory and historical consciousness of such folks, the knowledge that one is never safe so long as one lacks power and resources is a truism that must inform our analysis.

At the very least, it should give us pause when we presume a national unity, a collective brother- and sisterhood, or a common experience. Our experiences are not common, our treatment is not equal, and nothing about that has changed since the eleventh of September.

OCTOBER 2001

Don't Know Much about (Black) History

School Curricula and the Myth of a Common Narrative

Recently, Philadelphia became the first American city to require its high school students to complete a course in African American history as a condition of graduation. And predictably, there is already an outcry of opposition from certain whites, whose children compose less than 20 percent of the city's public school students. Though the white CEO of the school system has spoken forcefully to the effect that one cannot really understand American history without understanding black history, some less enlightened souls feel decidedly otherwise. Their complaints are nothing if not unoriginal.

Requiring African American history will be "divisive," they claim, further tearing the city apart, rather than uniting it. But what kind of argument is this? Are we to believe that standard American history has been unifying? The kind of history that largely ignores the contributions and struggles of persons of color in the United States? The history that too often paints an image of Africa suggesting there were no signs of civilization there before whites arrived, and thus that black history doesn't begin until slavery? The kind of history that relegates black folks to one month out of the year, and even then only teaches about a few prominent figures: Dr. King, Frederick Douglass, Harriet Tubman, and perhaps Rosa Parks?

Could it be that such a "standard" history has only been unifying for whites by and large, seeing as how it has presented history in a way that typically glorifies white leaders, European cultural contributions and traditions, and white perspectives on various historical events?

How unifying has it been for black folks to read about their history as if it were only a compendium of victimization narratives? To learn nothing of early African cultures and the ways in which many of their existing traditions stem from those longstanding folkways? To be given the impression that Africa is a vast jungle of uncivilized brutes, as contrasted with the ostensibly superior European nation-states that colonized and dominated it for so long? This, in spite of the rather overwhelming evidence that many African lands were far more advanced than those of Europe, well into the recently completed millennium.

And what is more divisive? The addition of African American history to the curriculum or the exodus of white families from the Philadelphia schools in the first place, in large part to escape integrated environments and to run instead to whiter suburban systems or private schools? That this resegregation has been far more divisive than black history could ever be should be obvious, but will certainly be missed by those white folks who think our perspectives are somehow independent of racial considerations or biases.

Of course, white folks often misunderstand what is and is not unifying. To many of us, whatever makes us feel good is seen as a source of unity, like July 4th. Back in 1987, during the two hundredth anniversary celebration of the Constitution, Supreme Court Justice Thurgood Marshall's observation that the nation's history was not merely the resplendent menagerie of greatness perceived by most whites brought down shit storms of outrage upon his head. He had injected "divisiveness," it was said, into a celebration that, in the absence of his own big mouth, would have been enjoyed by all.

Indeed, whites throw the unity concept around absent any real understanding of what it means. So after 9/11, for example, millions of whites (and pretty much only whites) slapped bumper stickers on their cars that read UNITED WE STAND. The lack of such automotive adornment on the vehicles of persons of color owes less to differences in patriotism per se, or shock and outrage over the events of that day, than it does to a recognition on the part of such persons that disunity is more common in this nation than unity, and a terrorist attack didn't change that. Wide racial gaps in income, wealth, and housing, along with persistent bias in the justice system, makes a mockery out of white pronouncements of unity, and renders utterly specious the notion that teaching black history (rather than merely living the white version) is what divides us.

Other voices in Philly claim that black history is too narrow a topic to be required. Presumably the themes therein won't be sufficiently broad to appeal to all students or offer them important historical lessons. The same argument was heard several years ago in San Francisco. At the time, a push for diversifying the literature curricula in schools was met with howls of protest, even from liberal whites, who insisted the addition of "too many" authors of color would crowd out "the classics." That the classics were only "classic" because white scholars had deemed them so—such a label had, in other words, not been due to some objective scientific standard by which great literature can be judged—escaped notice. That many of these classics were once considered junk fiction (like the works of Mark Twain for example) also went unremarked upon during the uproar. White critics of the plan complained that black and brown authors' stories wouldn't be "universal" enough in the themes they discussed, signifying the way in which Eurocentric thinking supplants rational thought. Such an argument assumes that white folks' perspectives are sufficiently broad to stand in as the generic human experience, while persons of color have experiences that are theirs alone, and from which whites can learn nothing. This is, truth be told, the essence of white supremacist thinking.

Related to the idea that black history is too narrow a subject matter, critics like Pennsylvania Speaker of the House John Perzel argue it is unfair to focus only on blacks. What about other groups? Perzel himself recently complained that when he, a Czech descended American, came through the Philadelphia schools, there was no class about his people's homeland: an argument that ignores the fundamentally larger role blacks have played in the development of the United States as compared to Czech immigrants. To reduce the black experience to just one of many, as if it were no different from any other immigrant group either in quantity or quality, is to give all the evidence one should require of the need for such a class to be mandated, and for some adults to be required to reenroll so as to take it as well. Of course American History classes should strive to tell the stories of those from all ethnic and national origin groups. But black history is especially important given the unique ways in which the black struggle for equality has defined the contours of American freedom (or the lack thereof) in every generation since the nation's founding.

Perzel then argues Philly students should focus on reading, writing, and arithmetic before dabbling in such extraneous classes as Black History. But this posits a false choice: as if one cannot learn to read, write, or compute and gain a historical grounding at the same time. Indeed, engaging the school's two-thirds black majority in an exploration of a history that has largely been invisible to them, and which directly relates to their lives, may result in more achievement in other areas precisely by engaging them in a more relevant pedagogical frame than the one currently offered. This is not to deny that literacy and broad-based achievement are the most important goals. Of course they are, and other initiatives underway in Philadelphia (like the expansion of accelerated and honors programs in all the city's schools, in an attempt to reach more kids who are capable but currently underperforming) can help that process along. But one boosts achievement best not by offering drill-and-kill standardized tests to kids, or teaching them outdated and monocultural history, but rather by engaging them where they are, with curricula that speak to their lives.

Even the students in the Philadelphia schools who aren't black may find the new material on African American history more interesting than having to rehash the information they've been fed since birth. This will be especially likely if the new course teaches, as it should, the ways in which nonblack folks have often worked with African Americans to forge a more equitable society, in the abolitionist movement, the civil rights movement, and in contemporary justice struggles. In other words, Black History need not be a history only of black folks, but a history of the ways in which the black experience has defined *all* of our lives, politically, culturally, and otherwise. That is, by definition, a multicultural history, albeit one told through the predominant lens of a particular group whose voices have long been ignored.

While some of the more thoughtful critics contend black history should be integrated throughout the existing history classes (and in this they surely have a point), the fact remains that it isn't, and there is no evidence to suggest it will be anytime soon. The choice at present is not between a well-integrated, multiple-perspective history curricula on the one hand, and African American history on the other. Rather it is between a largely Eurocentric history on the one hand (with occasional smatterings of "other" folks' narratives thrown in like an afterthought), or an attempt at a more honest and complete course offering on the other: one that can break down the white perspectivism that too often sullies our understanding of history and miseducates everyone's kids in the process.

Given that choice, the path ahead should be clear.

JULY 2005

Reagan, Race, and Remembrance:

Reflections on the American Divide

If one needs any more evidence that whites and people of color live in two totally different places, politically and psychologically, one need only look at the visual evidence provided by the death of Ronald Reagan. More to the point, all one needs to know about this man and his presidency can be gleaned by looking even haphazardly at the racial and ethnic makeup of the crowds flocking to his ranch or his library to pay tribute. So too will it be apparent from the assemblage lining the streets of DC for his funeral procession, or gathering in the Capitol Rotunda to pay respects to their departed hero.

They are, and will be—in case you missed it or are now waiting for the safest prediction in the history of prognostication—white. Far whiter, one should point out, than the nation over which Reagan presided, and even more so than the nation into whose soil he will be deposited within a matter of days. While persons of color make up approximately 30 percent of the population of the United States, the Reagan faithful look like another country altogether. As they gathered in Simi Valley—home of the fortieth president's library, as well as the jury that thought nothing of the police beating of Rodney King—one wonders if they noticed the incongruity between themselves and the rest of the state in which they live: a state called California, where people like them are slightly less than half the population now.

Doubtful. Most of them, after all, are quite used to never seeing black and brown folks, since the vast majority of whites live in communities with virtually no people of color around them, quite by choice, in fact.

That the mourners wouldn't notice the overwhelming

monochromy of their throng is no surprise. But it has been more than a little interesting that no intrepid reporter has thought to ask the obvious question about the racial makeup of those losing sleep over the death of Ronald Reagan, versus those who frankly aren't. After all, there are really only two possible interpretations of the sanguine reaction by people of color to Reagan's death: namely, either black and brown folks are poster children for insensitivity, or perhaps they know something that white folks don't, or would rather ignore. The former of these is not likely—after all, millions of black folks actually forgave George Wallace when he did a partial mea culpa for his racist past before his death—but the latter is as certain as rain in Seattle.

What white folks ignore, but what most African Americans can never forget, is how Reagan opposed the Civil Rights Act at the time of its passage, calling it an unwarranted intrusion on the rights of businesses, and never repudiated his former stand. Or that as governor of California, Reagan dismissed the struggle for fair and open housing by saying that blacks were just "making trouble" and had no intention of moving into mostly white neighborhoods.

Perhaps they have a hard time forgetting that of all the places Reagan could have begun his campaign for the presidency in 1980, he chose Philadelphia, Mississippi: a town famous only for the 1964 murder of three civil rights workers. And perhaps they recall that the focus of his speech that day was "states' rights," a long-standing white code for rolling back civil rights gains and longing for the days of segregation.

Maybe they have burned in their memories the way Reagan attacked welfare programs with stories of "strapping young bucks" buying T-bone steaks, while hardworking taxpayers could only afford hamburger, or how Reagan fabricated a story about a "welfare queen" from Chicago with eighty names, thirty addresses, and twelve Social Security cards, receiving over $150,000 in tax-free income. That Reagan picked Chicago as the site of this entirely fictional woman, and not some mostly white rural area where there were plenty of welfare recipients too, was hardly lost on African Americans.

Perhaps black folks and other people of color remember the words of former Reagan education secretary Terrell Bell, who noted in his memoir how racial slurs were common among the "Great Communicator's" White House staffers, including common references to Martin Lucifer Coon and "sand niggers."

Perhaps they recall that Reagan supported tax exemptions for schools that discriminated openly against blacks.

Perhaps they recall how his administration cut funds for community health centers by 18 percent, denying three-quarters of a million people access to services; how they cut federal housing assistance by two-thirds, resulting in the loss of about two hundred thousand affordable units for renters in urban areas.

Or how Reagan opposed sanctions against the racist South African regime, and even denied that apartheid, under which system blacks could not vote, was racist, noting that its policies were "more tribal than racial."

And it isn't surprising that few if any Salvadorans or Guatemalans who came to the United States in the 1980s, fleeing from violence in their countries, were to be seen placing flowers outside Reagan's library either. After all, the former were forced to seek refuge here precisely because Reagan was so intent on funneling money and arms to the murderous death squad governments who were responsible for killing so many of their compatriots, and the latter no doubt recall how Reagan brushed off the genocidal policies of Guatemalan dictator Rios Montt—a man whose scorched earth tactics, especially against the nation's indigenous, resulted in at least seventy thousand deaths—by saying he was getting a "bum rap" on human rights, and was instead a man of "great personal commitment" who was dedicated to "social justice."

That whites would view much of this as irrelevant, even whining or sour grapes on the part of communities of color, is only proof positive that for many if not most such folks, the opinions of, and even humanity of black and brown persons with whom they share a nation is of secondary importance to the fact that Reagan—as many have been gushing these past few days—"made them feel good again."

But how can healthy people feel good about a leader who does and says the kinds of things mentioned above? Obviously the answer is by denying that racism matters, or that its victims count for anything. Even more cynically, it is no doubt true that for many of them, it was precisely Reagan's hostility to people of color that made them feel good in the first place. By 1980, most whites were already tiring of civil rights and were looking for someone who would take their minds off such troubling concepts as racism, and instead implore them to greatness, however defined, and pride, however defined, and flag-waving.

Whites have long been more enamored of style than substance, of fiction than fact, of fantasy than reality. It's why we have clung so tenaciously to the utterly preposterous version of our national history peddled by textbooks for so long, and it's why we get so angry when anyone tries to offer a correction. It's why we choose to believe the lie about the United States being a shining city on a hill, rather than a potentially great but thoroughly flawed place built on the ruins and graves of Native peoples, built by the labor of enslaved Africans, enlarged by theft and murder and an absolute disregard for non-European lives. As Randall Robinson points out in his recent book, *Quitting America*, when such subjects are broached, the operative response from much of the white tribe is little more than "Oh, that."

Yes, white man, *that*—that exactly. That thing we were raised to gloss over, to speak of in hushed tones, as if by our diminished volume or failure to audibilize it, it would go away, that perhaps they would forget about it, and instead join with us in praise of our country, since praiseworthy is most definitely how so many of us envision it.

White people, especially those who are upper middle class and above, have no reason on earth to be aware of the truth, let alone to dwell on it. The truth is, after all, so messy, so littered with the bodies of dead Nicaraguans, and dead Haitians murdered by Duvalier while Reagan stood by him; so soiled by his support for Saddam Hussein. Better to ignore all that, and to go mushy before the pictures of Reagan in his cowboy hat, to remember a president who, for all of his murderous policies abroad and contempt for millions at home, at least never got a blow job in the Oval Office.

This is the twisted psychosis of growing up privileged, as a member of the dominant group, a group that must view their nation as fair and just, as a place struck off by the literal hand of God, as a place where average guys like Ronald Reagan can become "great leaders." As a place where an "aw shucks" smile and a profound lack of knowledge about the details of public policy (or even the names of foreign leaders) is not only *not* cause for embarrassment, but yet another good reason to vote for someone; where refusing to read up on important policy details prior to a key international meeting so one can watch *The Sound of Music* on TV is seen as endearing rather than cause for a recall.

This is why we get people like George W. Bush, for those who haven't figured it out yet. Oh sure, vote fraud and a pliant Supreme Court help, but were it not for the love affair white Americans have with mediocrity posing as leadership, things never could have gotten this far. It's why a bona fide moron like Tom DeLay can brag about not having a passport (because, after all, why would anyone want to travel abroad and leave "Amurka," even for a day) and not be seen as the epitome of a blithering idiot, and why he could probably be elected again and again in hundreds of white-dominated congressional districts in this country, and not merely in Texas.

Having to grapple with the real world is stressful, and people with relative power and privilege never know how to deal with stress very well. As such, they long for and applaud easy answers for the stress that occasionally manages to intrude upon their lives: so they blame people of color for high taxes, failing schools, crime, drugs, and jobs they didn't get; they blame terrorism on "evil," and the notion that *they* hate *our* freedoms: a belief one can only have if one really thinks one lives in a free country in the first place. In other words, delusion is both the fuel that propels people like Ronald Reagan forward in political life, and then makes a rational assessment of his legacy impossible upon his death.

I think this is why so many white people remember him fondly and are truly crestfallen at the thought of his physical obsolescence: simply put, much of white America *needs* Ronald Reagan, a father figure to tell them everything is going to be OK, a kindly old Wizard of Oz, to assure them that image and reality are one, even when the more cerebral parts of our beings tend toward an opposite conclusion. With Reagan gone, maintaining the illusion becomes more difficult. But knowing white folks—I am, after all, one of them, and have been surrounded by them all of my life—I have little doubt that where there's a will to remain in la-la land, we will surely find a way.

Reagan has been released from the lie, finally, and may his soul find peace among the millions of dearly departed victims of his policies around the world. Meanwhile, the rest of us must pull back the curtain on all phony heroes, Reagan among them, lest we create many millions more.

JUNE 2004

Rebels without a Clue:

Racism, Neo-Confederacy, and the Raising of Historical Illiterates

Here's a little experiment, in two parts.

First, pick pretty much any white person; then go up to them and mention the subject of slavery, and its consequences for blacks in the United States. Next, pull out a stopwatch and time how long it takes for them to say something to the effect of, "All that was a long time ago. Why can't we leave the past in the past and move on?"

And here's the second part: Come and spend a little time in my neck of the woods, the American South, and watch how long it takes for you to spot someone waving, wearing, or otherwise displaying (perhaps on their car) a Confederate flag. Now, having seen several, go up to their respective owners and tell them "All that was a long time ago. Why can't you leave the past in the past and move on?" And as they look at you blankly, or even angrily, and perhaps call you a Yankee or some such thing that they consider the vilest of slurs, ask them about slavery, and watch how quickly they turn to the very same "all that was in the past" line you just used on them, not realizing the irony, which was, after all, the point of this experiment in the first place.

You see, white Southerners (and, truth be told, whites generally in the United States) love to live in the past, so long as it's a past that makes us feel good and venerates us as heroes. So whether waxing emotional about the greatness of our founding fathers, or waving an American flag on Independence Day, or prattling on about some ancestor who died in battle at Gettysburg, the point is the same: to lift up the past and to remain stuck there, at least for a while. But let anyone suggest the less noble side of that same past and watch how quickly history gets relegated to the ashbin of the irrelevant.

Those who wave the Confederate flag, for example, insist they are merely trying to fondly remember part of their history. Yet if blacks (including, to be sure, more than a few Southerners) broach the subject of their ancestors' enslavement and its lingering effects on black America today, they are viewed as wallowing in pity. But what, other than wallowing, and most certainly pitiable, can we call those who insist on waving the standard of a defeated government, some 141 years after it fell? Really now, let us move on indeed!

Case in point: the recent flap in Burleson, Texas, involving two young women who were brought to their high school principal's office for displaying Confederate flags on their purses: a symbol that has been deemed disruptive and potentially racist by school officials. When Ashley Thomas and Aubrie McAllum were chastised by their principal for carrying the so-called Rebel Purses to school—gifts they had received for Christmas (and who says there's no Santa Claus?)—they decided to leave campus altogether, rather than submit to turning the purses over to school officials until the end of the day. Their respective parents, one of whom is a member of the Sons of Confederate Veterans, have threatened to sue, claiming that the girls' free speech is being violated. Aubrie's dad (the SCV member) goes further, insisting that a "heritage violation" has been committed. Yes of course, because you know how hostile those liberal North Texas principals can be toward anything Southern.

The school, which is 90 percent white, is now having to contend with legions of white students who have taken up the girls' cause, by plastering "censored" signs over their purses (be they rebel or not) and book bags, all the while caring quite little as to how the whole thing might feel for the statistical handful of blacks in the school.

Though the young women in question can be excused for their ignorance as to what the flag they chose to display means, the same cannot be said of their parents, who either should know, or do know the truth, but (especially in the case of Rick McAllum) choose to lie about it and push a sanitized, kinder, and gentler version of the Confederacy than history itself affords us.

Oh sure, neo-Confederates yelp at such a suggestion, insisting that the Confederate Battle Flag—the St. Andrew's Cross as it is technically known—has nothing to do with slavery or racism. In fact, they argue, since the flag was really only a battle standard, and not an official flag of the Confederate States of America, it can't even be seen as representative of the government itself. So, even if one accepts that the Confederacy was founded on the basis of racism and for the purpose of maintaining slavery—and indeed this was the position of their leaders, to a person, as will be seen below—the modern day Confederates insist that the battle flag only represents the noble and gallant efforts of their ancestors in warfare, and holds no deeper ideological or practical meaning than this. To hear the neo-Confederates tell it, the brave boys who fell on the fields of battle were not interested in slavery, as very few of them owned any slaves, but rather were fighting in defense of home and hearth, for regional pride and the heritage of their people, which they saw as threatened by an overzealous federal government.

But even as neo-Confederates try valiantly to duck the meaning of their iconography, their efforts flounder on the shoals of both common sense and history. After all, the idea that the motives of soldiers themselves—even if they do differ from the government for which they fight—somehow alter the underlying meaning of the battles in which they engage is fanciful in this or any other war. Soldiers, after all, are not the ones who determine either when they fight, or for what purpose they do so. As such, the notion that the Confederate Army fought for such noble principles as defense of homeland, or regional pride, or other similarly abstract notions amounts to little more than wishful thinking at best, and a deceptive fraud at worst. Armies fight for their respective governments, and for whatever purposes the elected officials of those governments choose to send them.

If the Confederate leadership said (and it did, with disturbing clarity and a complete lack of misgiving) that its reasons for secession had to do with the desire to maintain and extend slavery, and that white supremacy was its "cornerstone" (in the words of CSA vice president Alexander Stephens), then that is the purpose for which the soldiers were fighting. They could have thought they were fighting for mommy, teddy bears, and cornbread, but it wouldn't have made it so. Likewise, in the present, soldiers may think (and apparently some still do) that they are in Iraq to avenge September 11, but if so, this speaks only to their own self-delusion, and that instilled by their commander-in-chief. It says nothing whatsoever about why they are actually there, and why they may ultimately die. That soldiers find themselves the victims of a monstrous con, whether in the 1860s, or nearly a century and a half later, is regrettable to be sure, but it does not allow us to reinterpret the purposes to which their sacrifices were put, merely so that we may feel better about them, or about us.

This may be unsettling to those Southerners who feel compelled to honor "Ol' great-great-grandpappy Beauregard," or some such wretch of a patriarch, but their discomfort in having to confront the truth of the matter hardly makes it any less true. Fact is, great-great-grandpappy died for a lie: the lie of white supremacy, whether or not he believed in it (and of course, truth be told, he did, to the letter, so let us not kid ourselves). There is no honor in that, and nothing at all worth commemorating, except insofar as we may use the sacrificing of our kinfolk on the altar of such evil as an opportunity to resolve that we will do whatever it takes to smash that altar entirely.

No matter, the neo-Confederate will insist, now changing gears: The Confederacy itself was established not because of slavery, but rather for the purpose of defending "states' rights." And this is true, so far as it goes. But to claim that the war and secession were about states' rights in the abstract is to ignore precisely which right the South believed was being violated by their Northern neighbors. It was not, to be sure, the right to decide the proper recipe for a mint julep, nor to make sour mash whiskey in a backyard shed. Rather (and not a single historian worthy of the title denies it) the right they saw as imperiled was the right to maintain and extend slavery.

Since the rebel purse controversy has erupted in Texas, perhaps we would do best to reflect on what the leaders of that fair state had to say about their own decision to depart the Union to which they had only recently been accepted. Doing so leaves very little room for speculation as to their motives.

When Texas announced its secession from the United States, its leaders issued a "Declaration of Causes." Therein it was noted that Texas had been admitted to the Union "as a commonwealth hold- ing, maintaining and protecting the institution known as Negro slavery—the servitude of the African to the white race within her limits—a relation that had existed from the first settlement of her wilderness by the white race, and which her people intended should exist in all future time." The problem, or so the declaration claimed, was that the federal government had sought to exclude slavery from the newly expanding national territories to the West, in effect choking off the economic vitality of the region and "destroying the institutions of Texas and their sister slaveholding states." The declaration continued

> In all the non-slave-holding states . . . the people have formed themselves into a great sectional party . . . based upon an unnatural feeling of hostility to these Southern states and their beneficent and patriarchal system of African slavery, proclaim- ing the debasing doctrine of equality of all men, irrespective of race or color—a doctrine at war with nature, in opposition to the experience of mankind, and in violation of the plain- est revelations of Divine Law. They demand the abolition of Negro slavery throughout the Confederacy, the recognition of political equality between the white and Negro races, and avow their determination to press their crusade against us . . .

The Texas secession delegates went even further than those in most other Southern states, by declaring

> We hold as undeniable truths that the government of the various states and of the (federal) Confederacy itself, were established exclusively by the white race, for themselves and their posterity; that the African race had no agency in their establishment; that they were rightfully held and regarded as an inferior and dependent race, and in that condition only could their existence in this country be rendered beneficial or tolerable.

As if this were not all quite putrid enough, they pressed on:

> In this free government, all white men are and of right ought to be entitled to equal civil rights . . . the servitude of the African race, as existing in these states, is mutually beneficial to both bond and free, and is abundantly authorized and justified by the experience of mankind, and the revealed will of the Almighty Creator; as recognized by all Christian nations.

Of course, this was not merely the view of those in Texas who sought secession, but rather was representative of the views of all the Southern states that broke from the United States. Each and every state made clear their motivations behind leaving the Union, and in each and every instance the reasons given—and they were indeed the *only* reasons given—concerned the South's perception that the North was trying to undercut and eventually eliminate slavery. They specifically mentioned incitements to insurrection on the part of abolitionists, the refusal to enforce the Fugitive Slave Act and thereby return runaway slaves to their masters, and most prominently the concept that came to be known as "free soil," which would prevent newly acquired territories and new states from practicing slavery. This, it was claimed, would encircle the slaveholding South and devastate the region's economy by preventing slavery's expansion.

In the case of Texas, the brief ordinance of secession specified that the decision to secede had been made necessary by the hostility of the federal government to the property interests of Texas and its fellow slaveholding states: in other words, hostility to those states' maintenance of slaves as property, which was the only property in contention at the time.

To criticize the flag and the Confederacy in this way is simply a matter of historical accuracy, not, as the Sons of Confederate Veterans would have it, a "heritage violation." In fact, to suggest that critiquing the Confederacy amounts to a slur against Southern heritage is itself a slur against the Southland, in that it has the effect of linking the South and the Confederacy as if they were synonymous, when in fact they are not. After all, it is absurd to suggest that hundreds of years of the American South and its history can be represented by a symbol of an army, of a government that lasted a mere four years of that history.

Neither the flag in question nor the government for which its soldiers fought are representative of the South. To suggest otherwise is to write black people out of Southern history, since, to be sure, it is not *their* flag, even though blacks have been in the American South for at least as long, if not longer, than the vast majority of European subgroups. It is also to write out of that history the many white Southerners who opposed secession, so mightily in many cases that the Georgia secession vote had to be rigged, and troops had to be sent to East Tennessee to force white folks there to go along with breaking from the Union. West Virginia, indeed, broke away from Virginia over the secession issue, led by men and women who saw the cause of a Southern Confederacy as illegitimate.

To choose the Confederate battle flag as one's proxy for Southern heritage is to make a choice that is inherently ideological and fraught with baggage. After all, one could choose to celebrate any number of other things about the South. As a proud Southerner, I do, by celebrating the civil rights movement, which grew from the soil of the South and was led by brave black Southerners; or by celebrating the educational tradition of historically black colleges and universities, which symbolize the striving for knowledge on the part of persons denied access to higher education by the white majority; or by honoring white abolitionists, who actually numbered more, per capita, in the South than in the North. Or for that matter by celebrating the gastronomic traditions of the region, though indeed such indulgences are probably best if limited, for the sake of oneself and one's arteries.

In other words, Southern heritage means a good deal more than the Confederacy, and indeed, a good deal that is better than that: a tradition of struggle and triumph on the road to liberty, a tradition of music and literature and artwork, and any number of things one could venerate without having to honor a government that openly proclaimed its belief in racial supremacy and sought to hold millions of other human beings in bondage. It says something, and not something flattering, that so many people would prefer to celebrate the machinations of those who desired black servitude than the struggles of those blacks and their white allies, who struggled for freedom.

None of this is to deny that the young women in Burleson have the right to display a racist and offensive symbol such as the Confederate battle flag. They probably do, under any fair reading of the First Amendment. But this truth is hardly the point. After all, just because one has a right to do something, doesn't mean that it *is* right to actually then do it, or that we must call the thing good, once it is actually done. I have the right, after all, to stand in the middle of Central Park and shout racial slurs, but if I do so, it makes me an asshole, plain and simple. And I would certainly hope that someone would tell me so, and not allow my rights—which in this case would include the freedom to be an asshole—to somehow cow them into not exercising theirs, including, in this case, the right to tell me off.

So for the two young women in Burleson, the same is true:

They most assuredly are free, one supposes, to don a rebel flag, be it on their purse, on a shirt, or on a bumper sticker located on their cars, right between the one that says W: THE PRESIDENT, and the other one, which reads, BACK OFF OR I'LL FLICK A BOOGER ON YOUR WINDSHIELD. But that's not the point. The point, or rather the question, is this: If you know that a symbol you intend to display is deeply hurtful to a group of people—is viewed for understandable reasons, even if you disagree with them, as perhaps even terroristic—then what kind of insensitive slug must you be to decide to display that symbol anyway?

Liberty is not, in the final analysis, an argument for engaging in obnoxious or offensive behavior, just because one can. And the fact that one is free to be both obnoxious and offensive hardly suggests that when people choose to do so, they should then be seen as martyrs to a noble cause, or that others should join them in the act for which they are being criticized, or that still others should refrain from shunning them as the ethical reprobates they are, simply because, after all, they have a right to be just that.

And as my friend and fellow educator Paul Gallegos, of Evergreen State College, puts it: "Just because speech is free doesn't mean that it has to be worthless."

FEBRUARY 2006

Bill of Whites:

Historical Memory through the Racial Looking Glass

In 1992, white supremacist Jared Taylor lamented the ostensibly growing influence of people of color in the United States when he wrote:

> The old, standard history united Americans . . . It emphasized one point of view and ignored others. It was history about white people for white people . . . This served the country well, so long as Blacks and Indians did not have voices. All that changed [in] the 1960s. The civil rights movement gave voices to Blacks and Indians . . . It was the end of a certain kind of America.

To listen to Taylor, whites are no longer in control of the nation's dominant historical narrative thanks to a rising tide of multiculturalism forcing us to listen to the perspectives of others. Frankly, we should be so lucky.

In reality of course, the history we teach, learn, and remember is still largely a white-perspectived history, even though we rarely think of it as such. So used are we to perceiving race and identity as something only people of color have, we often neglect to notice when our own perspectives are intensely racialized, even as we try and pass them off as universal.

Case in point: a recent syndicated column by pundit Mark Shields, in which he extols the virtues of the 1944 Servicemen's Readjustment Act, popularly known as the GI Bill of Rights. It's a piece of legislation about which most of us have heard, and from which many we know, including family or friends, have likely benefited, signed by President Roosevelt so as to help returning soldiers from World War II reintegrate into civilian life via subsidized education and job training.

In his homage to the GI Bill, Shields explains that while higher education had previously been the preserve of the elite, with the passage of this government mandate, "all that changed immediately," as nearly eight million vets enrolled in college or job training. Additionally, he notes, veterans were extended favorable mortgage terms, allowing them to own a home for the first time. He concludes his Memorial Day essay by describing the bill as an example of "our ability to act for the common good."

Now, far be it from me to dispute the positive effects of the GI Bill. It was indeed, and still is, in more recent incarnations, a powerful example of what the state can do to provide opportunity when it chooses. Yet, what Shields fails to mention, perhaps because he doesn't know it himself, or it doesn't seem relevant to him, is that the GI Bill was hardly a universal triumph, and the same can be said of the VA and FHA loan programs implemented around the same time to expand opportunity for members of the working class. For the working class that was able to take full advantage of these programs was hardly representative: indeed, the benefits of these otherwise laudable efforts were received nearly exclusively by white folks, and white men in particular. Universal programs in name and theory were, in practice, affirmative action and preferential treatment for members of the dominant majority.

For blacks returning from military service, discrimination in employment was still allowed to trump their "right" to utilize GI Bill benefits. An upsurge of racist violence against black workers after the war, when labor markets began to tighten again, prevented African American soldiers from taking advantage of this supposedly universal program for readjustment to civilian life. And although 43 percent of returning black soldiers expressed a desire to enroll in school, their ability to do so was severely hampered by ongoing segregation in higher education, none of which the GI Bill did anything to reverse or prohibit. Especially in the South, where segregation was most severe, opportunities for blacks to take advantage of the educational component of the bill were harshly curtailed. As the opportunities were largely restricted to historically black colleges and universities with limited openings for enrollment, nearly as many black veterans were blocked from college access as gained access.

And finally, during World War II in particular, black soldiers often served under openly racist white officers, many of whom issued undeserved dishonorable discharges to blacks in uniform, thereby denying them the benefits of the GI Bill. Black soldiers, on average, received nearly twice the percentage of dishonorable discharges as white soldiers. And even those discharged honorably had to confront another formidable obstacle: the U.S. Employment Service, responsible for job placements. As author and professor Karen Brodkin has noted, the USES provided little assistance to black veterans, especially in the South, and most jobs they helped blacks find were in low-paying, menial positions. In San Francisco after the war, and even with the GI Bill to assist them, the employment status of blacks dropped to half their prewar status. In Arkansas, 95 percent of placements for African American vets were as unskilled labor.

So too with the VA and FHA loan programs for housing, both of which utilized racially restrictive underwriting criteria, thereby assuring that hardly any of the $120 billion in housing equity loaned from the late 1940s to the early 1960s through the programs would go to families of color. These loans helped finance over half of all suburban housing construction in the country during this period, less than 2 percent of which ended up being lived in by nonwhites.

Far from being a mere historical dispute, this issue is important for a number of reasons. First, it is valuable for whites to realize how often we falsely assume that our perspective is the perspective of everyone, and that we can speak to what it means to be an American with some kind of all-encompassing authority.

Humility on this score is in order, if we ever hope to address the internalized racist beliefs from which the larger community suffers. Secondly, with the attack on affirmative action being led by those whose mantra of "preferential treatment" implies that only black and brown folks have ever gotten special dispensation from the government, it's good to remind ourselves how long affirmative action for white men has been around. And finally, since whites have reaped the benefits of these "handouts," largely off-limits to people of color, and since many of those white beneficiaries and excluded nonwhites are still around, passing down wealth (or failing to do so) thanks to the restrictive nature of these programs, it seems apparent that a similar effort now, on behalf of those denied opportunity under the original bills, should be undertaken. That we should pass comparable legislation to improve the housing, educational, and employment status of Americans of color, who were for so long denied equity under programs that did these things for whites, is a matter of simple justice.

To not do so would be not only to continue privileging the white interpretation of history, but also to continue privileging whiteness itself. A columnist like Mark Shields can be forgiven for the white-blinders that blinker his analysis of the recent past, less so, however, those of us who allow that past to continue producing inequality in the present.

JULY 2000

Preferring Our Violence Wholesale:

Riots and Destruction in Black and White

I don't know why these things amaze me, but for some reason they always do. Before the ashes were even cool from the recent riots in Benton Harbor, Michigan, much of white America had decided that it knew what was behind all the mayhem, at least if the white folks who call in to talk radio are at all representative.

It wasn't the reason stated by the residents who had engaged in the destruction, of course: namely, a history of police racism, brutality, and misconduct, which they saw symbolized most recently by a high-speed police chase from a neighboring township ending in the death of a black motorcyclist. Of course not: That explanation, though not necessarily justifying mass violence, would still constitute a reason, and having a reason would mean that the rioters were something other than merely insane, and insane is how much of white America prefers to see our black and brown brothers and sisters.

To whites who called talk radio in the days following the riots, the violence by certain members of the Benton Harbor black community was indicative of cultural depravity, even a biological predisposition to violence: arguments that are never made when whites on college campuses riot, as they have done some three dozen times in the past several years.

In truth, the idea that blacks are more prone to violence and destruction than those of us who are white is so utterly incomprehensible as to boggle the imagination. After all, the people who incessantly wonder why blacks occasionally riot and wreak havoc in their own communities never ask why whites are so quick to wreak havoc in the communities of others. Indeed, the history of white violence done to nonwhites, to say nothing of that done to each other (think 1066, think the Holocaust, think Stalin's purges) makes one wonder how anyone could believe persons of European descent were especially peaceful.

It wasn't black people who destroyed one Indian village after another throughout this continent and wiped nearly one hundred million people off the face of the planet in the process. Black folks didn't lynch themselves, or cut off their own ears for souvenirs after burning their own bodies, or hanging themselves from tree limbs.

It wasn't black people who launched a war with Mexico in the name of Manifest Destiny, or conquered Hawaii, or laid siege to the Philippines at the turn of the last century, or planned, authorized, and carried out the terror bombings of Dresden, Tokyo, Hiroshima, and Nagasaki, knowing full well that the victims in each case would invariably be innocent civilians. It wasn't black people who created napalm and then decided to drop it on Southeast Asians.

It wasn't black people who drew up the war plans to bomb Baghdad's electrical grid in the first Gulf War, thereby rendering water treatment facilities inoperable, even though it was acknowledged that doing so would result in widespread disease and death. And with the exceptions of Colin Powell and Condi Rice—two black people who have long felt more at home in the presence of white elites than anyone who looks like them—it wasn't blacks who lied about Iraq's weapons of mass destruction so as to launch another war on that nation, resulting in the deaths of well over one hundred thousand civilians and the destruction of what economic infrastructure remained after a decade of sanctions.

For that matter, even violence in American cities has been the work of whites far more than blacks. Though it may not receive the same attention, the effect of white elite actions vis-à-vis our cities has been every bit as destructive as anything thought up by the residents of Watts, Miami, Cincinnati, or Detroit, let alone smaller towns like Benton Harbor.

When white political and corporate elites launched "urban renewal" in the 1950s and 1960s, the destruction wrought upon black peoples was immense. Hundreds of thousands of homes, representing one-fifth of all black housing in the United States, were destroyed to make way for office buildings, shopping centers, and parking lots. Afterward, only one-tenth of the property destroyed was replaced, forcing displaced families to rely on crowded apartments, the homes of relatives, or run-down public housing. Interstates were built through the heart of black communities in city after city, impacting not only housing but economic vitality as well, leaving a congested, loud, disorganized space behind. It is doubtful that the combined amount of property destroyed by blacks in urban riots comes anywhere near the amount of property destroyed by urban renewal, for the benefit of whites.

When white-run banks redlined black communities, refusing to loan money to any businesses or individuals within the borders of those communities, no matter their individual credit worthiness, the effect was as destructive to neighborhood well-being as any riot.

When banks continue to refuse loans in such places, only to turn around and grant the very same loans through their subsidiaries known as subprime lenders, and in the process charge three to five times higher interest than would be allowed through the bank itself, the effect on black people is economic violence.

When two-thirds of black children in extreme poverty test positive for elevated levels of lead in their blood, all because they have been exposed to lead paint in old, dilapidated buildings built by whites, the result is far worse than that from any aggravated assault.

In fact, white institutions have intentionally exposed black children to lead paint, as with recent revelations that Baltimore's Kennedy Krieger Institute, with the approval of officials from Johns Hopkins University, essentially used black families as guinea pigs for a study on lead abatement in the 1990s. The study, condemned by a Maryland Appeals Court judge, placed poor families of color in housing with varying levels of lead, without telling them the dangers of such exposure. Researchers used incentives like T-shirts, food stamps, and payments of $5 each to encourage families to move into contaminated housing, and then after periodic testing of lead levels in the children's blood withheld information on the extent of their poisoning until it was too late to prevent serious health effects. Indeed, if riots result in the burning of lead-infested buildings, or the places where such truly evil studies are concocted, we might more properly view such actions as the ultimate act of intraracial charity, rather than an irrational explosion of blind rage.

And it's not only in the inner city where white violence destroys the lives of people of color. When the government, in concert with white-owned businesses, strip-mines uranium on Native American soil, thereby helping to inflate the cancer rate among Navajo exposed to radiation by 1600 percent above the national average, the result is death and destruction as severe as any low-level retail violence done by the oppressed themselves.

When white doctors routinely underdiagnose patients of color with serious illnesses, or fail to recommend the same medical interventions as they do for white patients, even when they present the same symptoms, have the same kind of insurance, and come from the same economic background, black lives are lost in numbers that dwarf those lost in riots.

When companies that pollute in white communities receive fines from the EPA that are 500 percent higher than the fines received for polluting in black communities, the result is violence of an especially pernicious form.

In fact, studies have estimated that because African Americans, particularly those of low income, have less access to wealth and high-quality health care, and are more likely to be exposed to environmental pollutants, as many as seventy-five thousand blacks die each year above the amount that would be expected to die if wealth, health care, and pollutant exposure were equal to that of their white counterparts.

That most whites can't conceive of these things as violence is testimony not to the veracity of the charge, but rather our unwillingness to understand systemic racism and the harm it does to people every day. So in the white imagination, burning down a building out of anger at police brutality is violence, while destroying a building to make way for a mall is progress, as is chopping down old-growth forests, dumping toxic waste in streams and rivers, or burying the waste in communities of color.

That's the difference between the violence of the powerful and that of the powerless. Those with power have the capacity to work out our existential crises on the bodies and property of others; those without have to make do torching their own stuff, because they know that the moment they turn their frustrations on those who have remained privileged and sheltered, the power of the state will be turned against them full-force. And if that day ever came, most white folks wouldn't bat an eye, because we have nothing against violence; we love it; in fact, we glorify it, so long as it's being done by John Wayne, Rambo, Clint Eastwood, Tony Soprano, Andrew Jackson, Teddy Roosevelt, Lyndon Johnson, Richard Nixon, Ronald Reagan, George Bush, or his kid.

Body counts never bother us, and neither does destroying property, so long as the bodies and the properties are not ours.

JUNE 2003

Home Runs, Heroes, and Hypocrisy:

Performance Enhancement in Black and White

Barry Bonds is now the all-time home run king of Major League Baseball. This fact, since coming to pass in the fall of 2007, has caused many a white baseball fan to curse the heavens, having concluded that the San Francisco Giants' slugger used steroids for at least a few seasons in the early 2000s, in order to help obtain the record.

Most blacks, on the other hand, either doubt that Bonds used steroids or at least feel as though the allegations haven't been proven. So while most of black America cheered Bonds on during his chase of the prior record, set by Hank Aaron in 1976, large numbers of whites were wishing (often quite openly) for the aging star to be injured, or for pitchers to deliberately walk him, just to deprive him of the honor, even if it would mean walking in the winning run in an important game.

As for me, I have no idea whether or not Barry Bonds used anabolic steroids, knowingly or otherwise. What evidence I've seen seems to suggest that he did, though as of the time of this writing he has yet to have been proven guilty of the charge, or of perjury regarding the matter in a court of law. But for the time being, let's put aside the issue of whether Bonds is guilty of having used steroids. And let's put aside whether or not the steroids he's accused of using can really help a batter hit a ninety-five-mile-an-hour fastball (possibly thrown by a pitcher who was also juiced, given the ubiquity of steroids in the game in the 1990s and early 2000s, all with the knowledge of team owners). And let's also put aside the issue of how many additional home runs Bonds may have hit, which he wouldn't have hit anyway but for the steroids.[1] While all are important matters, there is a more fundamental issue to address when it comes to how Bonds is to be viewed in the history books. For how can white Americans call for Bonds to have his records marred by an asterisk, as so many are demanding, while continuing to revere the records and performances of their white baseball heroes of eras past—folks with names like DiMaggio, Williams, Ruth, and Cobb—who benefited from a much greater "performance enhancement" than that which steroids can provide: namely, the racist exclusion of black athletes from the major leagues?

Steroids vs. Segregation: Which One Provides More of an Unearned Advantage?

There is no denying that anabolic steroids can enhance athletic performance, primarily by allowing athletes to rapidly rebuild damaged muscle mass and recover more quickly from injury. Whether or not they can cause batters to hit balls for greater distance is an open question, to which no one has provided an answer. Although home runs increased across Major League Baseball during the era of unregulated steroid use (and have remained high by historical standards since the crackdown), there are several factors that could have produced that result, even without a single batter being juiced. As sports columnist Dave Zirin notes in his amazing new book, *Welcome to the Terrordome: The Pain, Politics, and Promise of Sports*, these alternative explanations include shorter fences in the dozen or so new ballparks built during this period; balls that many experts believe are being wound more tightly than in the past; better training equipment (including computer technology that allows hitters to graphically analyze their swings and make corrections quickly); and much smaller strike zones. The last of these—imposed on umpires by team owners around the same time as the steroid boom—has forced pitchers to throw into prime hitting zones, thereby guaranteeing that good hitters (and everyone agrees Bonds is one, with or without drugs) are going to hit more home runs.

In other words, it is impossible to know whether or not Bonds's home run spree in the years from 1999 to 2003 was due to steroid use, or whether he may have hit the same number even without them. But we do know one thing for certain: From 1887, when blacks were run out of white-dominated professional baseball leagues, until 1947, when Jackie Robinson first stepped onto a field for the Brooklyn Dodgers, every white baseball player for six decades had been protected from black competition. And protection from competition is the most profound form of artificial performance enhancement imaginable.

It was none other than Joe DiMaggio who said—having once faced Negro League great Satchel Paige in an exhibition game—that Paige was the greatest pitcher he'd ever come up against. But of course, in DiMaggio's 1941 season, during which he hit in fifty-six consecutive games for the Yankees (still a record), he wouldn't have to face Paige, or any other black pitching legends. Though Paige would go on to play in the major leagues, it would only be after reaching his forty-second birthday, and a full fourteen years after his legendary thirty-one and four record in 1934, during which season he pitched sixty-four consecutive scoreless innings and won twenty-one games in a row.

That black players were fully the equals of their white counterparts is hard to deny. Throughout several exhibition games, involving each league's All-Stars, the two leagues split games roughly fifty-fifty. Considering that the Negro League teams had fewer resources to develop players and typically carried smaller rosters (with weaker benches), this was no small feat. Had certain players been allowed in the majors, there is little doubt but that white record holders, then or now, would have faced longer odds when it came to recording their feats. Pitchers like Smokey Joe Williams (who shut out the 1915 National League champion Philadelphia Phillies in an exhibition) or Paige (who was able to pitch three shutout innings in the major leagues at the age of sixty, in a special 1965 appearance with the Kansas City A's) would have wreaked havoc with the bats of white players, had they been given the chance.

By the same token, sluggers like Josh Gibson, Buck Leonard, and Oscar Charleston (who hit .318 with eleven home runs in fifty-three exhibitions against white major leaguers, and is considered the fourth best player in history by baseball historian Bill James) would have easily vied for many of the records set by whites, some of which stand to this day. This would have been especially true had they been able to play in homer-friendly Yankee stadium, which originally had home run fences down the right and left field lines that were less than three hundred feet from home plate, so as to accommodate the likes of Babe Ruth. (As a side note, it's interesting how no one ever suggests Ruth's accomplishments should be looked at skeptically because he was swinging at fences that I was able to reach routinely at the age of fifteen.)

And speedsters like Cool Papa Bell, given the chance, would certainly have challenged Ty Cobb's record of stolen bases, long before Lou Brock ultimately obliterated it in 1978 (since eclipsed by Rickey Henderson). Not to mention, had players like Monte Irvin, Larry Doby, Roy Campanella, or Don Newcombe—who ultimately played major league ball but got their start in the Negro Leagues—been able to start their big league careers earlier, who knows what records they might have set?

One thing is certain though: All of the records set by white players prior to 1947 are tainted. Any time that someone is protected from competition (be that someone an athlete or a corporation), those who are protected get to shine, without having to prove themselves against the full range of possible talent. Barry Bonds, on the other hand, even if juiced by steroids, had to compete against the best (many of whom were no doubt also using such medicinal enhancements), and as such, enjoyed far less of a relative boost in his career than white players did for nearly half of the twentieth century.[2]

And No, It's Not Different: The Absurdity of the "Segregation Was Legal" Excuse

Confronted with the argument that maybe Williams, DiMaggio, and especially Babe Ruth wouldn't have been as good had they been required to play against black players, most white folks fall back on what they consider their trump card, which to them seems to differentiate the performance enhancement of steroids from the performance enhancement of white privilege and institutionalized favoritism. Namely, they suggest, Barry Bonds broke the rules, while Ruth and company merely played within the boundaries of the rules, as they existed at the time. While most everyone acknowledges that racism in baseball was a shameful stain on the game, you'll often hear it said that segregation was "just the way it was." The implicit argument here is that we shouldn't lower our estimation of white players due to segregation, since they weren't the ones who enforced the color barrier, but rather just played by the rules as they found them.

But there are several things about this argument that are wrong, illogical, or ethically indefensible. To begin with, during the period of Bonds's alleged steroid use, there was actually no rule against steroids in major league baseball. So, in point of fact, Bonds, assuming he used steroids, did not break the rules of the game. Yes, using the substances without a prescription is illegal, but we don't take records away from players for breaking the law. If we did, we'd have to erase pitcher Doc Ellis's perfect game in 1970, which he claims to have tossed while tripping on acid. We'd have to disregard the performance of Keith Hernandez, who has admitted to using cocaine during his years on the field, and who once suggested that upward of 40 percent of all players were using blow. Or what of Willie Mays and Willie Stargell (two of the game's all-time greats), who were accused in the mid-'80s of providing amphetamines to players? Should we erase their records as well? Or what of Ruth, who once tried injecting himself with sheep hormones to get an edge on the competition, and who kept right on drinking, even in the age of prohibition, when booze was outlawed?

Even worse, the argument that segregation was "just the way it was" implies that we are not under any obligation to challenge injustice unless we ourselves created it, and that if we collaborate with it, we bear no moral responsibility for its perpetuation. But what kind of moral standard is that? By that logic, folks who stood by and remained silent during Jim Crow, during lynchings, during the Holocaust of European Jewry or American Holocaust of indigenous persons did nothing wrong. By that logic, we should teach our children that whenever they see an injustice, so long as it benefits them, they should go along to get along. But any parents who taught their kids such a thing would be shirking their responsibilities as moral guides.

The truth is, had even a handful of the top white players refused to play until the major leagues were integrated—especially in the 1920s, '30s, or early '40s, by which time the sport had become "America's pastime"—it is almost certain that the color barrier would have fallen more quickly. After all, it was in large part because of the demands of nineteenth-century great Cap Anson, a player-manager, that blacks were booted from the game in the first place. Players did have power. They were the ones fans came to see and for whom they paid good money. There is no way that baseball could have remained all-white if Babe Ruth or Lou Gehrig had said they were sitting down until blacks were allowed to play. Had Gehrig ended his long-standing record of consecutive games played because of opposition to racism, it would have been one of the most important sports stories of all time. That he didn't, and that no white players had the courage to take this step, is far from inconsequential and calls into question their character, whether or not white fans are prepared to hear this uncomfortable truth. In other words, whites, by knowingly protecting themselves from some of the game's greatest players, "cheated" every bit as much as Bonds may have, via the use of anabolics. That the method for cheating was institutionalized, so that the rules themselves amounted to fraud, and that racial cheating was given the imprimatur of law hardly provides moral cover for the practice's ethical failings, and the failings of those who took advantage.

Oh, and not to put too fine a point on it, but in parts of the country (including most of the Northeast) the laws of the local communities actually prohibited segregation by race. Of course, northern cities ignored these laws, and persons of color were subject to intense racism there, as in the South. But if our concern is the law, and how the law was for segregation (and how therefore players can't be accused of having broken the rules), we should remember that teams like the Yankees were essentially *breaking* local and state law by keeping blacks off their squads. So perhaps we should erase the records of the Yankees, erase the Babe, erase Ted Williams's 1941 season in which he hit .406 for the Red Sox, another team in a Northern city with laws against segregation, but which remained segregated anyway (and in Boston's case, they were the longest holdout against black players due to the legendary racism of their owner).

But Is It Racism? Demeanor and Double Standards in the White Imagination

Of course, there is still the question of whether or not those whites who were rooting against Bonds, or who want to see that asterisk by his name, feel the way they do because of racism. On this point, honest people can truly disagree. After all, many of the white fans who disparage Bonds love other black athletes, including the man who Bonds overtook. That Aaron set the mark of 755 homers without any enhancements, without short fences, without juiced balls, and despite the hostility often dispensed to black players during his heyday suggests to many (myself included) that Aaron's accomplishments are, in many ways, more impressive.

And of course, there are reasons to dislike Bonds having nothing to do with his race. Among the most often cited is his generally hostile attitude to the press and the public. But here is where the issue of race becomes especially interesting as it relates to white folks' estimation of Bonds. Fact is, just because whites love certain black athletes doesn't mean that racial animosity or racism is not in the equation on the occasions when they feel decidedly otherwise. Racism can indeed be operating when whites respond negatively to the "attitudes" of persons of color, if they fail to do so when encountering the same attitudes from whites. Studies have found that when people of color act in ways that trigger negative group associations in the minds of whites, those whites often react in a much harsher manner than when a white person evinces the same attitude or behavior. The white athlete who is arrogant or ill-tempered is seen through an individual lens, while the black athlete who does the same is seen as a representative of a larger racial group, and deemed threatening, angry, maybe even violent.

So Roger Clemens can deliberately throw at the heads of batters, to either back them off the plate or in retaliation for a player on his team being hit by a pitch, and no one seems to care, let alone accuse him of aggravated assault with a deadly weapon (which a ninety-seven-mile-per-hour fastball surely is). And pitcher Randy Johnson can act like an ass, even pushing a New York cameraperson upon his arrival to the Yankees several years back, and yet have few fans turn on him. As long as he was producing, his attitude was overlooked, as with basketball coach Bobby Knight, baseball coaches Earl Weaver and Leo Durocher, or, for that matter Ruth, Ty Cobb, and Mickey Mantle, who were, according to pretty much everyone who knew them, utter bastards. So if there is a racially differential way in which Bonds's rudeness is interpreted, in comparison with any number of white athletes (think John McEnroe, as one final example), then there are few ways to interpret the difference other than as a racial matter.

Additionally, if whites respond negatively to blacks whose demeanor is seen as hostile or arrogant but respond well to blacks who seem less gruff, it may well be that the first of these has to do with the way in which certain behavior prompts negative stereotypes in white folks' minds. Once prompted, white racial hostility may be triggered in this kind of situation, even though it wouldn't be deployed against blacks whose behavior ran counter to white folks' preconceived biases. Far from mere speculation, it is precisely the difference in white perceptions of some blacks relative to others that prompted Branch Rickey to choose Jackie Robinson as the instrument of integration in baseball, over other equally or more talented black ball players. Though Robinson was no sellout, as is often alleged, he was clearly more accommodating to the racial taunts it was feared he would (and often did) receive from white fans. Rickey realized that certain black players would rub whites the wrong way, thanks to racism, but that Robinson would project the kind of image that would be less likely to trigger latent biases on the part of white fans.

Whites have long demonstrated a preference for gregarious and smiling black folks ever since the days of slavery, when such characters reinforced white assumptions about the fairness of the society. If black folks play by the script set up by whites—don't be angry, don't question authority, don't be arrogant (read: uppity), don't be political (like John Carlos and Tommie Smith at the 1968 Olympics, or Muhammad Ali, whose reputation with many whites was forever tainted by his anti–Vietnam War commentary), and don't purposely seek to tweak white folks' racial fears (as with fighter Jack Johnson, who often taunted whites about his white female companions)—then everything will be OK. But if blacks deviate, or cop a "to hell with you" attitude, whites often see it as a racial challenge in ways we wouldn't if another white person did it, and react angrily.

So whites loved Michael Jordan and Magic Johnson (understandably of course, given their talent), but detest many of today's younger, amazingly capable, but often brash black ballers, and not only the ones who have been in trouble with the law. For that matter, whites never much cared for Kareem Abdul-Jabbar either, after he became a Muslim and changed his name from Lew Alcindor. Kareem was seen by many (still is) as unfriendly, brooding, and arrogant, and this perception has hurt his ability to land a much deserved and desired coaching gig anywhere in the NBA, despite his demonstrated basketball genius.

Conclusion: Letting Go of the Mythology of Baseball's Glory Days

As a final thought, it's hard to avoid the conclusion that at least part of white America's anger at Bonds's accomplishments is in keeping with white folks' general anxiety over the loss of a mythologized past, one in which a supposedly more innocent, decent society held sway, folks played by the rules, and all was right with the world. While black folks know this world never existed, at least for them, white folks' hagiographic history tends to gloss over the racial injustices of past eras, rather choosing to hold these eras up as the "good old days" of mom, apple pie, *I Love Lucy*, and Radio Flyers zooming down snow-covered hills.

This romantic notion of our national past is especially strong when it comes to baseball. Whites wistfully praise the accomplishments of the 1927 Yankees, even though, in terms of sheer strength and talent, they would get their clocks cleaned by even a mediocre team in the present, largely due to better conditioning routines in the modern era. Babe Ruth was an overweight, out of shape drunk, whose home runs were hit disproportionately in a stadium with fences that were set at a distance more appropriate for high school kids. Our glorifying of these faded icons speaks more to the nostalgic tendencies of whites, adrift in a culture that, although still dominated by folks like us, isn't completely defined by those like us any longer. As society changes, those who always benefited most from the traditional arrangement naturally resist the seismic shifts in national consciousness, to say nothing of demographics. If you think the falloff in fan support for Major League Baseball isn't related to the increasing Latinization of the sport at the highest levels, in other words, then perhaps you'd like to purchase my beachfront property in Missouri.

In the final analysis, it is not Barry Bonds who is the problem, but white sports fans, longing for those olden days, irrespective of the injustices that defined them. The problem is white folks who want and apparently need black athletes to pander to our tastes, kiss our asses, and tell us how wonderful everything is with the system and society in which we live. Too bad for us. Bottom line: Barry Bonds is a better hitter than any white ball player who ever lived, period, end of story. And he is equal to Aaron and Mays if not better overall. And if you don't like that, pick up a bat and try to be better. Good damned luck.

AN EARLIER VERSION OF THIS ESSAY WAS
PUBLISHED IN JUNE 2007

---

1 Bonds's critics claim that only steroids could have produced the slugger's seventy-three home run season of 2001, since his highest total prior to that time had been forty-nine in the course of a year. Yet what they conveniently ignore is how white ball players often have remarkable years, unduplicated over the lifetimes of their careers. So, for instance, Roger Maris (who held the record for single-season home runs, at sixty-one, from 1961 until 1998, at which point Mark McGuire and Sammy Sosa both surpassed him) had hit only thirty-nine home runs the year before his record. The year after, Maris hit only thirty-three, and then hit only seventy home runs over a five-year period, beginning in 1963 and ending with the 1967 season. Indeed, roughly one-fourth of Maris's career home runs occurred in that single magical season, out of a total career that lasted twelve years.

2 It should be noted that steroids would likely be of more direct benefit to pitchers than to hitters, which is something to keep in mind since Bonds likely faced many steroid-enhanced pitchers during the years of his alleged use. After all, steroids allow players to have shorter down time in the case of injury, which is especially important to pitchers, who by definition are in on every play when they're on the field. Wrenching your arm forward a hundred times a game or throwing utterly unnatural curve balls takes a toll on pitchers, which toll can be dramatically lessened by anabolic steroids. Which is all to say that Bonds's use (assuming it happened exactly as alleged) may well have only placed him on an even keel with many of the pitchers he faced. While the commonality of use hardly makes it acceptable to use steroids, it does suggest that the comparative advantage Bonds would have obtained from steroids would have possibly been quite small.

MEASURING THE COSTS

Overclass Blues:

Class, Race, and the Ironies of Privilege

The first word of this article's title does not exist according to the spell-check program on my computer and the dictionary on my desk. Underclass? Yes, both sources recognize and can define that term. Yet neither acknowledges that any word with the prefix "under" is by definition relative, and that there must be an "over" somewhere in the equation, with which it can be contrasted. As such, the good folks at Webster's inform us that the underclass refers to those who are "below subsistence level" in terms of income (we used to call them poor). However, they don't seem to think that if those with too little constitute an underclass, perhaps those with too much constitute an overclass, no doubt because there is no such thing as "too much" in the United States, where excess is applauded and sought out with reckless abandon.

The underclass, social scientists tell us, is made up not merely of the poor, but those trapped in a cycle of poverty, pathology, addiction, and dependence, particularly on welfare programs, drugs, or both. They are to be pitied, perhaps, feared always, regulated and controlled to be sure. The underclass supposedly have different values than the rest of us: They live for the moment (this is called having a "short-term orientation"); they engage in destructive behaviors at alarming rates (things like substance abuse, violence, or other criminal endeavors); they take a lackadaisical attitude toward school; they don't want to work hard and prefer government handouts to honest labor; their families are a tangle of dysfunction.

Yet many of these things are common not only among those struggling to survive but also among those who don't struggle for much of anything, those who, if our dictionaries reflected basic intellectual honesty, would be called the overclass; those of privilege in the upper echelons of the nation's class structure.

The wealthy and specifically their corporations rely heavily on government handouts—subsidies totaling more than $100 billion annually, far more than all the money spent on poor folks. Without these taxpayer-funded gifts, these companies and entire industries would not be able to remain competitive in the so-called free market, the meaning of which is apparently "free money," at least for them.

As for laziness and an aversion to work, one really can't find better examples of that than among the rich heirs to family fortunes: Take Paris and Nicki Hilton for example, whose paparazzi-covered lives seem to consist of nothing but one party after another, interrupted occasionally by a photo shoot. Poor folks who don't work are parasites, while rich people who don't work are cover story material for glamour magazines.

More broadly, the wealthiest Americans get at least half of their income not from work at all, but from the money they already have, in the form of rent, dividends, and interest payments. Yet few people would be willing to suggest the obvious: that these folks are less hard-working by definition than the typical waitress, housekeeper, garbage collector, or even mother on "welfare," trying to keep a roof over the heads of herself and her kids.

As for short-term orientations, what could be more emblematic than a corporation's quarterly profit and loss statement, and the mindset that places short-term profits ahead of long-term fiscal stability? Dot-com bust, anyone? That sure as hell wasn't underclass

twentysomething youth from the so-called ghetto setting up sweet-
heart compensation packages for themselves, without regard for a
long-range business plan. Short-term orientation is supposedly why
the poor squander money on lottery tickets, preferring the long shot
of get-rich-quick over the daily grind of steady employment. But
when moral czar, author, and former secretary of education William
Bennett blows several million dollars in casinos it's just a hobby,
passing the time, or entertainment. Such behavior is never viewed
as evidence of a flawed value system. The fact that the wealthy who
gamble could spend their money feeding hungry people instead of
amusing themselves at slot machines is not apparently proof of their
narcissism, but if the poor engage in the very same behavior, they
are viewed as "different" from the rich, rather than mimicking them.
Likewise, if the rich gamble with other people's money via specula-
tive investments, junk bonds, Savings and Loan rip-off schemes, or
shady accounting à la Enron, this is not seen as evidence of a class
flaw, and it isn't usually punished nearly as harshly as the typical food
stamp fraudster.

As for devaluing education, wasn't it President Bush—he of the
privileged prep school and Yale set—who bragged to graduates of
his alma mater that he had been a C student, and that there was
nothing wrong with such mediocrity?

Destructive behavior? Well let's see: It isn't the poor who start
wars, incinerate cities, or pollute the environment with toxic waste.
It is those with power—by definition not the "underclass"—who
develop weapons of mass destruction, or impose deadly sanctions
on countries they don't like.

Even closer to home, the affluent engage in more than their
fair share of destructive activity. Suburban schools have equal or
higher rates of violent and property crime annually than urban
schools, according to the Departments of Education and Justice,
even though the former tend to be doubly privileged: mostly
white and mostly affluent. Whites (the group with racial privilege
in the United States) are far more likely to drive drunk, have a rate

of child molestation and sexual violence against children that is pushing double the rate for blacks, and are equally or more likely to use drugs than blacks or Latinos. In fact, white high schoolers are more likely to use every category of drug than blacks, according to the National Institutes on Drug Abuse and data from the Centers for Disease Control.

It also isn't poor folks of color creating computer viruses that have caused over $65 billion in damages worldwide. Instead, it is almost always upper middle class, white suburbanites. Yet, as an AP story on the latest Internet meltdown noted, criminal prosecutions of the high-tech thugs wreaking all this havoc are few, penalties are minimal, and only a handful of people have ever been imprisoned for such behavior. Interesting, considering how utterly premeditated virus creation is, far more so than typical street crime, which regularly lands its perpetrators in jail for long stretches, even when the damage is minuscule by comparison.

Our unwillingness to label destructive behaviors by whites and those in the upper classes as a character flaw typical of the group as a whole, while we readily do so for people of color and the poor, speaks to our culture's insipient racism and classism. And our lack of an adequate language to critically examine the behaviors of the society's haves also leads us to ignore the warning signs or potential dangers posed by such persons, to themselves and others.

It is blindness to the concept of the overclass that explains in large part the inability of most commentators to properly analyze a just-released study from Columbia University. According to the report, from the National Center on Addiction and Substance Abuse, the key risk factors for drug, alcohol, and tobacco use among teens are too much stress, boredom, and too much money. As for too much money, well, that's obviously not an underclass problem. And boredom too is more common among those in sterile, uninspiring suburbs, at least if one believes what an awful lot of youth say about their own lives. Which brings us to the issue of stress. On the one hand, one would think that dealing with poverty, racism, crumbling schools, and dilapidated housing, as is common for the stereotypical member of the underclass, would be pretty stressful. Yet, all data indicates it is whites and those with money who are more likely to drink alcohol, use drugs, or smoke cigarettes. So what's going on, and what really explains the findings of the Columbia study?

Clearly it is not absolute levels of stress that correlate with these self-destructive behaviors, since kids driving their own Acuras and SUVs hardly deal with more pressure than those who are homeless, or desperately poor, or simply black for that matter. Rather, it must be the relative inability of the affluent—of the overclass—to *deal* with their stress that is to blame. It is the lack of coping skills among those with resources that gets them into trouble. Whereas those who face oppressive conditions must, as a matter of survival, learn to deal with these conditions from an early age, those who have been pampered and provided for don't learn the same lessons because they never have to. If their grades drop, they pay for tutors; if they wreck their car, they get it fixed or get another one; when they screw up, someone is usually there to bail them out, whether through drug rehab, anger management counseling, or other forms of expensive therapy. But all that cushioning also leaves them strangely vulnerable to dysfunction. Not to romanticize suffering or oppression, of course, but what studies like that from Columbia indicate is that the folks we have been taught to fear and loathe often have more self-control than those in our own families.

So even though blacks and Latinos are more likely than whites to report having been offered drugs in the past month, or having had drugs made available to them, they are less likely to actually use drugs than their white counterparts. Even though persons who are in marginal economic conditions would have every reason to anesthetize themselves with alcohol, persons at the bottom of the economic pyramid are half as likely to drink as those with annual incomes above $75,000 and more than twice as likely to completely abstain. Among youth, despite targeted liquor and tobacco advertising in poor communities and communities of color, whites are three times more likely than blacks to binge drink, and three and a half times more likely to smoke cigarettes regularly.

Despite the oppressive conditions of racism and economic marginalization, the poor are less likely to commit suicide, as are people of color, and indeed studies going back fifty years have found that suicide is linked more to having one's previously high status threatened than to absolute hardship. In other words, unemployment and financial struggle are correlated with self-destructive tendencies, not only or even mostly for the poor or people of color but also and heavily for whites and those who are affluent, and who find themselves unable to deal with temporary setback.

So before we go casting about for evidence of social pathology among those at the bottom, we would do well to recognize the factors, environmental and cultural, that exist among those at the top, and which also are likely to correlate with dysfunction: too much money, too much power, and a mentality of entitlement and expectation that can leave a person dangerously ill-equipped to deal with the real world.

Privilege is dysfunctional, in other words, just as surely as its polar opposite. To be the favored, the top dog, the one who always gets what one wants is to create unrealistic expectations that often can't be sustained, and a kind of self-centeredness that can eclipse whatever personality disorders some folks claim to find among the poor. This kind of narcissism breeds excessive risk-taking, lack of empathy, delusions of grandeur, and the kinds of abuses of power that only those on top can possibly manifest.

And this is a truism that holds not only for people but nations: the powerful, the empire, held together by a reigning mythology of not only self-righteousness but invincibility. The kind that says "We spend $300 billion on defense and no one can mess with us," until a few $5 box cutters and nineteen guys with a bone to pick show us otherwise, that is.

None of this is to say that we should now pity the rich, or cry tears for the racially privileged or men who reap the benefits of patriarchy, or any other dominant group. It is merely to say that if we are going to truthfully analyze what is wrong with our culture, and the environmental influences on certain behaviors, we should begin with the folks at the top, not the bottom, for as the old saying goes, the fish tends to rot from the head down.

SEPTEMBER 2003

Collateral Damage:

Poor Whites and the Unintended Consequences of Racial Privilege

A few years ago, a young woman who was an antipoverty organizer in rural Kentucky asked me how she could infuse her work with an antiracist analysis. She knew there was a need to address the link between institutional racism and white privilege on the one hand, and economic oppression on the other, yet she was aware of the difficulty of relating these issues to the lived experiences of the mostly white poor with whom she was working. After all, how does one explain (indeed is it even proper to bring up) the existence of white privilege among poor whites, for whom the idea of privilege must seem remote? And how could she make poor whites realize the need to fight racism against people of color when they have, to put it mildly, their own problems?

I thought seriously about her questions and promised to get back to her with some ideas, then, as often happens, I got side-tracked and never got around to responding. Yet I continued thinking about the issue, finally concluding that not only is it proper to address white privilege among the white poor, but indeed it is critical to do so, if we ever wish to address not only the misery faced by too many people of color but even that felt by the white poor themselves. For poor whites, as I'll explain below, are victims not only of a class system that views them as expendable but also a racial caste system that favors them, and yet whose favors come at an enormous cost.

Of course, to suggest that poor whites reap the benefits of skin color when they suffer so terribly in class terms seems preposterous to some. But privilege is not merely a monetary or absolute concept, rather it is also relative, and it is this relative meaning of privilege that concerns us here. The white poor, for example, clearly reap certain privileges vis-à-vis the poor of color, beginning with the more positive way in which they are typically viewed.

Consider the early imagery of the poor in the United States, and what various changes in that imagery over time have wrought in terms of the nation's views toward persons in poverty. Not all that long ago, the poor in this country were typically thought of and represented as white, especially white and rural. Images from the Great Depression or the Dust Bowl were among the first mass-distributed visuals of the poor in the United States and, along with early 1960s media attention to conditions in Appalachia, helped frame poverty in a way that was just as likely to conjure up visions of whites as anyone else. In line with the mostly white representation of the poor came a significant degree of sympathy for those in poverty. During the Depression and for several decades after, most Americans viewed poverty as something that was in large part the result of forces beyond the control of the poor themselves.

But by the 1970s, the discussion of poverty had shifted dramatically, thanks in large part to a transformation of media imagery. Whereas in 1964, only a little more than one-quarter of all media representations of poor people in the United States were representations of blacks, by the early 1970s, over 70 percent were, according to Martin Gilens in his book, *Why Americans Hate Welfare*. Likewise, by the early 1970s, three out of every four stories on so-called welfare programs featured African Americans. This shift in imagery of the poor corresponded with a growing backlash against antipoverty efforts and the poor themselves, who increasingly became the targets of political scapegoating and were rarely seen as victims, but rather perpetrators of social decay.

Importantly, the white poor, despite their economic condition, generally escaped the full weight of this emerging invective and were not the ones typified as the harbingers of social pathology. Even though roughly 40 percent of the long-term poor and welfare-dependent "underclass" is white, virtually all media stories discussing the underclass—inevitably in highly critical ways—have portrayed people of color, with few if any exceptions.

The white poor, despite the growing backlash, have been able to remain the "salt of the earth" in the eyes of most, buffeted by circumstances not of their own making. In the 1980s, the farm crisis left thousands of white families on the margins of economic survival and needing government support at record levels (on top of the agricultural subsidies they had already been receiving for years). Yet few blamed the farmers themselves, recognizing instead the larger structural forces at work. This in contrast to the lack of slack cut to the inner-city poor, even though they too were facing economic forces beyond their control: deindustrialization, the loss of manufacturing jobs, and outsourcing to poor nations by companies seeking higher profits, to say nothing of plain old-fashioned racism.

This difference in the way the poor are viewed based on race is indicative of racial preference: an advantage and immunity extended to the white poor, irrespective of class status, which leaves them several steps above the poor of color in the public's estimation, and thereby more likely to garner support, be it in the form of charity or government expenditure. This is one reason why the whiter one's state is demographically, the more generous one's welfare system is likely to be. States with an overwhelmingly white population tend to have far stronger safety nets for those in need, and have imposed far softer cuts and sanctions under the rubric of welfare reform.

And yet, these benefits and privileges have a flip side, one that demonstrates just how harmful racism against people of color (which generated those privileges in the first place) can be, even for the persons who reap the benefits of it in relative terms. In other words, white racial privilege and its corollary (antiblack and antibrown racism) have blowback effects on whites, especially the white poor, and these blowback effects render the white poor a form of "collateral damage" in the ongoing oppression of their darker brethren.

First, because the poverty and welfare issues have been racialized, the white poor have been rendered largely invisible. On the one hand, this extends the privilege of not being the ones scapegoated for the problems of the underclass; but on the other hand, personal invisibility renders one's very real suffering invisible as well. And if the white poor are off the radar screen because the public is so angrily focused on the supposed depredations of the black and brown poor, it will become harder to address the economic needs of the white poor too.

Secondly, to be white and poor in a nation that is rooted in the notion of white domination and supremacy is to fail to live up to that society's expectations, and to fail to live up to those expectations—which because of racial privilege are higher for whites than for others—is to render oneself vulnerable to a special kind of stigma. It is to be an exceptionally spectacular screwup, which can lead one to not only be shunned by other whites but to develop a crippling amount of self-doubt as well. In other words, it's bad enough to be poor and black, but to be poor and white in a land where white folks are expected to excel is to forever brand oneself with a scarlet *L,* for "loser." Here too, the system of white privilege grants benefits on the one hand, even to the white poor, who can remain one step above the poor of color, but still sets up many whites for a fall. It generates expectations that can be sustained for most, but which for some will fall flat, to their absolute detriment. That society provides extra opportunity for whites to make it is a privilege to be sure; but for those who fail, the promise becomes an especially cruel hoax, precisely because of its magnitude.

Third, to the extent the public identifies poverty and welfare efforts with blacks, that same public will become increasingly hostile to the provision of income support needed by all persons in poverty, including whites. Studies have found that the public perceives the poor to be much blacker than they are, and that the public perception of blacks and their work ethic is the single strongest predictor of their attitudes toward income support programs.

In other words, if whites think of blacks (especially poor blacks) in negative terms—a kind of racism that provides privilege to the white poor, who can be viewed as more deserving than those of color—this racism will translate into calls for safety net cuts, thereby endangering the well-being of the very whites who benefited in relative terms from the racist imagery in the first place. So once again, privilege has a downside: In this case, it brings with it a more frugal welfare state and system of support for all the poor, because that privilege is the side effect of racism, and that racism limits support for public assistance generally.

Finally, a system of white privilege encourages the white poor not to form alliances with poor and working class people of color, since such a system encourages those whites to think of their race as all they have, when their economic condition is so miserable. The failure then to form such alliances renders the collective strength of poor and working class people below what it would otherwise be, and thus harms all those who could benefit from such an effort.

Historically, this is how both racism and the class system have been maintained, by playing off whites against people of color, offering the former just enough advantage in relative terms to keep them from aligning with the poor of color and rebelling on the basis of their absolute condition. In the 1700s, this meant ending indentured servitude and placing poor whites on slave patrols, among other things, so as to make them, at least partially, members of the same team as the elite. In the mid-1800s, it meant Southern aristocracy convincing poor whites to ally with the cause of secession and the maintenance of slavery, even though the latter drove down the wages of all low-income whites, since they would have to charge for their labor, while black property could be made to work for free.

When people are poor, a little boost is sometimes all it takes to divide them from their natural allies. White privilege has been that boost. In fact, ironically, white privilege matters more to the poor than the rich. When one is rich, after all, one has enough money to stay warm and buy security. But when one is poor and white, skin is all one has left, and it takes on larger-than-life meaning.

If we ever hope to eradicate the class injustices of poverty and relative deprivation, we must confront directly the racism and institutional privilege that has for so long prevented the class unity needed for such an end. Racism cannot be viewed as it often is on the left, as secondary to the "real issue," which in the minds of white leftists is typically class. The fact is, the issue is both, and without a frontal assault on racism and white privilege, there will be no end to the class system, because there will never be the necessary coalition building needed to fundamentally challenge the existing system of domination and subordination that immiserates poor whites and poor persons of color alike.

OCTOBER 2003

School Shootings and White Denial

I can think of no other way to say this, so here goes: An awful lot of white folks need to pull our heads out of our collective ass. Two more children are dead and thirteen are injured, and another community is scratching its blond scalp, utterly perplexed as to how a school shooting the likes of the one in Santee, California, could happen. After all, as the mayor of the town said on CNN: "We're a solid town, a good town, with good kids; a good church-going town; an All-American town." Well, maybe that's the problem.

I said this after Columbine and no one listened, so I'll say it again: Most whites live in a state of self-delusion. We think danger is black or brown, not to mention poor, and if we can just move far enough away from "those people," we'll be safe. If we can just find an "all-American" town, life will be better, because "things like this just don't happen here."

Well excuse me for pointing this out, but in case you hadn't noticed, "here" is about the only place these kinds of things *do* happen. Oh sure, there's plenty of violence in urban communities too. But *mass* murder, wholesale slaughter, kill-'em-all-let-God-sort-'em-out kinda craziness seems made for those "safe" white suburbs or rural communities. Yet the FBI insists there is no profile of a school shooter. Come again? White boy after white boy after white boy decide to use their classmates for target practice, and yet there is no profile? In the past two years, thirty-two young men have either carried out mass murder against classmates and teachers or planned to do so, only to be foiled at the last minute. Thirty of these have been white. Yet there is no profile? Imagine if these killers and would-be killers had nearly all been black. Would we still hesitate to put a racial face on the perpetrators? Doubtful.

Indeed, if any black child, especially in the white suburbs of

Littleton or Santee, were to openly discuss plans to murder fellow students, as happened at Columbine and Santana High, you can bet somebody would have turned them in and the cops would have beat a path to their door. But when whites discuss murderous intentions, our racial stereotypes of danger too often lead us to ignore it. They're just "talking" and won't really do anything, we tell ourselves. How many have to die before we rethink that nonsense? How many parents, mayors, and sheriffs must we listen to describing how "normal" their community is, and how they can't understand what went wrong?

I'll tell you what went wrong and it's not TV, rap music, video games, or a lack of prayer in school. What went wrong is that white Americans ignored dysfunction and violence when it only seemed to affect other communities, and thereby blinded ourselves to the chaos that never remains isolated forever. That which affects the urban "ghetto" today will be coming to a Wal-Mart near you tomorrow, and was actually there all along, merely hidden by layers of privilege that allow most white folks to cover up our own pathologies. What went wrong is that we allowed ourselves to be lulled into a false sense of security by media representations of crime and violence that portray both as the province of those who are anything but white like us. We ignore the warning signs, because in our minds, the warning signs don't live in our neighborhood, but across town, in that place where we lock our car doors on the rare occasion we have to drive there. That false sense of security, itself the result of race and class stereotypes, then gets people killed, and still we act amazed.

But our children are no better, no more moral, and no more decent than anyone else. Dysfunction is all around us, whether we choose to recognize it or not, and not only in terms of school shootings. For example, according to the Centers for Disease Control's Youth Risk Behavior Survey, and the Monitoring the Future report from the National Institutes on Drug Abuse, it is *our* children, and not those of the urban ghetto, who are most likely to use drugs. White high school students are *seven times* more likely than blacks to have used cocaine and heroin, *eight times* more likely to have smoked crack, and *ten times* more likely to have used LSD. And no, I don't simply mean that there are seven, eight, or ten times more white users than black users (since these disproportions would largely be due to the fact that there are simply more whites in the country); rather, I mean that on a per capita basis, the rates of usage in the white community are anywhere from 600 to 900 percent higher. What's more, it is white youth between the ages of twelve and seventeen who are more likely to sell drugs, and it is white youth who are twice as likely to binge drink, and nearly twice as likely as blacks to drive drunk, and white males are twice as likely as black males to bring a weapon to school.

Yet I would bet there aren't one hundred white people in Santee, or most anywhere else who have ever heard a single one of the statistics above, because the media doesn't report on white dysfunction; or rather, when they do, it is not in a fashion that leads one to recognize the dysfunction as explicitly white.

A few years ago, *U.S. News and World Report* ran a story entitled: "A Shocking Look at Blacks and Crime." Yet never has any media outlet discussed the shocking whiteness of these shoot-'em-ups. Indeed, every time media commentators discuss the similarities in these crimes, they mention that the shooters were boys who got picked on, but never do they seem to notice a certain highly visible melanin deficiency. Color-blind, I guess.

White-blind is more like it, as I figure these folks would spot color pretty quickly were some of it to stroll into their community. Indeed, Santee's whiteness is so taken for granted by its residents that the mayor, in that CNN interview, thought nothing of saying on the one hand that the town was 82 percent white, but that on the other hand, "This is America." Well that *isn't* America, and it especially *isn't* California, where whites are only half of the population. This is a town that is removed from America, from its own state, and yet its mayor thinks *they* are the normal ones, so much so that when asked about racial diversity, he replied that there weren't many of different "ethni-tis-tities." Not a word. Not even close.

I'd like to think that after this one, people would wake up, take note, and rethink their stereotypes of who the dangerous ones are. But deep down, I know better. The folks hitting the snooze button on this none-too-subtle alarm are my own people after all, and I know their blindness like the back of my hand.

MARCH 2001

We Are All Collateral Damage Now:

Reflections on War as Emotional Botox

I remember the first time I ever visited inmates on Tennessee's death row. What struck me about the experience was not so much the solemnity or the pall of pending execution that hung over the place like a threatening storm cloud; nor was it the incredible humanity and even decency of several of the condemned (even those whose crimes had been truly horrific), though that too was unsettling. What rattled me most were the expressions of the guards; or rather, the lack of expression. There was an emptiness, an affect devoid of all visible emotion; not a cruelty, mind you, but something quite a bit worse, as if they had all been required to take Botox injections daily to smooth out the lines and creases of everyday life. The facial flatness was made all the more distracting by the words conveyed by these same guards, which words bespoke a numbness running far deeper than their outer epidermal layers and reaching seemingly well into the inner chambers of their souls.

As one guard put it, he had to dispense with the feelings he had developed for the men he was guarding, men who he acknowledged were amazing painters and poets, and far different than the stereotypical image one tends to have of those who wear the label of "murderer." In order to do their jobs, these guards had been forced to separate the inmates from the common circle of humanity of which they were a part, to accept their disposability in the eyes of the state, to view them as less than the men they are.

I think it no exaggeration, and indeed perhaps a profound understatement of somewhat embarrassing proportions, to suggest that ignoring the essential humanity of another living soul, especially when that humanity is so glaringly obvious, does something to a person, and what it does is never a good thing. Just as slave owners had to make themselves numb to the pain of their chattel, so too did they ultimately become numb to their own pain: the pain of women trapped in oppressive patriarchal conditions; the pain of their children, who never could quite understand how to split their emotions between love for the black women who literally raised them and the fear and loathing they were supposed to feel for black men.

That war inspires a similar emotional schism should be obvious. We are not born, after all, with a natural desire to dominate and oppress and kill others of our species. We are born with an instinct to survive, but since so much oppressive and murderous behavior has little to do with legitimate self-defense (and thus this same survival instinct), there is clearly something that happens to allow people to bomb, shoot, maim, and then assess the damage and do it all over again, and as with the prison guard or slave owner, whatever this thing is, is never good.

For terrifying proof that war turns people into something considerably less gentle and precious than their better selves, one need not look far nowadays. While we certainly should make note of and rejoice in the proliferation of conscious, feeling, very un-numb anti-war voices around the globe, let us also rightfully acknowledge and mourn the capitulation to violence and death on the part of quite a few others, and the apparent majority of Americans, especially those who are white: a subject to which I will return.

First, and this should be apparent, bombing another nation requires believing that those with different citizenship from your own are disposable. Whether the dead are civilians "accidentally killed" by errant "smart" bombs, or soldiers slaughtered intentionally to "shock and awe" the survivors into surrender, the only way one can accept the taking of lives in such a fashion is to ultimately believe that said lives are worth less than your own. It requires a belief that their children are less precious in the eyes of God, or that if equally precious, their deaths are yet an acceptable cost of doing business in the modern world. We might not want to admit this, but it doesn't take much searching to find confirmation. I hear it in the words of those who write to me calling for a bloodbath in Iraq, and who, when asked how many people they are willing to exterminate to make themselves feel safe, answer without hesitation or the slightest sense of irony, "As many as it takes." Something tells me that they weren't like this when they were seven or eight years old, and no one seems too interested in discovering exactly what it was that transpired in their lives between then and now that turned them into willing genocidists. But I would like to know, and I think we all might benefit from such information.

Something has to happen to make one say, as a colleague of mine did in 1986 as we bombed the home of Muammar Quadaffi, "Well, we might not have gotten him, but at least we killed his daughter, and she probably would have grown up to be a terrorist someday." Something has to happen to make one gleeful at the thought of global war, as were the two men driving by our antiwar protest in Nashville this week, waving the American flag and shouting "Korea is next" out the window, not specifying *which* Korea, or perhaps not knowing that there are two, or perhaps not caring. Something has to happen to make one so bitter, angry, hateful, and ravenous as to drive by that same protest where people are merely calling for peace and yell through a face contorted by rage if not a mental breakdown, "Bomb, bomb, bomb, kill, kill, kill," as I also witnessed this week.

But even more frightening than the rush to ugly and violent rhetoric such as that discussed above is the more voluminous shift to reserved and unaffected acceptance. After all, something also has to happen in order to allow us to label dead children "collateral damage," a term we would consider an offense of the highest order if used to describe our own loved ones, but which we are told to accept without hesitation when applied to someone else's family on the other side of the globe.

Something terrible has to happen in order to allow us to watch blandly the high-tech, video-game-like coverage of this war on CNN, or MSNBC, or Fox; to read calmly the bold fonts that are the script of choice for the networks as they promote mass death and destruction; to note without comment the little clock in the right-hand corner of the screen counting down the minutes and seconds left until the Bush-to-Baghdad ultimatum runs its course and bombing can commence. One can almost imagine someone rigging a bejeweled glass ball in Times Square to count down the final seconds, like Dick Clark counts them down at New Year's.

But perhaps that sounds a bit too cynical, and if there is one thing I wish not to be it is cynical. Even at this late hour in the evolution of our species, I believe in the fundamental goodness of other people. If I didn't believe this before the birth of our daughters, I certainly do now. Bringing children into the world is, after all, a visceral statement of hope if ever there was one; it's an insistence that the world does not have to be taken as one finds it; it's a promissory note to the future, a demand that we can and must carry on. No, if there are cynics in this scenario they are not those who raise their voices against the bland discussion of nation-wrecking. The cynics are those who discuss this nation-wrecking in such a fashion over a latte. They are those who nod in agreement, or perhaps wishful thinking, as they hear Donald Rumsfeld—who is frankly a man for whom the term cynic was created—insist, "We did not ask for this war," though indeed we did *exactly* that, at least until it became obvious that asking wasn't getting us anywhere, and so permission was no longer needed. They are those so practiced at self-deception that they can listen without laughing or experiencing a deep and revolting shame as this same man claims that one of the goals of this war is to allow for the lifting of sanctions and the rebuilding of Iraq, albeit a million or so deaths too late.

They are those who breathe a sigh of relief at the steady and reserved (though oh so reassuring) promises of the gaggle of retired generals paraded by the media, to the effect that "this is precision bombing," so not to worry. Residential neighborhoods are safe. Of course, al-Qaeda didn't target residential areas on 9/11 either per se, but I'm figuring that didn't make anyone feel much better.

Don't get me wrong. I am not trying to draw a moral distinction between those of us already against this war and those favoring it. I am not saying that we are better, more ethical, more righteous, or in any way superior people. I have no doubt that at various times we too have experienced this kind of numbness or turned our heads to atrocities. Indeed, in a society with such atrocities happening regularly—and almost always without the active consent or even input of the masses—it is unlikely that we could conceivably avoid such things from time to time. No one is at all times the perfect resistance fighter. Collaboration is virtually built in to the modern world. But the fundamental egalitarianism of our species' weaknesses is no cause for celebration. That we all fall short several times a week is no source of comfort, but rather a reason for the redoubling of our efforts to un-numb those who are anesthetized at this time, just as we would hope that they would do the same for us in our less noble moments. For the costs really couldn't be much higher.

Today I received an e-mail message from someone who described herself as a suburban soccer mom, who was utterly opposed to the insanity of this slaughter. It was nice to read such a thing from someone who most would probably expect to be first in line at the yellow ribbon and American flag giveaway: Such is the nature of our stereotypes, including my own. Of course my pleasure at reading her righteous screed was tempered by the story she told therein, in which she recounted being asked by a store clerk how she was doing, replying "awful," and after explaining this response as being related to the extant bombing, being told by the same clerk that "at least we're safe here and we don't have to go through all that."

Putting aside the obvious problem that we weren't "going through" 9/11 before 9/11 either, and thus one never really knows when payback is sneaking up on you, there is a more subtle weakness to the clerk's assurance. Namely, when one can offer such a dispassionate logic in the face of havoc, that same person should at least be clear that they are indeed *going through it*, if by "it" we mean death. Death, after all, can come to a person long before the heart stops beating, and this I mean not as hyperbole. Death is indeed not merely a physical state. In its less blatant form, we have all suffered small types of death from time to time. Indeed, in a world filled with injustice (as well as much human kindness, it should be noted), one can hardly expect otherwise.

At the more extreme end, if one needs further confirmation that breathing souls can be deadened, one need only look at the faces of those white men and their sandwich- and lemonade-making wives, standing beneath the lifeless bodies of black men swinging from oak trees in old photos of lynchings to see what I'm talking about. There is no sign of life in their eyes, even though they must surely be as awake as they had ever been at that moment—the smell of flesh burned before the final hanging would all but assure as much. Yet the picnic carried on as planned, and the flies were shooed away with the swat of a hand, by genteel souls who probably thought against all evidence to the contrary that those same flies had only come for the chicken salad. And no, I am not implying an exact equivalence between pro-war forces in the present and those whites who participated actively in the murder of blacks across this country. I am merely noting the general phenomenon, and asking about trajectories and continuums, and wondering what good fortune separates us from those who can participate in such evil and keeps us from giving in to our baser instincts? We need to know the answer to this question too.

And speaking of white people, it is at times like these that I can say without fear of contradiction that I wish my nation were run by black folks. For although African Americans are assuredly capable of violence on a widespread scale, as with those of us more melanin-deprived, it is nonetheless true that they seem to be a bit less sanguine about the notion of mass death, wholesale killing, or scorched earth. While the vast majority of whites, especially men, say they support the war on Iraq even if it results in thousands of Iraqi civilians losing their lives, less than 20 percent of blacks feel the same. And while most Latinos support the war when asked to cast a simple yes or no vote, when the prospect of large-scale civilian death is raised, support plummets among them as well, down to less than one-fifth. Only white men, in fact, continue to support the war no matter how many people have to die.

Perhaps it is because being the dominant group in a society as drunk on power as ours allows one to never have to second-guess one's actions. Perhaps it is because being on top of the shit pile means never having to say you're sorry. Or maybe it's because white American males have yet to have our asses handed to us by a stronger foe. Unlike white Brits, or Germans, or the French, or Russians, who know what it means to be blitzed, firebombed, conquered, and made the subject of an extermination campaign, white American males think our dicks are simply bigger. Or perhaps we don't think this, but figure we can make up for any inadequacy by building the biggest missiles and saying things like "Don't mess with Texas." We build so-called daisy-cutter bombs as a form of technological Viagra: compensation for our moral impotence.

Black and brown folks, on the other hand, know what it's like to be the victims of mass murder. Whether in the Middle Passage that cost tens of millions of African lives, or the ninety-three million indigenous souls purged to make way for the conquest of the Americas, some people have been experiencing shock and awe for a long time; so long, in fact, that nothing white men do anymore seems all that shocking to them. Except, perhaps, for the persistent ability of those same white men to believe that the worm will never turn, that the other shoe will never drop. The unwillingness to grasp the simple and terrifying truth of the phrase "What goes around comes around," or, if you prefer, James Baldwin's prescient rendering, that "people ought not be surprised when the bread they have cast upon the waters comes floating back to them, poisoned."

It is long past time to put down the Botox and syringe. Time to feel again.

MARCH 2003

Rethinking Superiority:

Reflections on Whiteness and the Cult of "Progress"

As of this coming year, high school students in Philadelphia will be required to take a course in African American history in order to graduate. In a recent column, I lent my support to the new prerequisite, and responded to those who have attacked the plan, most of whom have criticized such a course for being "divisive," or too narrowly focused, or otherwise a distraction from the presumably more important (and unrelated) work of reading, writing, and arithmetic.

Having grown accustomed to hostile e-mails in response to my Internet-based essays, I was utterly unsurprised by the missive I received shortly after the first piece went up on my website a few weeks ago. Therein, the author attacked the black history requirement, offering reasons for his objections that I suspect were far more honest than those put forth by most, and which reasons were also considerably more racist in both tone and content. Indeed, his racial hostility virtually leapt off the page when he insisted, among other things, that no sub-Saharan African nation had developed a wheel prior to contact with whites and that ancient Egypt (which he grudgingly admitted was, as with modern-day Egypt, located in Africa) wasn't really African in the sense of being a black nation. Finally, he self-confidently proclaimed that "blacks have contributed between nil and zilch" to American history, and thus were unworthy of any classroom attention, let alone an entire course dedicated to their nonachievement. To be more specific, my detractor insisted that blacks have contributed no technological advances, no scientific discoveries, and no other inventions that would merit a class on black history.

There is much one could say here, and perhaps some will

question why I would even bother to respond at all. Yet the regularity with which such bombast finds its way into my web browser suggests that letting it slide will hardly make such views go away. At the very least, this kind of vapid argumentation points up a number of disturbing conclusions about the people who forward it, and those who believe it—and let us be clear, with regard to the last bunch, the numbers are far greater than are willing to say so openly. Bottom line: Racists almost always tell you more about themselves than about the people they seek to denigrate, and this is no exception to that rule.

First, let us take note of what appears to be an ironclad truism: Those who rush to herald the superiority of their own group have themselves rarely accomplished anything. Rather, they seek to live vicariously off the achievements of others with whom they share nothing more than some distant national or ethnic lineage. They are singularly unimpressive, in most cases, when it comes to professional or personal greatness, however defined—and certainly as defined by their own terms. Along these lines, I feel confident that had my e-critic ever done anything in the fields of science and technology, such that he could point to his own life as evidence of white superiority, he would have told me so.

But of course, it is never the inventor who proclaims his or her work to be evidence of ethnic or genetic superiority; it is not the great playwrights or sculptors who announce to the world that their art signifies the racial or cultural supremacy of the group to which they belong. Only life's losers seek out evidence of their own brilliance or potential in the works of others. Only those who secretly harbor suspicions of their own inferiority feel compelled, as a general rule, to insist upon how much better than *you* they are. Real superiority, measured along whatever axis one may choose, tends to demonstrate itself without the need of cheerleaders.

As for my electronic adversary, it's not as if anything he said was really new. Racists have long sought to dismiss the contributions made by folks of color—not only those made to science, art, and literature but even the importance of the manual labor to which millions were largely limited under slavery and apartheid. Several years ago, neo-Nazi David Duke dismissed the contributions made by black workers to the growth of the American republic by suggesting that horses could have done the physical labor performed by slaves.

Putting aside the matter of how horses can harvest crops or build levees, without which the homes and lands of the white planter class would have been washed away, there is another, more pressing issue. That others *could* have done the work in question hardly matters: The fact is, others *didn't*; black slaves did, and that makes all the difference. Lots of folks *could* do lots of things. I could pick up the garbage every week in my own neighborhood and haul it to the city landfill; but I don't. Three guys do: two black, one white, none of them, presumably, with my level of formal education, but whose contribution to the community in which I live is absolutely indispensable; more so, indeed, than my own. That I could do their job is beside the point. I don't, and unless they do it, my block is screwed. But under the logic of elitists, their contribution is minor, while the stockbroker who may (against my wishes) choose to move into my neighborhood would be considered a model and vitally important citizen.

Getting back to the point: Had it not been for that unimpressive labor on the part of blacks, the American Revolution itself would not have happened, dependent as it was on profits from industries that relied on slave labor. In that sense, to suggest that blacks have contributed nothing to American history is a logical absurdity because in the absence of black labor there would have *been* no USAmerican history to which they (or anyone else) could have contributed.

As for black folks' supposed lack of achievement in terms of technology, science, and the like—as well as the utterly specious claim about the lack of the wheel in preslavery Africa—I could spend several thousand words referring readers to the evidence on this subject, compiled by African and European scholars alike, which demonstrates both the racism and absurdity of such positions. But for those truly interested in this material—and that would exclude pretty much anyone inclined to take my critic's diatribe seriously—you would be better served to seek out the information yourself, seeing as how it will be far more adequately presented therein than I could do here. You can begin with the works of Cheikh Anta Diop, Molefi Asante, and Walter Rodney, among others, and for those whose racism leads them to dismiss black scholars on these subjects, you can always examine the voluminous writings of Basil Davidson, one of the most respected Africa scholars in modern history, who is decidedly both white and British.

But for my purposes, I would suggest a different approach to these kinds of slurs on persons of African descent: one that does not focus on a tit-for-tat comparison of the accomplishments of whites and blacks, Europeans and Africans, in an attempt to tally up the ledger and proclaim one or the other the historical victor. Nor would this approach spend considerable energy seeking to prove even those things which are eminently provable, such as the fact that there were several African civilizations (including sub-Saharan) in existence while Europeans were still, for all intents and purposes, shitting in the woods. Rather, I would argue that the entire basis for comparison offered by racist commentators is flawed, the paradigm under which greatness is being assessed is problematic, and the premises underlying the slanders upon Africa and the accolades for Europe are wrongheaded. In short: the Europhile interpretation of what constitutes cultural superiority and accomplishment is itself subjective, and more than that, terribly stultifying as a measure of human worth.

To suggest that we should gauge the legitimacy of a culture based upon its technological achievements is to elevate the importance of things over and above the importance of people. It would require that we extend the label of "superior" to any culture with advanced technological prowess, even if that technology were put to use in such a way as to exterminate others, or ultimately in such a way that led to the extinction even of the culture that created it. We would be forced to conclude that *any* technological advance whatsoever, no matter how dysfunctional, makes the group to which its creator belongs superior and more worthy of praise than others. So instead of viewing the creation of nuclear weaponry (a technological "contribution" to be sure) as evidence of a fundamentally pathological and destructive tendency among the whites who brought it forth, we are expected to praise the genius behind it, taking no note of the consequences now made possible by such progress. By contrast, hunter-gatherer societies that nurture respect for one another, mutual interdependence, compassion, and cooperation—and who by and large engage in little or no predation against others or the land base upon which they depend—would be considered inferior in this cosmology. That such an approach for rank-ordering societies would be morally and ethically absurd should be obvious, but won't be to those who have bought into the white supremacist view of things.

Furthermore, the "great man" paradigm of historical analysis—which is what my attacker's e-mail was promoting—by definition constitutes an assault on the dignity and worth of the vast majority of the globe's inhabitants, including almost all citizens of even the most advanced nation-states. After all, few of us will ever invent anything of note, compose a symphony, discover a cure for a deadly disease, or manage to accomplish any of the other things that the "great man" theorists extol as the only important human victories. By the standards of ruling class history, most Americans, of whatever race, are essentially useless, and have accomplished nothing. Likewise, entire cultures (and not just black and brown ones) come up short in such an analysis. Iceland, for example, has lots of folks who would be considered white, and very few who wouldn't be, yet they have hardly made a huge mark in the worlds of science, technology, or literature; so too for any number of Central European nations. What we think of as European civilization is really quite limited: composed of the historic, scientific, and artistic achievements of only a handful of nations, and even then, involving only a small fraction of the persons of those states, most of whose citizens have been little more than peasants for the bulk of recorded history. Thus, if we suggest that technological achievements or contributions are what mark a people as having history worth knowing, then we would have to teach almost nothing about Finland, as with Cameroon—a coupling most racists would reject, but which their own taxonomy of relevant history makes necessary.

Beyond all this, it was actually the next part of the angry e-mail that struck me as especially worthy of discussion, the part after its author claimed that blacks had contributed nothing to American history. This was the part where he proffered the opinion that rather than contribute, blacks had "merely survived American history." The snide remark was made as if to suggest that survival, even of the hideous racial history of this land—from being bought and sold, to raped, to having fingers cut off for learning to read, to being lynched, or to being relegated to the lowest-rung jobs and living in the poorest neighborhoods—counted for nothing; as if surviving such history (even if we accept the nonsensical proposition that this was all black folks had managed to accomplish) was no more impressive than chewing gum and walking at the same time.

Imagine, to survive attempted cultural and physical genocide does not, on this view, merit wonder or amazement, let alone a class to discuss how such a thing could be possible: this, in a nation that has made surviving a few weeks on an island with television cameras and emergency medical assistance at the ready something for which the last person standing should be rewarded one million dollars; in a nation where surviving the consumption of raw pig snouts or bull testicles might well win you $50,000 on *Fear Factor*. Since when has survival been seen as such an unimpressive accomplishment? Does not surviving the concerted attempt to destroy or at least subjugate one's people say something about the character of those who manage the feat? Does not leading a struggle for freedom and the advancement of human dignity suggest that the persons in question have made a substantial contribution to the nation in which they live, and indeed the world? By what moral, ethical, or practical standard could one fairly argue otherwise?

Interestingly enough, it was once believed that survival of one's racial group demonstrated the group's superiority, and as such, blacks would die off, unable to make it in a world where their biological defects would cause them to go the way of the dinosaur. Whites, it was argued, were superior, and this was proven—or so the argument went—by the way in which whites survived any obstacle thrown in our paths: the journey to the new world, harsh winters in the colonies, wars with the indigenous peoples of the Americas or with Mexico. What marked peoples of color as inferior was their presumed *inability* to survive, especially blacks after emancipation, who were thought incapable of fending for themselves absent the guiding hand of their masters. Now, seeing as how predictions of black extinction have fallen flat, and given the ways in which African Americans have thrived when given full opportunity to do so, racists have, by necessity, changed their story. Now survival, as my electronic interlocutor would have it, means nothing, and is certainly not the evidence of superiority that his predecessors in the cult of white supremacy thought it to be. How very convenient for him: changing the tune to fit the bias.

To suggest that surviving the predatory ways of one's captors and oppressors counts for less than the oppressor's success at developing gadgets and commodities (but even then, only after having stolen the land, labor, and mineral resources of other peoples first) is to turn technology into a fetish. It is to conclude that the person who creates instruments that clear-cut forests more speedily, that remove minerals from the earth more expeditiously, and then belch poisonous by-products into the air once the minerals are converted to energy is superior and worthy of more praise than the person who merely survives the destruction but contributes far less to it. By the logic of such objects fetishism, we should praise Dow for giving us napalm and view them as more worthy of historical reverence than the Vietnamese civilians who merely survived the trenches, the product of all that white male genius burned into their backs. We should spend more time in class ruminating on the technological aptitude of the folks who create torture devices (think shock batons or genital clamps hooked up to car batteries) than we should to the victims of their torture, who do nothing except occasionally survive the depravity of the first bunch. Oppenheimer gets the praise, while the citizens of Hiroshima become a historical footnote.

It all makes sense, once you accept the internal logic of a culture fascinated by death and destruction, especially its ability to produce both with such amazing alacrity. Mere survival isn't nearly impressive enough, as it doesn't portend the kicking of anyone's ass, and what good are people who don't destroy and displace others? Mere survival implies passivity; it's too feminine (God forbid) in a culture that values and venerates the masculine, and even then in only its most pathological manifestations. Men (real men at least) don't just survive; real men create, they build, they destroy others who get in their way; real men steal others' land, rape others' bodies, make the world over in their image, consider themselves God, and then proceed to act as though their delusional messianism were an indication of strength rather than their own spiritual depravity.

How cut off from your own humanity must you be to suggest that technology and other inventions are the ultimate measure of human worth? After all, a robot is capable of making any of the things that those who worship technology might consider evidence of cultural superiority. But no robot can be programmed to lead a struggle for human freedom, democracy, or liberty. No robot can be made to raise a child into an adult, or write a novel filled with pathos and irony, or any human feeling whatsoever. No robot can nurse a sick puppy back to health, solve any of a thousand moral dilemmas faced by real people everyday, write a screenplay that can make us cry, or devise something as lofty as the Universal Declaration of Human Rights. To thus consider technology, ultimately *stuff*, as the evidence of a culture's superiority, is to engage in the ultimate auto-dehumanization; it is to utterly miss the point of creation, whether seen as a God-given gift or an act of nature.

Surely, superiority in any meaningful sense is located less in one's ability to create and destroy than in one's ability to empathize and to stop doing the things one is doing that wreak havoc on the planet and one's neighbors. To develop the capacity to kill and maim on a grand scale is not a sign of superiority; to be capable of saying you're sorry, even for making the effort, might well be, but good luck finding anyone among the masters of the universe willing to do *that*.

And so as not to engage in too extreme a version of anthropocentrism, no robot can accomplish even that which bees accomplish everyday: pollinating plants that bring forth fruit, nuts, and berries, and thereby keeping the chain of life trotting along. In other words, even creatures to which we typically extend little if any credit for their intelligence are more important to life on this planet than even the most impressive pile of technological junk upon which we are fixated at any given moment. And if that pile of junk threatens our survival—either because the extraction of the minerals needed to produce it has degraded the ecosystem or because the machine itself has as its purpose the bringing of death, as with guns, bullets, or bombs—then we might more properly view its creators as either crazy, evil, or both; we should certainly not consider them superior, unless our twisted concept of superiority involves the ability to extinguish life on the planet; unless the will to omnicide has come to represent, for us, the pinnacle of human achievement.

Sadly, perhaps that's the problem: Perhaps we really do define superiority this way. The ability to rape the earth, to destroy that which either God or nature (or both) has given us, places us in some sick way above God, at least in our minds. By our actions we seem to be saying that although God may have been able to create the world in just six days, we can and will destroy it, if not as quickly, just as completely. Unless we figure out a way to pull the brakes on this runaway train known as "white Western civilization," and thereby derail its headlong rush into the abyss from which it will never likely recover, all that genius, all that refinement, and all that self-congratulation regarding both will ultimately prove to be our undoing. At which point we will stand merely as the most spectacular failure in the history of mankind, and one for which there will be no propagandistic spin available, even for the most creative racist left standing.

SEPTEMBER 2005

Conclusion:

Being In (But Not *Of*) This Skin

However much we may not have known it up to now, white Americans have a choice to make. It is the choice between collaboration and resistance, silence and protest, complacency and agitation. It is the choice between accepting the way things are or insisting, indeed demanding, that we can and must do better. It is the choice, in short, between whiteness—in which direction one finds likely social, cultural, and economic destruction—and humanity. And how we resolve these choices may make the difference in years to come between war and peace, opportunity and misery, safety and danger, and in the very existence of life on the planet. White supremacy and its consequences—and one can count among these resource exploitation, unbridled capitalism, militarism, and colonialism—have pushed our world to the brink of self-annihilation. Unless those of us called white opt for resistance and alliance, standing shoulder-to-shoulder with persons of color around the globe and saying "enough," it is a very open question as to whether or not any of us will survive in the long run. Every society that has tolerated the kind of inequality tolerated in the United States—every society in which the few have sought to hoard resources to the exclusion of others, as is so common here—has eventually crumbled. Were it not for our hubris, perhaps we would be less likely to believe that somehow we were immune to the trajectory taken by those past empires; perhaps we'd notice that we're not so special or different after all.

But we don't see it, at least most of us don't. Not yet. But we will. The only question is whether we'll come to see the reality of our condition before it's too late, or only as we begin the steep decline that lies just over the cliff whose precipice we are rapidly approaching. On that question, the jury is still out. But knowing that we have the choice, and understanding the seriousness, indeed gravity, of inaction may yet spur enough of us to join in resistance, having come to understand the difference between being *in* this skin and *of* this skin. We are in it, to be sure, and over that we have never had control. But we are not *of* it. We are made of more, and better stuff, than that.

We are made of the same stuff as John Brown, as the Grimké sisters, as John Fee, as Ellsberry Ambrose, as William Shreve Bailey, as Lydia Marie Child, and as Anne Braden. The blood and history that courses through us is not only that shared by slave owners and members of lynch mobs; so too is it the blood and history of abolitionists and freedom riders. When we forget that, we not only compromise our own humanity, but we sacrifice the promise of what Dr. King called "the beloved community" on the altar of racial particularism. This we do to our own detriment.

So what is it going to be? Which path, which road shall we travel? The path of silence and collaboration is well trod, and it is perhaps an easier road, in that it asks very little of us and allows—for a time at least—a certain degree of smooth sailing, seeing as it permits us to remain oblivious, to go about our lives and not bother with such mundane subjects as white supremacy and privilege. But that road is ultimately a road to nowhere, or at least nowhere we'd really want to be. To choose it is to embark on a fairly bland and uneventful journey, right up until the end, at which point the destination will not seem nearly worth the effort. It would be akin to taking a slow, predictable boat ride over the River Styx, forgetting for a moment what lay on the other side.

The path of resistance is assuredly more difficult, with far more bumps—the kind that can occasionally knock one out of the ox cart altogether, or flatten one's proverbial tire. But those bumps build character, they build muscle, they build determination. To flail against them, unsure as to the ultimate outcome but hopeful that enough will take the same path as to pick us up when we fall, is to learn what it means to become fully human. I say "become" human because to think that one is already human based solely on one's status as a member of *Homo sapiens* is to make a category mistake. Our humanness is, and always has been, so much more than a biological notion; it is inherently spiritual, metaphysical, *bigger* than flesh and blood and those twenty-three chromosomes.

Speaking of which, I, like most people, have pondered over the years what it is about us as members of the human species that makes us so special. Why are we here? For what purpose? And, to put it simply, for what reason was I born a person, rather than, say, a parakeet, or a meerkat, or, for that matter, a single-celled paramecium? It is a matter of little effort to dispense with any notion that somehow our species' specialness comes from higher-order mental powers, or the notion that we are in some way smarter than others. If anything, we may be the least intelligent species on the planet. We are the only one, after all, that has ever concocted weapons capable of ending life on earth, and we are the only one that engages in such massive predation against our own land base. In short, when it comes to intelligence, parakeets, meerkats, and paramecia may well have us beat by a mile.

After careful consideration, and after thinking about what sets humans apart from other species (in a positive and not horrifyingly negative way), I came to realize that there was really only one thing separating us in a way that was flattering to the human side of the equation: We are the only species (at least the only one I know of) that has ever organized itself in struggle for collective liberation. This is not to be confused with altruism, for other species exhibit altruistic and charitable tendencies in abundance; rather, I am speaking of collective liberation efforts to end oppression and exploitation. Even the animal rights movement, one must note, had to be organized by people. Bunnies and chimps and mink have never been capable of doing it themselves. This is no indictment of those other animals, by the way, just a way of indicating that indeed there is something about the human animal that is different, and perhaps in a good way—perhaps in the way that ultimately matters most.

And yes, it's true that the collective liberation for which humans, and only humans, have fought has only been necessary because those same humans first managed to screw things up, by way of oppression and exploitation. So yes, we are, as a species, a bit like the parent with Munchausen syndrome by proxy, which causes caregivers to make their children sick on purpose, so they can then rush in and save them. But whatever the case, and however much we have caused damage, the fact that we can, if we choose, fight to undo the damage, to make amends, to repair a broken world, still matters. And if it is that—and *only that*—which separates us from the other creatures of this world, then who are we to fail in that solitary endeavor? How can we refuse to do the one thing that really makes us special and sets us apart? How can we walk the road of silence and collaboration and yet justify to ourselves the oxygen that, in so doing, we thieve from others who could put it to more productive use?

We are here for a very short time, so short in the greater scheme of things that it's almost incomprehensible. In that brief moment, that blip on the screen, that blinking of a cosmic eye—which, relative to the history of the world, is a far less significant amount of time than the time it took me to write this sentence is to my own life—we had best do something to justify our presence. Whether one believes in God (however defined) or whether one is sure that this is all there is, either way, it stands to reason that the prudent course is to hedge one's bet. If there be a creator, then surely we must strive to be accountable for our actions in the face of such an entity. And if there is not, then the clock is ticking, and it is the only one we have—a thought that should spur us on, even more than faith perhaps, to make our time on this earth worthwhile.

It is, in the end, really as James Baldwin put it many years ago in *The Fire Next Time*, when he noted:

> Life is tragic simply because the earth turns and the sun inexorably rises and sets, and one day, for each of us, the sun will go down for the last, last time. Perhaps the whole root of our trouble, the human trouble, is that we will sacrifice all the

beauty of our lives, will imprison ourselves in totems, taboos, crosses, blood sacrifices, steeples, mosques, races, armies, flags, nations, in order to deny the fact of death, which is the only fact we have. It seems to me that we ought to rejoice in the fact of death—ought to decide, indeed, to *earn* one's death by confronting with passion the conundrum of life. One is *responsible* for life: It is the small beacon in that terrifying darkness from which we come and to which we shall return. One must negotiate this passage as nobly as possible, for the sake of those who are coming after us.